FEDERAL GOVERNMENT

Federal Government

K. C. WHEARE

FOURTH EDITION

Issued under the auspices of the
Royal Institute of International Affairs

A GALAXY BOOK
NEW YORK OXFORD UNIVERSITY PRESS 1964

CONTENTS

Part I
WHAT FEDERAL GOVERNMENT IS

Part II
WHEN FEDERAL GOVERNMENT IS APPROPRIATE

Part III
HOW FEDERAL GOVERNMENT SHOULD BE ORGANIZED

Part IV
HOW FEDERAL GOVERNMENT WORKS

Part V
REVIEW

WHAT FEDERAL GOVERNMENT IS

Chapter I

THE FEDERAL PRINCIPLE

1

AN inquiry into the working of federal government begins of necessity with some discussion about the meaning of the term. For the term 'federal government' is used very loosely in political discussions and it is seldom given a meaning which is at once clear and distinct. To be sure, most of those who use it agree in this, that they have in mind an association of states, which has been formed for certain common purposes, but in which the member states retain a large measure of their original independence. But although they agree in this, they differ about the particular form or type of association of states which they think it proper to describe as a federal government. Thus it comes about that the term has been applied alike to the Austro-Hungarian Empire, to the German Empire of 1871–1918, to the League of Nations, to the United States of America, and to the Union of South Africa—all of them associations of states, but each differing from the other in the form which that association has taken. Where common usage differs so much, the academic man must be careful not to adopt too rigid a definition. But he is entitled to inquire whether a more restricted use of the term 'federal government' is not justifiable.

The modern idea of what federal government is has been determined by the United States of America. Not that the Constitution of 1787 which established and regulates this association of states described it as a federal government. Indeed the words 'federal' or 'federation' occur nowhere in the American Constitution.[1] None the less it has always been called the 'Federal Constitution',[2] and nowadays everybody regards the United States as an example of federal government. Many consider it the most important and the most successful example. Any definition of federal government which failed to include the United States would be thereby condemned as unreal. It would seem sensible, therefore, in seeking a legitimate and convenient definition of federal government, to begin by examining the Constitution of the United States.

The Constitution of the United States consists of the original document of 1787 and more than a score of amendments. It can be studied

[1] The word 'confederation' occurs once, but not as a description of the union. Article 1, Sect. X directs that 'no state shall enter into any treaty, alliance or confederation'.
[2] S. E. Morison, *History of the United States*, Vol. I, p. 87.

from a variety of points of view. Our interest in it at present is limited to one particular point of view, namely as a document which regulates an association of states. We examine it in order to discover what sort of association it regulates. What is the fundamental characteristic of the United States considered as an association of states?

The answer seems to be that the Constitution[1] of the United States establishes an association of states so organized that powers are divided between a general government which in certain matters—for example, the making of treaties and the coining of money—is independent of the governments of the associated states, and, on the other hand, state governments which in certain matters are, in their turn, independent of the general government. This involves, as a necessary consequence, that general and regional governments both operate *directly* upon the people; each citizen is subject to two governments. It is not always easy to say what matters are within the spheres of the general and the regional governments respectively. The words of the Constitution are sometimes ambiguous, contradictory or vague. But however vague the Constitution may be about where the line is to be drawn, it is quite clear on the point that, once granted that a government is acting within its allotted sphere, that government is not subordinate to any other government in the United States. If we examine the American Constitution we must conclude that, as a matter of law there laid down, the field of government is divided between a general authority and regional authorities which are not subordinate one to another, but co-ordinate with each other. In the words of a modern American historian,[2] the general government 'is a government supreme within its sphere, but that sphere is defined and limited. As the tenth amendment made clear in 1791, "the powers not delegated to the United States by the Constitution, nor prohibited by it to the states, are reserved to the states respectively or to the people". The states are co-equally supreme within their sphere; in no legal sense are they subordinate corporations.' The principle of organization upon which the American association is based is that of the division of powers between distinct and co-ordinate governments.

It is fair to mention at this point that not all Americans in 1787 would have accepted this view of the nature of their Constitution. Indeed, when the Constitution first came into operation and for many decades thereafter, a strong body of opinion asserted the view that the general government established by the Constitution was intended to be not the equal and co-ordinate partner of the state governments but their agent and to this extent their subordinate.[3] It was not until

[1] I must emphasize that I am referring to the whole of it—original document and amendments

[2] S. E. Morison, op. cit., Vol. I, p. 88.

[3] The chief exponent of this view was John C. Calhoun, of South Carolina, who was Vice-president of the United States, 1825–32, and thereafter Senator. The classic statement of his view is found in 'The Exposition of 1828', a manifesto published by the legislature of South Carolina to justify its proposal to nullify an act of Congress. See below, pp. 86–87, 122–5. The exposition is found in Calhoun, *Works*, Vol. VI.

after the American Civil War of 1861–5 that this view was finally discredited. Moreover, there existed in the original Constitution of 1787 one provision at least which lent colour to the view that the general government was subordinate. This was the provision that members of the upper house of the general congress, the senators, were to be chosen by the legislatures of the states. This meant that one part of the general legislature was to some degree dependent upon the government of the states.[1]

To these considerations my answer is that the view I have taken of the Constitution seems to me the correct view, because, in spite of this one admitted exception in the case of the Senate, the *predominant* principle of the original constitution was that of a co-ordinate division of powers.[2] The exception in the case of the Senate was important, but it was not decisive. After all, the Senate was a part, not the whole, of the general legislature. It was an exception; the general rule, I maintain, was that of co-ordinate division. Further, whatever may have been the correct analysis in 1787, time was to prove that the principle which would prevail was the principle of co-ordinate division. The Civil War settled that question. An amendment of the Constitution in 1913[3] completed the process formally by making the election of senators a matter for the people of the states, not for the legislatures, and thus removed the exception to the rule. The modern Constitution recognizes a co-ordinate system, and, as I have explained already, it is of the modern Constitution that I am speaking.

2

But, it may be said, even if it be admitted that this principle of organization is a characteristic of the United States, considered as an association of states, is it legitimate to claim it as a *distinguishing* characteristic? Does it mark off the United States from other associations of states which are sometimes classed with it as examples of federal government?

Perhaps the best way to begin an answer to this question is to look at the form of association which the American states had adopted in the years before the Constitution of 1787 was drawn up. For, as is well known to students of American history, the present Constitution of the United States is not the only Constitution of the United States that ever was. When the American Colonies began their resistance to Britain, they drew up in 1777 the Articles of Confederation of the United States of

---

[1] James Wilson, one of the delegates from Pennsylvania to the Convention at Philadelphia which drew up the Constitution, expressed this opinion. See Max Farrand, *Records of the Federal Convention*, Vol. I, p. 413.

[2] My view of the nature of the Constitution has the support of most modern American historians, for example, S. E. Morison and H. S. Commager, *The Growth of the American Republic*, Vol. I, pp. 171–3. It is in line with the views expressed at the time by such men as James Wilson (see Farrand, op. cit., Vol. I, p. 413,) and James Madison (ibid., Vol. II, p. 93).

[3] Amendment XVII.

America.[1] These Articles of 1777 differ in an interesting way from the Constitution of 1787.

Like the Constitution of 1787 they provided that a Congress of the United States was to have sole and exclusive power of determining upon, among other things, peace and war, sending and receiving ambassadors, treaties and alliances, coinage, and, with certain exceptions, the government and regulation of the land and naval forces. But at the same time care was taken that Congress, in exercising these and all its powers, should not be independent of the state governments. Congress itself consisted of one house only and this was composed of delegates appointed from each state for one year in such manner as the legislature of each state determined. These delegates were recallable before the year of office expired. Each delegation, though varying in number from a minimum of two to a maximum of seven, had only one vote. It was inevitable therefore that the delegates should be appointed by the legislature and executive of their state, and be closely controlled by them. Further, though Congress was to decide upon the amount of money to be spent on defence and war, the legislatures of the states were to impose and collect the taxes; and though Congress was to decide the number of the land forces and make a requisition from each state for its quota, the legislatures of the states were to appoint the regimental officers, to raise the men, clothe, arm and equip them in a soldier-like manner at the expense of the United States, and they were to be the final judges as to whether any extra men above the allotted quota should be raised, if Congress called for them. The form of government which resulted was described by a great contemporary, Alexander Hamilton, in these words: 'In our case the concurrence of thirteen distinct sovereign wills is requisite, under the Confederation, to the complete execution of every important measure that proceeds from the union.'[2]

The principle of organization upon which this American association of states was based was that of the subordination of the general government to the regional governments. It is illustrated by the degree to which the general government was authorized to operate upon the state governments only and not directly upon the people. When, after some experience of this form of association, it was decided that it was inadequate, a new form of association, based upon a different principle, was advocated and finally embodied in the Constitution of 1787. The difference between the present Constitution of the United States and the Articles of Confederation lies in the fact that the present Constitution replaces the principle of the general government being subordinate to the regional governments and dependent upon them, by the principle of the general and the regional govern-

---

[1] Printed in A. P. Newton, *Federal and Unified Constitutions* and H. S. Commager, *Documents of American History*.

[2] *The Federalist*, No. XV. Everyman Ed., p. 73.

ments being co-ordinate and independent in their respective spheres. The characteristic which we have discovered in the present American association of states is quite clearly a characteristic which distinguishes it from its predecessor.

3

We reach the same conclusion if we compare the Constitution of the United States with those of other associations, mentioned at the outset of this chapter, which are often grouped with it as examples of federal government. Consider first the Austro-Hungarian Empire under the *Ausgleich* or Compromise of 1867 which lasted until 1918.[1]

In 1867 Hungary, which had enjoyed very little autonomy in the Habsburg Empire, was granted a considerable measure of independence by the Emperor Francis Joseph, and a Dual Monarchy—the Empire of Austria and the Kingdom of Hungary—was established.[2] Three services common to Austria and Hungary were recognized in foreign policy, war, and the finance involved in administering these two. A minister common to both countries was to be appointed to control each of these services. These ministers were to be appointed by Francis Joseph as the Emperor of Austria and the King of Hungary—but they were to be responsible also to what were called the Delegations. The Delegations—or Imperial Representative Assembly—were two bodies of sixty members each, one chosen by the Austrian Parliament, the other by the Hungarian Parliament, two-thirds from the lower house and one-third from the upper. They were to be summoned by the Emperor to Vienna and Budapest alternately, to vote the common budget, which they were to discuss and vote upon separately, or, in case of disagreement, to vote in joint session without discussion. Other matters of common interest were to be arranged either between the Austrian and Hungarian cabinets or by special deputations. The Delegations did not make laws. Any legislation needed to give effect to the decisions was to be passed by the separate parliaments. On the legislative side, therefore, Austria-Hungary was no more than a league or confederation. Austria and Hungary acted as separate states with a common sovereign.[3] But on the administrative side, the possession of a common sovereign imported something of the marks of a unitary state. All ministers and officials and the whole military and naval establishment were responsible to the Emperor-King. The difference between this system and that of the

---

[1] Bryce calls it a federal government in his *Studies in History and Jurisprudence*, Vol. I, p. 393, note; but he does so rather as an afterthought.

[2] It is as well to say at once that the following short account of the Dual Monarchy is inevitably misleading. No summary can suggest the complications of the problem of government under the Habsburg Monarchy and it is the complications which were important. I have derived much help from two articles by R. W. Seton-Watson in *The Slavonic Year Book*, Vol. XIX. The reader may find assistance also from Wickham Steed, *The Habsburg Monarchy* and A. J. P. Taylor, *The Habsburg Monarchy, 1809–1918*. The great classic on the system is L. Eisenmann, *Le Compromis Austro-Hongrois*.

[3] There was no common citizenship, however.

United States is apparent. The Delegations never in fact met together, so that they were never a single assembly. They did not hold the actual legislative power. On the administrative side there was a mixture of controls. In so far as the ministers for the common services were controlled by the Delegations—and this control could not be considerable, because the Delegations met for a fortnight only in a year—the general government of Austria-Hungary was subordinate to the Austrian and Hungarian Parliaments. But in so far as the Emperor-King held and exercised the supreme executive power, the general and regional governments, unlike those of the United States, were not independent governments. The Austro-Hungarian Empire was at once a league and a unitary state; the United States is not.

The Constitution of the German Empire of 1871–1918 is often described as federal.[1] It also was formed upon a principle which is distinct from that embodied in the Constitution of the United States. The Empire of 1871[2] was an association of twenty-five states, varying in size from Prussia which had a population of 33 million down to Schaumburg-Lippe with 42,000. It was governed by an Emperor, a Council of the Confederation, and an Imperial Diet (Reichstag). On the legislative side the Council was the important body. It consisted of representatives of the governments of each of the associated states, varying in number from seventeen for Prussia to one for most of the other states. Although each representative had one vote, all the representatives from any given state had to vote as a single delegation, and in consequence were likely to be under close control by their governments. The Council was thus dependent upon the state governments and in particular upon one—that of Prussia. For Prussia not only held seventeen votes out of a total of fifty-eight, but the King of Prussia was the German Emperor, and the Prime Minister of Prussia was the Imperial Chancellor and President of the Council of the Confederation. Prussia's great strength and prestige enabled it to command the support of others. There was here none of that independence of general from regional governments which is the characteristic of the Constitution of the United States.

If the Austro-Hungarian Empire and the German Empire were organized upon the principle of a dependence of the general upon the regional governments, it does not need any argument to show that this principle was clearly embodied in the League of Nations. Indeed it is clear from a study of the Covenant of the League and from its practice[3] that it was a league of states not a league of nations, and its organs—the Council and the Assembly—were composed of repre-

---

[1] For example, Bryce, in his *Holy Roman Empire*, calls it a federation. But he says it is 'a Federal Monarchy, whose peculiar constitution makes it unlike all other monarchies and all other federations'. See Chapter XXIV. The Constitution is printed in Newton, op. cit.

[2] For accounts of the system see F. Kruger, *Government and Politics of Germany* (1915); A. L. Lowell, *Government and Politics of Continental Europe*, Vol. I, and K. Loewenstein in *Governments of Continental Europe* (1940), edited by J. T. Shotwell.

[3] See A. E. Zimmern, *The League of Nations and the Rule of Law*.

sentatives of the governments of the member states. A root principle in its organization was that decisions upon most matters of importance would not be binding upon a member without its own consent. Here was a degree of dependence upon the sovereign wills of the associated states which surpassed that of the Articles of Confederation of 1777, and the difference in principle between the Covenant of the League and the Constitution of the United States is correspondingly great.

The Constitution of the Union of South Africa,[1] as also that of the Republic which succeeded it in 1962,[2] embodies quite a different principle of association from those of the Articles of Confederation, the Austro-Hungarian Compromise, the German Imperial Constitution or the League Covenant, but it also is a principle which differs from that of the United States. In South Africa the regional governments are subordinate to the general government. When the self-governing colonies of the Cape, Natal, the Orange River and the Transvaal united in 1909, they established a parliament for the whole union and four elective councils, one for each of the uniting colonies, now provinces of the Union. These provincial councils were empowered to make ordinances on a list of subjects set out in the Constitution. The list included education (other than higher education), agriculture, hospitals, municipal institutions, roads and other matters of a local or private nature. But these ordinances were subject to the approval of the Union Government and they were valid only in so far as they did not conflict with an act of the Union Parliament. That parliament had power to override the provincial councils at any time, to increase or decrease their powers, or to abolish them altogether. And the position remained the same in the 1962 Constitution of the Republic of South Africa. There is clearly no question here of regional governments being co-ordinate with the general government as in the United States.

It is apparent, then, that there is found in the Constitution of the United States a principle of organization which distinguishes it as an association from those other associations of states so far discussed which are sometimes grouped with it as examples of federal government.

4

But to all this the practical man may say: It is clear enough that there is a difference between associations of states organized so that the general government is dependent upon the regional governments or vice versa and associations, like the United States, where the general

---

[1] The text will be found in Newton, op. cit. See also H. J. May, *The South African Constitution* a second edition of W. P. M. Kennedy and H. J. Schlosberg, *Law and Custom of the South African Constitution;* and H. R. Hahlo and E. Kahn, *South Africa, The Development of its Laws and Constitution.*

[2] See supplement, *The New Constitution* to Hahlo and Kahn, op. cit.

and regional governments are co-ordinate. But is it a difference of sufficient importance to justify us in placing the United States in a separate category among associations of states? Is not this just one of those distinctions which theorists draw and politicians ignore?

To this question the history of the United States itself suggests an answer. After experience from 1781[1] of a Constitution based upon one principle the practical men who were working the American government drew up in 1787 a Constitution based upon another principle.[2] They thought that the difference between the two principles was the difference between an inadequate, ineffective and unpractical government and a government capable of regulating the common concerns and preserving the general tranquillity of the United States. Three of them—Alexander Hamilton, later to be Secretary of the Treasury under President Washington, John Jay, first Chief Justice of the Supreme Court of the United States, and James Madison, later president of the United States—collaborated in 1787–8 in writing a series of public papers, the whole object of which was to convince people that the principle embodied in the Constitution of 1787 was one which was not only different from the principle embodied in the Articles of Confederation of 1777, but that the difference was so important that it contained in itself the only hope of good government for the American association of states. That is the whole argument of the papers, published as *The Federalist*. Whether they were right or wrong is not the question here. What their book illustrates is that they regarded the difference in principle of the Constitution of the United States as an important practical difference.

There is some evidence from the other side. The opponents of the Constitution of 1787, themselves also 'practical politicians', violently and often bitterly objected to the principle of the new Constitution. They preferred that of the old. They saw just as clearly as Hamilton and his colleagues that the difference in principle was of fundamental importance.[3] Nor did the struggle end with the adoption of the Constitution. A long controversy, which was not finally closed until after the Civil War of 1861–5, continued between those who regarded the general government as the agent of the states and those who maintained that it was or ought to be an independent government.[4] Indeed it took 'the terrible exercise of prolonged war', in Woodrow Wilson's phrase,[5] to resolve the conflict between the two principles. From the history of the United States alone, it would seem clear that the prin-

---

[1] It was in this year that the Articles of Confederation came into effect.

[2] The story may be read in A. C. McLaughlin, *Confederation and Constitution*; R. L. Schuyler, *The Constitution of the United States*, and C. Warren, *The Making of the Constitution*.

[3] The argument can be studied best in Max Farrand's *Records of the Federal Convention* (4 vols.).

[4] The greatest example of the controversy was the debate in the Senate in December 1829 and January 1830, between Senator Hayne of South Carolina, who supported the former view, and Daniel Webster who supported the latter. For Webster see Birley, *Speeches in American History*, Vol. II.

[5] *Epochs of American History: Division and Reunion, 1829–1889*, p. 254.

ciple embodied in the Constitution of 1787 is a distinct principle of association, that this distinction is a distinction with a difference, and that this difference is important.

The example of South Africa illustrates the same point. When the delegates from the four colonies met together in 1909 to frame a form of association, they discussed the principle upon which it should be established. There were some, chiefly from Natal, who advocated the principle of the United States. But it was deliberately rejected by the delegates of the other colonies who, rightly or wrongly, thought it an inferior principle to the one they chose, viz. subordination of the regional governments to the general government. These practical politicians saw the difference of principle involved and they thought it of practical importance.[1]

Or listen to this conversation. One morning in the early summer of 1911, five prime ministers sat round a table at the Foreign Office in London and discussed the best form of association for the self-governing portions of the British Empire. There had been a good deal of talk at that time about what was vaguely called 'Imperial Federation'. On this particular occasion, Sir Joseph Ward, Prime Minister of New Zealand, had initiated a discussion with a resolution that an Imperial Council of State should be set up advisory to the Imperial Government. We have a record of what was said.[2] These are extracts from it.[3]

Sir Joseph Ward: '. . . My opinion is that there ought to be established an Imperial Council or an Imperial Parliament of Defence, in the interests——'

Sir Wilfrid Laurier, Prime Minister of Canada: 'There is a difference between a council and a parliament. What do you propose, a parliament or a council? I want a proper definition of what you mean, because you have proposed neither so far.'

Sir Joseph Ward: 'I prefer to call it a Parliament of Defence. . . .'

Sir Wilfrid Laurier: 'But you say "Council". Is it a council, or is it a parliament? It is important we should know exactly what is the proposal. . . .'

Sir Joseph Ward: 'I prefer to call it a parliament. . . .'

Sir Wilfrid Laurier: 'Very good then; now we understand what you mean.'

Sir Joseph Ward: 'I prefer to call it a parliament, although I admit there is a good deal in the name.'

Sir Wilfrid Laurier: 'There is everything in the name.'

Mr. Fisher, Prime Minister of Australia: 'Would it not be as well to amend your resolution on these lines?'

---

[1] See, for example, E. A. Walker, *Lord de Villiers and his Times*, and Sir E. H. Walton, *The Inner History of the National Convention of South Africa*. The whole story is told in fascinating detail in L. M. Thompson, *The Unification of South Africa, 1902–1910*.

[2] *Minutes of Proceedings of the Imperial Conference*, 1911 (Cd. 5745), pp. 46 ff.

[3] Ibid., pp. 55 ff.

Sir Joseph Ward: 'No, I do not propose to amend it; if it is necessary afterwards I shall have no objection.'

Sir Wilfrid Laurier: 'You propose a council in your resolution, but you advocate a parliament.'

Sir Joseph Ward: 'You can call it a council if you like.'

Mr. Asquith, Prime Minister of the United Kingdom: 'We want to know what you call it.'

Sir Joseph Ward: 'It is a Parliament of Defence that I am suggesting. I have no objection to its being called by any suitable name. . . .'

General Botha, Prime Minister of South Africa:[1] 'How is such a Council to be appointed? Who will decide what matters are to come before it? What authority is to be vested in it? To what representative body is such a council to be responsible? These are only a few of the questions which crop up immediately, and it seems to me that no satisfactory reply can be given to them.'

Here again practical men stress the difference between a 'parliament' and a 'council', between a body with authority to decide and a body with authority to advise, between a general government and a general conference. And, said Sir Wilfrid Laurier, 'there is everything in the name.'

5

It seems justifiable to maintain, therefore, that the difference in principle between the form of association embodied in the modern Constitution of the United States and the other forms of association which have been discussed, is an important and a practical difference; so important, indeed, that it justifies us in placing the United States in a separate category among associations of states. And, further, since the United States is universally regarded as an example of federal government, it justifies us in describing the principle, which distinguishes it so markedly and so significantly, as the *federal principle*. By the federal principle I mean the method of dividing powers so that the general and regional governments are each, within a sphere, co-ordinate and independent.

This restriction of the word 'federal' to the sense just defined may be objected to by some students on historical grounds. They will point out, quite correctly, that the authors of *The Federalist*, for example, use the words 'federal' and 'federation' to describe both the system set up by the Articles of Confederation of 1777[2] and that proposed by the Constitution of 1787. The fact is that up to 1787 the word 'federal' signified little more than a league of states resting upon the good faith of the parties,[3] and it was the natural description of the Articles of

---

[1] Ibid., at p. 69.

[2] See the first sentence of *The Federalist*; 'After an unequivocal experience of the inefficiency of the subsisting federal government, you are called upon to deliberate on a new constitution for the United States of America.' Or the beginning of No. XXII—'the existing federal system'.

[3] Morison, *History of the United States*, Vol. I, p. 87.

Confederation. Indeed what the authors of *The Federalist* claimed for the Constitution of 1787 was not that it substituted a federation for a league but that it substituted an efficient federation for an inefficient federation. At the same time the new constitution which they supported established a government based, as they themselves asserted, upon a different and a novel principle, the principle of a division of powers between general and regional governments each independent within a sphere. And although, if the strict usage of the time had been followed, it would not have been called 'federal' at all,[1] it *was* called 'federal' and the government which it established upon this new principle was called 'federal'. As this government developed, the new principle became firmly established, and with the end of the Civil War in 1865 it became the accepted doctrine of the Constitution. The choice of the student is therefore to say one of two things. He may say that 'federal' has widened its meaning since 1787 so far that it includes both principles of association—that of 1777 and that of 1787. Or, he may say, as I do, that since these two principles are distinct and different principles, and that since the United States is nowdays generally regarded as a federal government, it is appropriate to confine the use of the term 'federal' to that principle embodied in the government of the United States under the Constitution of 1787. And perhaps there is something not unfitting in choosing as the federal principle that principle which the authors of *The Federalist* advocated; and in choosing it principally on the ground that the Constitution which embodied that principle and which they supported has by its success spread the fame of that principle in the world. For the federal principle has come to mean what it does because the United States has come to be what it is.

6

It is proper to add that this definition of the federal principle is not accepted as valid by all students of the subject. Some authorities find the essence of federalism in some different principle. There are those, for example, who hold that the federal principle consists in the division of power in such a way that the powers to be exercised by the general government are specified and the residue is left to the regional governments. It is not enough that general and regional governments should each be independent in its own sphere; that sphere must be marked out in a particular way. The residuary powers, as they are called, must lie with the regional governments. On this view a government is not federal if the powers of the regional governments are specified and the residue is left to the general government. By this

---

[1] Thus the opponents of the Constitution of 1787 are represented in *The Federalist* as saying that the Constitution does not propose a federation at all but a '*consolidation*' of states. The 'federal' form, they say, 'regards the Union as a Confederacy of sovereign states; instead of which, they have framed a national government which regards the Union as a consolidation of the states'. The authors of *The Federalist* do not accept this restriction of 'federal'. See No. XXXIX, Everyman ed., p. 192.

test the Constitution of the United States embodies the federal principle because it names certain subjects over which the general legislature has control and it provides that powers not so delegated to the general government remain with the states.

In my view this test of federalism concentrates on a relatively superficial characteristic of the American Constitution. The essential point is not that the division of powers is made in such a way that the regional governments are the residuary legatees under the Constitution, but that the division is made in such a way that, whoever has the residue, neither general nor regional government is subordinate to the other. It is true that the question where the residue of power is to rest is an important question in framing a federal government. It may affect the whole balance of power in a federation. It is likely also that when previously sovereign states federate, they will wish to hand over to the new general government certain specified, limited and enumerated powers only and will wish to keep the rest for themselves. They will not want to sign a blank cheque. But these points are not essential to the federal principle. They may be usual characteristics of governments which are federal, but they themselves do not make a government federal.

A similar sort of test for the federal principle was applied by Lord Haldane in the course of his judgement in the case of *Attorney-General for the Commonwealth of Australia v. Colonial Sugar Refining Company Ltd.* in 1914.[1] Then he said that the natural and literal interpretation of the word 'federal' confined its application to cases in which states, while agreeing on a measure of delegation of their powers to a common government, yet in the main continue to preserve their original constitutions. The word could only be used loosely, he thought, to describe states which agree to delegate their powers with a view to entirely new constitutions even of the states themselves. For this reason Lord Haldane declared that Canada was not a true federation because the British North America Act, 1867, created not only a new common government but also new provincial governments whose powers were confined exclusively to a list of subjects enumerated in Section 92 of the Act.[2] The United States and Australia on the other hand, he said, was truly federal, for the state governments, after the establishment of a common government, continued unaltered except in so far as they had surrendered certain specified and limited powers to the common government.

Here again, in my opinion, this criterion of the federal principle misses the important point. And the important point is whether the powers of government are divided between co-ordinate, independent authorities or not.[3] This division can be made either by marking off

---

[1] [1914] A.C. 237 at 252–4.
[2] Lord Haldane's views are criticized in Kennedy, *The Constitution of Canada*, Chapter XXIII.
[3] Kennedy, ibid., p. 412.

the powers of the general government and limiting it to them, and then saying that, with this exception, the regional constitutions are to go on as before and that the powers of the regional governments are limited to what is left; or the division can be made by marking off and limiting the powers of both general and regional governments and thus creating new constitutions for them all. Both methods can achieve the kind of division of powers which is characteristic, in my view, of the federal principle. Circumstances will decide which method is to be adopted.

A third definition of the federal principle is that which distinguishes it by saying that in a federal government both general and regional governments operate directly upon the people, whereas in a league or confederation it is the regional or state governments alone which operate directly upon the people; the general government operates only upon the regional governments.[1] This definition appears at first sight to get some support from the experiences of the United States. For it is true that one striking difference between the system under the Articles of Confederation of 1777 and that under the Constitution of 1787 was just this difference which has been mentioned. The authors of *The Federalist* laid stress upon it. 'The great and radical vice in the construction of the existing Confederation,' they wrote, 'is in the principle of *Legislation* for *States* or *Governments*, in their *Corporate* or *Collective Capacities*, and as contra distinguished from the *Individuals* of which they consist.'[2] The general government set up by the Constitution of 1787 was to operate directly upon the people just as did the regional governments.

Now there is no doubt that this difference in the mode of operation of the general government is a difference which distinguishes a federation from a league or confederation. But it is not sufficient in itself to distinguish a federation from some other forms of association. It does not distinguish the Constitution of the United States from, for example, the Constitution of the Union or of the Republic of South Africa, or of any other devolved or decentralized system. For in South Africa the general government and the provincial governments all operate directly upon the people, just as do the general and regional governments of the United States. Yet, as I have shown,[3] there is a difference between the two constitutions, the difference that in South Africa the regional governments are subordinate to the general government, and in the United States they are co-ordinate. This difference is what is fundamental, and this is the difference that provides the real distinction.

The point may be explained in this way. In a Constitution such as that of 1777, the general government is dependent to some degree

---

[1] Bryce uses this criterion in *Studies in History and Jurisprudence*, Vol. I, pp. 392, 408–9. J. S. Mill makes reference to it in *Representative Government*, c. XVII.
[2] *The Federalist*, No. XV (Hamilton).
[3] See above, p. 7.

upon the regional governments. One example or illustration of this dependence[1] was that the general government in some important matters did not operate directly upon the people but operated upon and through the regional governments only. But this fact is just an illustration of a deeper principle of organization, the principle of subordination of the general government to the regional governments. This is the fundamental and distinguishing characteristic of the confederation; the indirect operation of the general government is just an illustration of it. Similarly in the case of a federation, the fundamental principle is that general and regional governments are co-ordinate. The fact that both operate directly upon the people is an illustration of this principle, but it is not enough in itself to ensure that they are co-ordinate, as the example of South Africa shows. What is necessary for the federal principle is not merely that the general government, like the regional governments, should operate directly upon the people, but, further, that each government should be limited to its own sphere and, within that sphere, should be independent of the other.[2]

---

[1] See above, p. 4.

[2] My definition agrees substantially with the views of Freeman, *History of Federal Government in Greece and Italy*, p. 12; Jethro Brown, *Law Quarterly Review*, July 1914, p. 305; Kennedy, *Constitution of Canada*, e.g. pp. 407–8; Quick and Garran, *Annotated Constitution of the Australian Commonwealth*, p. 333; W. Harrison Moore, *Constitution of the Commonwealth of Australia* (2nd ed.), p. 68; Dicey, *Law of the Constitution* (9th ed.), Chapter 3, e.g. p. 144. Sir Robert Garran's short definition quoted in the *Report of the Royal Commission on the Australian Constitution* (1929) is perhaps the best there is: 'A form of government in which sovereignty or political power is divided between the central and the local governments, so that each of them within its own sphere is independent of the other.' (p. 230). Among criticisms of my definition which has appeared since the first edition of this book, the most constructive and fruitful are found in A. H. Birch, *Federalism, Finance and Social Legislation* (1955) and M. J. C. Vile, *The Structure of American Federalism* (1961). An exhausting dissection was undertaken by S. R. Davis in *Australian Journal of Politics and History*, Vol. I, No. 1.

Chapter II

FEDERAL CONSTITUTIONS AND FEDERAL GOVERNMENTS

1

THE federal principle has been defined rigidly in the preceding chapter. It may seem indeed that this approach to the study of federal government has been too academic. Yet the fact is that this principle, which is characteristic of the way in which the government of the United States is organized in its Constitution, is a distinct and different principle of organization and it is entitled to a distinct and different name. Whether I have been wise to allocate the name 'federal' to it is open to dispute. But I shall hope that the reasons already given are sufficiently persuasive to convince the student that this is a possible and practical definition.

If, then, the federal principle may be defined along the lines set out in the preceding chapter, what are we to mean by a federal constitution and a federal government? Are we to confine the terms to cases where the federal principle has been applied completely and without exception? It would not be sensible to do this. After all, the Constitution of the United States itself, as originally drawn up, contained at least one exception to the federal principle in that the Senate was composed of representatives selected by the legislatures of the states. Thus a part of the general government of the United States was dependent to some extent upon a part of the regional governments. This exception to the federal principle was maintained in law up to 1913. Yet the American Constitution from 1787 to 1913 was and must be called a 'federal Constitution'.[1] For the federal principle was predominant in it. That is the criterion. Is the federal principle predominant in the constitution? If so, that constitution may be called a 'federal constitution'. If, on the other hand, there are so many modifications in the application of the federal principle that it ceases to be of any significance, then the constitution cannot be termed federal. This appears to be the most instructive and reasonable way in which to use the term 'federal constitution'. It seems essential to define the federal principle rigidly, but to apply the term 'federal constitution' more widely.[2]

[1] See pp. 2–3 above.
[2] Freeman, in his *History of Federal Government in Greece and Italy*, adopted a similar method. His 'federal idea' (p. 3)—'the complete division of sovereignty', 'the government of the federation and the government of the state have a co-ordinate authority, each equally claiming allegiance within its own range' (p. 12)—is similar to my 'federal principle'. And he makes the same use of it. But he uses the term 'federal government' more loosely than I do. Too loosely, I think, even allowing for the fact that his approach is historical and therefore (as he says, p. 2) justifiably wider than that of the political scientist.

2

Adopting this method, then, which are the federal constitutions? The Constitution of the Commonwealth of Australia enacted in 1900 is perhaps the most obvious example, at any rate in the form in which it was originally enacted, before later amendments modified it.[1] The Australian Constitution established a government for the whole of Australia which, within a sphere, was enabled to exercise powers independently of the governments of the states; while the latter, within a sphere, were authorized to act independently of the government of the whole Commonwealth.[2] Neither state nor Commonwealth government acting alone could alter the scope of the other's power as laid down in the Constitution. In personnel as in powers both Commonwealth and state parliaments were to be independent of each other. Each was to be elected directly by the people. The respective cabinets were to be responsible each to its own parliament. Both Commonwealth and state parliaments were to be limited in their powers, but not by each other; they were to be co-ordinate with each other, but they were to be subordinate to the Constitution. And, while the Constitution of the United States had been silent on the point, the Constitution Act of Australia declared that the people of the associating colonies were to form a 'federal Commonwealth'. The Australian Constitution of 1900 was clearly an example of a federal constitution.

3

Two other examples—Switzerland and Canada—do not appear so obvious. The Swiss Constitution of 1848[3] follows the American Constitution in many respects. In two matters it contains a modification in the strict application of the federal principle. First of all it provides[4] that the upper house of the general legislature—the Council of States—shall be composed of two representatives from each of the cantons and that these representatives shall be paid by their cantons and their period of office and method of election shall be determined by their cantons. This admittedly creates a small degree of dependence, particularly as in some cases the cantonal representatives are elected by the cantonal councils themselves. But it will be appreciated that this degree of dependence does not prevent us from describing the Swiss Constitution as federal. For the extent of dependence is less than what was found in the Constitution of the United States up to 1913. For the Swiss Council of States, unlike the

[1] It is printed in, for example, A. P. Newton, *Federal and Unified Constitutions*, H. E. Egerton, *Federations and Unions in the British Empire*, and in an abridged form, in W. I. Jennings, *Constitutional Laws of the Commonwealth*, Vol. I. Reference to authorities on the Australian Constitution will be found in the select bibliography at the end of this book.
[2] The details of the allocation of powers are more complicated than this. See below, Chapter V.
[3] Printed in French in Newton, op. cit., and in English and German in Christopher Hughes, *The Federal Constitution of Switzerland* (1954). For further references see select bibliography at the end of this book.
[4] Arts. 80–83.

American Senate, is probably the least influential organ in the Swiss general government and, moreover, it is only a minority of the cantons which elect representatives through cantonal councils.[1]

The second modification upon the strict application of the federal principle in the Swiss Constitution tends in the direction of unitarianism, and not, as does the first, in the direction of control by the regions over the general government. The Swiss courts are required by the Constitution to treat all laws passed by the general legislature—the Federal Assembly—as valid, though they may declare cantonal laws to be void on the ground that they transgress the field allotted to the cantons in the Constitution. The result of this is that the general legislature might pass laws on cantonal subjects and these laws might go into effect and thus modify the distribution of powers between general and cantonal governments laid down in the Constitution. In the United States or Australia an attempt is made to prevent this by allowing the courts, when so invited, to declare that laws which are beyond the powers of the general or regional legislatures are void. Does this difference between the Swiss Constitution and those of the United States and Australia require us to say that the Swiss Constitution is not federal? I do not think so. We must admit that there is an omission in the Swiss Constitution so far as the machinery for giving effect to the application of the federal principle is concerned. But it does not follow from this that it was the intention of the framers of the Swiss Constitution that the general legislature should be permitted to make laws on any subject it chose. On the contrary its powers are carefully enumerated. And it does not have the last word legally. For the Swiss Constitution provides[2] a system of referendum whereby, on the demand of 30,000 voters or of eight cantons a law passed by the general legislature must be submitted to the people for approval. It is the people which has the last word as to whether a law of the general legislature shall go into effect.[3] It may be that this method of ensuring that the general government keeps within its own proper sphere is not completely effective, but it is clear that the principle on which the Swiss Constitution is drawn up is that there is a sphere allotted to general and regional governments respectively, and that they are expected to keep within that sphere, and that neither is to have the last word in deciding the extent of that sphere.

4

The case of Canada is more difficult. The Canadian Constitution—the British North America Act, 1867, and certain subsequent

---

[1] Four cantons use this method—Berne, Fribourg, St. Gallen, and Neuchâtel—and nll except Fribourg prescribe one year as the term of office. Fribourg prescribes four years. This is the usual term in most of the cantons where direct election by the people is employed, though a few prescribe three.

[2] Art. 89.

[3] This does not apply to federal resolutions (arrêtés), a common mode of legislation, which to a large extent can be withheld from referendum.

amending acts—divides the powers between provincial and Dominion legislatures in such a way that the provinces have exclusive legislative control over a list of enumerated subjects, and the Dominion has exclusive legislative control over the rest, which, 'for greater clarity', were enumerated also, though not exhaustively. The legislatures of Dominion and provinces are distinct in personnel from each other; neither has power to alter the Constitution so far as the distribution of powers is concerned. That power belongs to the United Kingdom parliament alone. The Courts may be invited to declare Dominion or provincial laws void on the ground that they transgress the field allotted to the respective legislatures by the Constitution. So far the federal principle is rigidly applied. But there are certain important exceptions. The executive of the Dominion has power to disallow any Act passed by a provincial legislature, whether or not the act deals with subjects falling within the legislative field exclusively assigned to the provinces. Further the Dominion executive appoints the Lieutenant-Governor of a province, that is, the formal head of the provincial government. It can instruct the Lieutenant-Governor to withhold his assent from provincial bills and to reserve them for consideration by the Dominion executive, and it may refuse assent to such reserved bills if it thinks fit. Finally, appointments to all the important judicial posts in the provinces are in the hands of the Dominion executive. These are all unitary elements in an otherwise strictly federal form of constitution. They are matters in which the regional governments are subordinate to the general government, and not co-ordinate with it.

These are substantial modifications of the federal principle. Consider the powers of disallowance and of veto alone. They mean that, as a matter of law, the Dominion executive could prevent a provincial legislature from making laws upon its own allotted subjects, if the Dominion executive happened to disapprove the policy involved in the laws. The powers of disallowance and veto are quite unrestricted in law.[1] They extend to financial legislation as much as to any other. The Dominion executive could prevent a province from raising revenue or spending money if it disapproved of its financial legislation. Could there be a more powerful weapon for centralizing and unifying the government than this? It is true that the Dominion parliament cannot itself legislate upon provincial subjects; it can only prevent the provincial legislature from doing so. In this respect the Canadian Constitution differs from that, for example, of South Africa, where not only may the executive of the Republic veto provincial ordinances but the parliament of the Republic can itself also legislate upon provincial matters. The federal principle is not completely ousted, therefore, from the Canadian Constitution. It does

---

[1] This had been disputed but was settled by the Supreme Court of Canada in 1938 by their decision in *In re Disallowance and Reservation* (1938), S.C.R. 71.

find a place there and an importance place. Yet if we confine our-
selves to the strict law of the constitution, it is hard to know
whether we should call it a federal constitution with considerable unitary modifications, or a unitary constitution with considerable federal
modifications. It would be straining the federal principle too far, I
think, to describe it as a federal constitution, without adding any
qualifying phrase. For this reason I prefer to say that Canada has a
quasi-federal constitution.

But the matter cannot be left at that. The law of the constitution is
one thing; the practice is another. What do these unitary elements
amount to in practice? The power of disallowance has not been a
dead letter, but at the same time it has been used sparingly.[1] Sometimes the Dominion executive has taken the view that disallowance
should not be used unless a provincial act is obviously *ultra vires*.
So exercised it could become part of the machinery to ensure observance of the federal principle in the Constitution. However, as this
function can be performed by the Courts in Canada, and as they are
less likely to be interested parties than the Dominion executive, it
would be better to leave questions of *ultra vires* to them. But the use
of the power of disallowance has not been confined to cases where a
provincial act was thought to be *ultra vires*. It had been used also to
nullify legislation of which the Dominion executive did not approve.
The power of veto has been similarly used to destroy provincial bills.
As late as 1937 both disallowance and veto were used by the Dominion to destroy legislation by the province of Alberta where a 'social
credit' government of unorthodox economic views was in power.

The powers of disallowance and veto, therefore, are not dead.
But it is clear that the Dominion executive is careful not to use
them frequently. Such use would be most unpopular among the
people of Canada who desire to be left alone in the exercise of their
own provincial powers. So far these legal powers which might turn
Canada into a unitary state have been subordinated to the federal
principle in practice.

Constitutional custom goes further. It is true that the law of the
Constitution empowers the Dominion executive to appoint the
Lieutenant-Governor of a province and that by law the Lieutenant-
Governor appoints the ministers of the province. But by convention
the system of cabinet government prevails in the Dominion and
provinces of Canada. The Lieutenant-Governor is bound by the
convention that he must appoint as his ministers only such persons
as can command a majority in the provincial legislature.[2] 'It is the

---

[1] For an account of the way in which the powers have been exercised see W. P. M. Kennedy,
The Constitution of Canada, Chapter XXIII, E. Forsey, *Canadian Journal of Economics and
Political Science* (1938), Vol. IV, pp. 47 ff.; Harlow J. Heneman, *American Political Science
Review* (1937), No. 1; *Report of the Royal Commission on Dominion-Provincial Relations*
(referred to hereafter as the *Rowell-Sirois Report*), Book I, pp. 49, 253–4. And see below, pp.
224–5.

[2] On this topic see John T. Saywell, *The Office of Lieutenant-Governor* (1957).

provincial legislature and electorate which decide who shall form the effective executive government of the province; and the Dominion executive must accept their choice. Similarly, although the Dominion executive appoints the principal provincial judges, it has exercised these powers with discretion and has not attempted to pack the courts with partisans opposed to provincial powers. The fact is that Canada is politically federal and that no Dominion government which attempted to stress the unitary elements in the Canadian Constitution at the expense of the federal elements would survive.

From what has been said, it seems justifiable to conclude that although the Canadian Constitution is quasi-federal in law, it is predominantly federal in practice. Or, to put it another way, although Canada has not a federal constitution, it has a federal government.

5

This distinction is important. For it must be stressed that if we are looking for examples of federal government, it is not sufficient to look at constitutions only. What matters just as much is the practice of government. A country may have a federal constitution, but in practice it may work that constitution in such a way that its government is not federal. Or a country with a non-federal constitution may work it in such a way that it provides an example of federal government. The experience of Canada has illustrated this. Its constitution is, as a matter of law, not completely federal; it is quasi-federal. But its constitution in practice, its system of government, is federal predominantly. For the student of the working of federal government, it is obvious that the practice of the constitution is more important almost than the law of the constitution. It is usually convenient to begin with the law, as a basis of classification. But before a country with a federal constitution can be regarded as providing an example of federal government, the practice of the constitution must be discovered. It is for this reason that I have headed this chapter not 'Federal Constitutions' only, but 'Federal Constitutions and Federal Governments'. And as it is the working of federal government which I propose to study, it will follow that it is those countries which provide examples of federal government and not those which provide examples of federal constitutions merely that will be considered in later chapters.

This consideration of law and practice leads me to describe Canada as an example of federal government, although its constitution is only quasi-federal. I regard the United States, Switzerland and Australia as examples of countries with federal constitutions and federal governments, although in the case of Australia, as will be seen in later chapters, tendencies are at work which may make it necessary soon to describe its constitution and its government as quasi-federal.

But here it would seem that the list ends. The remaining examples that come to mind seem to be cases of countries which have either federal constitutions but not federal governments, or quasi-federal constitutions but not federal governments, or constitutions and governments which are not federal at all. Something must be said of these examples, however, to justify the classification that has been asserted.

6

Some Latin-American states provide us with examples of federal constitutions. There is the Brazilian Constitution of 1891[1] in which the federal principle is embodied predominantly. Powers are divided between general and state legislatures. Some matters are given to the general legislature exclusively, a few to both general and state legislatures concurrently, and the rest remain with the states. The general legislature is composed of two houses both elected directly, the Senate containing, as in the United States of America, an equal number of representatives for each state and the Chamber of Deputies representing the states in proportion to their population. But in spite of much that is federal there is one provision in the Constitution which seems to me to destroy almost all its federal character and that is the process of amendment.[2] For the Constitution can be amended by the general legislature provided that it is approved by two-thirds majorities in both chambers in two successive years. This would seem to place the regional governments at the mercy of the general legislature. There is, it is true, a safeguard in the Constitution that 'bills having for their object the abolition of the federal republican form of government, or of the equal representation of the states in the Senate, cannot be introduced for discussion into the Congress.'[3] Perhaps this safeguard might be thought to compensate for the unitary elements in the amending power. But whether we are to call the Brazilian Constitution of 1891 a federal constitution or not, there seems to be general agreement among students of its working that in practice its federal aspects were usually neglected.[4] Centralization has usually predominated over federalism,[5] or there have been intervals of internal dissension among certain of the states, when the general government was weakened and when actual civil war has occurred. Brazil does not provide a working example of federal government.

[1] It remained in force until the revolution of 1930. Iti s printed in Newton, op. cit. The best treatment in English is H. G. James, *The Constitutional System of Brazil* (Washington, 1923). In 1934, 1937 and 1946 new constitutions were promulgated, each less federal than its predecessor. The Constitution of 1946 is printed in R. H. Fitzgibbon (ed.), *The Constitutions of the Americas*.
[2] Art. 90.
[3] Art. 46.
[4] This is the opinion, for example, of P. A. Martin writing on 'Federalism in Brazil' in *The Constitution Re-considered* (ed. Conyers Read); and Frank Tannenbaum in *Political Science Quarterly*, Vol. LVIII, September 1943.
[5] This is the thesis of Ernest Hambloch, *His Majesty the President, a Study of Constitutional Brazil* (London, 1935) and, allowing for his exaggeration, his case seems established.

The Argentine Constitution of 1853 was a federal constitution.[1] The upper house of the general legislature was admittedly elected by the legislatures of the constituent provinces, but apart from this the federal principle was generally embodied. Amendment of the Constitution, though initiated by the general legislature, was vested in a convention called for the purpose.[2] But here again the federal principle was not applied substantially in practice. Intervention of the general government in the affairs of the regional governments was common and has been described as one of the abuses of Argentine political practice. On the whole Argentina provides an example of decentralized government, not of federal government.[3]

The Mexican Constitution which was adopted in 1857 and re-enacted with amendments in 1917, embodies the federal principle to a similar degree. It is based largely on the Constitution of the United States. Yet Mexico provides little for our purpose. A recent student writes that 'Federalism has never existed in fact in Mexico. It is an undisputable commonplace that the Mexican nation is now and always has been federal in theory only; actually it has always been centralistic'.[4] The federal principle is embodied to a substantial degree in the Venezuelan Constitution of 1936. Yet in Venezuela also we get little evidence of the working of a federal government.[5]

In practice, then, these republics of South America have oscillated between periods of centralization, under a strong executive, and of regional independence when the claims of the general government are largely ignored. The federal system has not found the conditions necessary for its firm establishment in the Latin-American republics.[6]

The Constitution of the Austrian Republic of 1920 was federal. It introduced some interesting variations into the method of allotting powers as between general and regional governments. There was a fourfold division.[7] Legislative and executive powers in some matters were vested in the general government; for certain other matters legislative power only was with the general government, while executive power was with the provinces; in other matters again, legislative power in respect of principles was vested in the general government, and the enactment of executive decrees and executive power was vested in the provinces. For the remaining unenumerated matters, legislative and executive power remained with the provinces. An examination of the subjects thus allotted shows that few matters of

[1] See S. P. Amadeo, *Argentine Constitutional Law*, a study in the application of judicial review in Argentina.
[2] Art. 30.
[3] C. H. Haring in *The Constitution Re-considered* (ed. Conyers Read). See also A. Kirkpatrick, *History of the Argentine Republic*.
[4] J. Lloyd Mecham on 'The Origins of Federalism in Mexico' in *The Constitution Re-considered*.
[5] C. H. Haring, loc. cit. A new constitution was adopted in 1947.
[6] See, for example, Frank Tannenbaum, loc. cit.; H. G. James and P. A. Martin, *The Republics of Latin America* (1923) and A. F. Macdonald, *Latin American Politics and Government* (1949). The reasons for the failure are not fully understood.
[7] Arts. 10–15.

importance are left for the independent control of the provinces. In most matters they are agents and subordinates of the general government. And in the distribution of financial powers the general government also had the greater share. There was a sphere, it is true, where the federal principle applied and to this extent Austria had a federal constitution. But this sphere was so small, and, after a constitutional amendment of 1929, so insignificant, that there was little experience to be discovered from Austria of the working of federal government.[1]

7

It is more difficult to express an opinion about the Constitution of the German Republic—the Weimar Constitution of 1919–33—and the Constitution of the U.S.S.R. of 1936.

The Weimar Constitution[2] embodied the federal principle to some extent. There was a division of subjects between general and state legislatures, with the residuary powers passing to the states. Some subjects like foreign affairs, defence and customs were given to the general legislature exclusively; others were given to general and regional legislatures concurrently but with the proviso that general prevailed over regional legislation in case of conflict. There was a Supreme Court to settle constitutional disputes between general and state legislatures. But there were modifications. There was one which suggested a control of the states over the general legislature. It was provided that the upper house, the Reichsrat, was to be composed of representatives of the states, appointed by the state governments. This was similar to the provisions of the Imperial Constitution of 1871. But in this case the control amounted to very little, for in the Weimar Constitution, unlike that of 1871, the Reichsrat was the less important house. It was in the Reichstag, elected by the universal suffrage of the people, that the chief power lay. Moreover, the representatives of the states were allowed to vote freely and were not required, as in the Constitution of 1871, to vote as a single delegation. This modification of the federal principle would not of itself prevent us from describing the Weimar Constitution as federal.

Nor need a second modification, which placed the power of amending the Constitution in the hands of the general legislature acting alone. For when we consider that the Reichsrat was composed of representatives of the governments of the states, and when we discover also that the Constitution provided that the Reichsrat, if it disagreed with the Reichstag on a proposal for constitutional amendment, could force a submission of the proposed amendment to a referendum of the people, we can see that the states had some control over the amending process.

[1] See Mary MacDonald, *The Republic of Austria, 1918–1934*, espec. pp. 30–38 56–58. The Constitution is printed in an appendix.
[2] It is printed in Newton, op. cit.

But there are two other aspects of the Constitution which seem to embody a more serious modification. There are, firstly, the provisions governing the financial relations of the general and state governments.[1] From a reading of these provisions it would appear that it is legally within the power of the general legislature to determine what the financial resources of the states are to be and in fact to control their whole means of independent existence. This is a great modification of the federal principle. In the second place the scope of the powers conferred upon the general legislature is so wide that it is difficult to see what topics of any importance are left to the regional governments, if the general legislature chose to exercise its powers to the full. For whenever it did pass a law within its sphere of operation that law overrode state law in so far as they conflicted.[2]

Of the Weimar Constitution it is hard to say whether it is quasi-federal, like the Canadian Constitution, or not federal at all but highly decentralized, like the South African Constitution.[3] But if the Constitution of the German Republic was quasi-federal, what of the government? Here the answer seems clear. The practice of the general government was progressively unitary. The financial powers alone provide a good example of this. They were used to bring state finance under the control of the general government. The states were soon made dependent.[4] The Weimar republic does not provide us with an example of federal government.[5]

The Constitution of the U.S.S.R. of 1936[6] seems to merit a similar description. It is quasi-federal. It contains a division of powers between the All-Union government and the governments of the constituent republics. But the power of amending the Constitution is vested in the general legislature, the Supreme Soviet of the whole Union, both houses of which are elected by the people, though the upper house is organized to represent constituent republics and the lower according to population. This modification is perhaps by itself conclusive in allocating the Constitution to the class of quasi-federal. But Article 19 contains what appears to me a decisive provision. It declares that the powers of the All-Union authorities include the 'confirmation of the unified state budget of the U.S.S.R. as well as of the taxes and revenues which go to form the All-Union, the republic and the local budgets'. Here is an assertion in law that, in respect of finance, the regional governments are subordinate to the general government, not co-ordinate with it.

[1] Arts. 8 and 11.
[2] Art. 13.
[3] The same may be said of the Constitution of the Federal Republic of Germany, 1949.
[4] See an article by Mabel Newcomer on 'Fiscal Relations of Central and Local Governments in Germany under the Weimar Constitution' in *Political Science Quarterly*, Vol. LI, No. 2.
[5] See two articles on 'German Political Institutions' by Lindsay Rogers and others in *Political Science Quarterly*, Vol. XLVII, Nos. 3 and 4; F. A. Ogg, *The Governments of Europe*; and K. Loewenstein in *The Governments of Continental Europe* (ed. Shotwell).
[6] It is printed in S. and B. Webb, *Soviet Communism*.

And finally, Article 14 gives to the All-Union legislature such comprehensive powers over almost all spheres of life that it leaves little to the constituent republics, if the All-Union chooses to exercise them to the full. Nor do the amendments made in the Constitution in 1944, by which the constituent republics were given powers in respect of military affairs and foreign relations, make a substantial alteration in the legal position. For although it was enacted that 'each Union republic has its republican military formations'[1] and that the republican supreme soviets had the right to 'establish the procedure of the creation of military formations of the Union republics',[2] it was also enacted at the same time that the Supreme Soviet of the Union had exclusive jurisdiction over 'the establishment of the directing principles of military formations in the Union Republics'.[3] Thus the grant of power to the regions was accompanied by an assertion of the directing and overriding power of the general government. Similarly, in the case of foreign relations, while it is enacted that 'each Union republic has the right to enter into direct relations with foreign states, conclude agreements with them, and exchange diplomatic and consular representatives with them',[4] it is also enacted that the All-Union government has exclusive authority to regulate 'the establishment of the general character of relations between the Union republics and other states'.[5] There is no doubt of the reality of the grant of power to the regions in these amendments, but it is a grant upon the principle of decentralization, of delegation from the centre, and not upon the federal principle. The general government remains potentially supreme in military and foreign affairs.

The best way in which to make allowance for these factors and at the same time to recognize the fact that the federal principle does find a place in the Constitution of the U.S.S.R. is to describe it as quasi-federal.

But here again, as in the case of the Weimar Republic, there is an example of a quasi-federal constitution, but is there an example of federal government? It is not easy to give a reliable answer. The workings of Russian government are not easily understood by students from outside. In particular, satisfactory information upon the working of the *federal* aspects of the Constitution of 1936 has been practically unobtainable. There are many, also, who approach the study of Russian government in a spirit of such enthusiasm that they refuse to believe that the practice of the Constitution of 1936 could be different from its law. The Constitution describes itself as federal and it envisages a federal government. To deny therefore or even to doubt that the Russian government is federal in practice is, in the eyes of such enthusiasts, to brand oneself as anti-Russian. Yet it seems quite probable that the U.S.S.R. does not provide an example

---

[1] Art. 18 (b).   [2] Art. 60 (e).
[3] An addendum to Art. 14 (g).   [4] Art. 18 (a).
[5] An addendum to Art. 14 (a).

of federal government, but of highly decentralized government. If the full powers conferred by Article 14 of the Constitution upon the All-Union Government are exercised in practice—and there seems every reason why they should be—very little of the federal principle remains in the government of the U.S.S.R. The Constitution of 1936 has had little chance to operate under normal conditions. The demands of war and preparation for war have made the predominance of the All-Union Government inevitable. For these reasons I do not propose to consider the U.S.S.R. in subsequent chapters as an example of the working of federal government.

8

After the end of the Second World War, federalism became fashionable, particularly in the British Commonwealth, as a means of solving or softening the problems of government of countries attaining or about to attain their independence. How far the federal features in these constitutions and governments justify us in calling them federal constitutions or federal governments, however, is not easy to say.

In the Basic Law of Western Germany which was adopted in 1949 and came into effect in 1950 there are certainly federal elements, but they are associated with certain other elements, familiar from the earlier German constitutions, which make it fairly clear that Western Germany has a 'quasi-federal' Constitution. The powers given to the general legislature in the exclusive list and potentially in the concurrent list cover almost all subjects of importance. Administration of the law, it is true, is very largely in the hands of the regions (Länder) but the general government has extensive powers to direct and supervise the regional governments in the execution of the laws of the general legislature. The regional governments are represented in the Bundesrat, the upper house of the general legislature, by delegates appointed by the executive governments of the Länder and subject to instruction, recall and replacement by these governments. The lower house, the Bundestag, represents the people as a whole. The general legislature is therefore, in some degree, dependent upon the governments of the regions. The powers of the upper house are by no means negligible, and include the power to veto constitutional amendments. The regions, therefore, in the West German system, have an important influence on the working of the general government of the country but it is difficult to say that they exercise that influence through a strictly federal system, at any rate as that system has been known and worked in the United States, Switzerland, Canada and Australia.

The Constitution of the Republic of India which came into force on January 26, 1950 has federal features though it does not in fact claim that it establishes a federal union. There is, however, a division of legislative powers between the parliament of the Union and the parliaments of the states and this division can only be altered with the agreement both of the parliament of the union and the parliaments of not less than one-half of the constituent states. On the other hand the powers granted in the exclusive Union list and in the concurrent list cover, as in Western Germany, almost all subjects of importance and what is left to the exclusive authority of the states tends to be of subordinate concern. What makes one doubt that the Constitution of India is strictly and fully federal, however, are the powers of intervention in the affairs of the states given by the Constitution to the central government and parliament.

To begin with, the parliament of India may form new states; it may increase or diminish the area of any state and it may alter the boundaries or name of any state.[1] It is true that a bill to alter the area or boundaries or name of any state may not be introduced until the legislature of that state has had an opportunity of expressing its views thereon, but in contrast, for example, with the constitutions of of the United States[2] and of Australia[3], the *consent* of the legislature of the state is not required. The very existence of the states depends, therefore, on the parliament of the Union.

There are also important emergency provisions[4] which enable the government and parliament of the Union to convert the union into a unitary state if it believes that the situation warrants it. The President of India may, if he is satisfied that a grave emergency exists whereby the security of India or any part of it is threatened, whether by war or external aggression or internal disturbance, issue a proclamation to this effect. Such a proclamation expires after two months unless it is approved by the parliament of the Union. The effect of the proclamation is to give the executive of the Union power to control the executives of the states and the parliament of the Union power to legislate upon any matter irrespective of whether it is within the competence of the states.

The President of the Union has powers also, if he is satisfied that the government of a state cannot be carried on in accordance with the provisions of the Constitution, to direct that the government of the state be, in effect, taken over by the executive and parliament of the Union. And there are in addition other similar powers of intervention and direction in the Constitution which reduce the independence of the states. It seems clear that, after allowing for the federal features of the Indian Union, it can only be concluded that the Constitution is quasi-federal.[5]

What of the government itself? Is it in practice, so far, federal or not? It is to be noted that the powers of reorganization and intervention possessed by the Union have been exercised in practice. The

---

[1] Art. 3.   [2] Art. IV, 3.   [3] Section 124.   [4] Arts. 249, 352–60, and 371.
[5] See D. N. Banerjee, *Some Aspects of the Indian Constitution*, espec. Chapter IV.

state of Andhra was created in 1953, state boundaries were reorganized primarily on linguistic lines in 1956, and the state of Bombay was divided, again on linguistic lines, in 1960. It is true that these changes were the result of strong regional pressure and were not imposed by the central authority of its own volition. But it need not always be so. Intervention by the Union to suspend the government of a state occurred in Assam in 1958 and in Kerala in 1959. When China invaded India in 1962 a proclamation of emergency was issued by the President and approved by the parliament of the Union. Though it is difficult to assess the position, it seems reasonable to conclude that in practice the government, like the Constitution of India is quasi-federal, not strictly federal. To say this is not, of course, to suggest a criticism of the Constitution or the government. A quasi-federal system may well be most appropriate for India.

The Constitution of Rhodesia and Nyasaland, formed in 1953 of the three territories of Southern Rhodesia, Northern Rhodesia and Nyasaland, was federal and the system worked in practice also as a federal government. The powers given to the parliament of the federation, either exclusively or potentially, were considerable, but some significant powers remained with the three territories whose existence in no way depended upon the will of the general government. The difficulties which the federation encountered in the ten years of its existence arose not from the fact that it was a federal union but from the fact of its being a union at all. The African population was unwilling to be associated with a union in which political power was concentrated in the hands of the European inhabitants of the territories. As a result the political history of the federation was concerned with the struggle for power between African nationalists and Europeans, and provided little material for the study of the normal working of a federal system.

In 1957 two unions which claimed to be federal were established in the British Commonwealth. The Constitution of the West Indies was strictly federal. Its most striking characteristic, perhaps, was the smallness of the powers granted to the general parliament, in particular in the financial field, where, for example, it was denied the power effectively to levy customs duties or a general income tax. In practice, as in law, the general government proved weak, and the West Indies provided, in the short history of its existence until it was dissolved in 1962, an example almost of confederate government rather than of even quasi-federal government. Of the West Indies, as indeed of Rhodesia and Nyasaland, we can say that we may learn something about when federal government is appropriate and what are the prerequisites of successful federal government, but we can learn practically nothing about the actual working of a federal government.

The Federation of Malaya, also established in 1957, has had a longer life and contemplates adding further territories to itself. The Constitution resembles that of India in containing emergency provisions[1] which permit the federal system to be converted temporarily into a unitary system if the general government and the parliament are satisfied that a grave emergency exists whereby the security or economic life of the federation or any part of it is threatened, whether by war or external aggression or internal disturbance. These provisions have been invoked on more than one occasion. Added to this the list of powers given to the general parliament exclusively is very great, though it must be added that those given to the states exclusively, particularly Muslim law, Malay custom and land are important. On the whole, however, it must be suggested that the Constitution and the government of Malaya come nearer to being quasi-federal rather than strictly federal.

The Nigerian Constitution of 1960 purports to establish a federation and it clearly bears many of the characteristics of that system. Here again, however, emergency powers are given to the parliament of Nigeria which, when invoked, suspend the division of legislative powers between the general and regional governments.[2] As exercised in 1961, for example, they led to the suspension of the government of the Western Region and its direct administration under the general government. Apart from emergencies, however, the Nigerian Constitution grants very considerable powers to the regions and safeguards their powers and function in the normal working of the system of government. It is too soon yet to judge whether, in practice, Nigeria will provide an example of federal government or not. Its short history so far has illustrated the strength of the emergency provisions more than the strength of federalism.

9

Of other constitutions which have described themselves or have been described as federal, some words must be said. It will be clear from the discussion in the preceding chapter that I do not regard the federal principle as present to a sufficient degree in the Articles of Confederation of the United States of 1777, in the Austro-Hungarian Compromise of 1867, in the German Imperial Constitution of 1871, or in the Covenant of the League of Nations, to give them the name federal. Nor in the practical working of these constitutions was federal government produced. The predominant principle in practice as in theory was the subordination of the general governments to the regional governments or, in the case of Germany, to one regional government, the Prussian. The same must be said of the Charter of U.N.O.; of the Swiss Constitution before 1848;[3] of the German

[1] Art. 149–150. [2] Art. 65, 66, 80.

[3] See W. E. Rappard, *La Constitution fédérale de la Suisse, 1848–1948*, Chapters 1–7. Newton, op. cit., prints the text of earlier Swiss Constitutions.

Constitution from 1815 to 1867; of the North German Confederation of 1867–71 ;[1] and of the United Netherlands.

Of this latter something must be said, perhaps, if only out of respect to Freeman who described it as a federal government in his *History of Federal Government in Greece and Italy*, although he admits that its claim is doubtful. Indeed his chief reason for including it is, as he says, 'the important place which the United Provinces once filled in European history, and the curious and instructive nature of their political institutions. . . .' The Constitution of the United Netherlands is found in the Union of Utrecht of 1579.[1] In it the associating provinces declared that they were 'allied, confederated and united together forever to remain in every way and manner as if all were but one single province. . . .' This suggests the establishment of a strong, independent general government, but a closer examination of the document does not support it. The States-General of the United Netherlands was composed of representatives from the Estates of each province; each delegation had one vote and it was closely controlled by the appointing body. The general government was therefore not distinct in personnel from the provincial governments. The control went further. For although, according to the words of the Union of Utrecht, the States-General had exclusive control over foreign affairs and the military and naval affairs of the Union, and although it appointed ambassadors, the Captain-General of the Union, and other important officials, and exercised a strong supervision over finance, yet in all important decisions upon matters of peace or war, treaties and finance, the common advice and consent of all the seven provinces was needed. 'A single province, however small, could, by obstinate opposition, block the way to the acceptance of any given proposal.' In consequence the States-General with all its powers 'possessed only a derived, not an inherent authority'. It was in reality 'a gathering of deputations from the seven sovereign provinces'.[3] The principle upon which this association was formed was clearly that of the dependence of the general government upon the regional governments. It found its successor in the United States, not in the present Constitution of 1787 but in the Articles of Confederation of 1777, which resemble the Union of Utrecht very closely.[4]

It will also be apparent from what has been said already that the constitution and government of the Union of South Africa may not be called federal. The principle embodied in the Union is that of the

---

[1] There are short accounts of German developments in Bryce, *The Holy Roman Empire*; K. Loewenstein in *The Governments of Continental Europe* (ed. Shotwell); A. L. Lowell, *Governments and Parties of Continental Europe*, Vol. I.

[2] Printed in translation in Newton, op. cit.

[3] Edmundson, *History of Holland*, p. 112. A similar account is given in *The Federalist*. No. XX. The reader who is interested will find it worth while to look at Sir William Temple's *Observations on the United Provinces* (1673).

[4] Cf. the words quoted from *The Federalist* on p. 4 above.

subordination of the regional governments to the general government. Although the provinces are interfered with as little as possible, the powers of supervision are exercised when necessary, and the whole existence of the provinces depends on the good will of the Union Parliament. Similarly, the Constitution of India of 1919 and the government it established were not federal.[3] Under its terms the provinces of British India were given powers by the general government, with the consent of the Secretary of State for India and the two houses of the British parliament, to legislate upon a list of subjects of considerable variety and extent. But these powers were to be exercised subject to the supremacy of the legislature of the general government. And, to take a final example, the relation between the parliament of the United Kingdom and that of Northern Ireland cannot be described as federal. It is true that the people of Northern Ireland are subject to two governments, one at Stormont, near Belfast, the other at Westminster, just as people in an American state are subject to two governments. But the two governments for Northern Ireland are not co-ordinate. Although the Government of Ireland Act, 1920—which contains the Constitution of Northern Ireland—says that the parliament of Northern Ireland has powers to make laws for the peace, order and good government of Northern Ireland except in respect of certain enumerated subjects like defence, external affairs, customs duties and the succession to the throne, it goes on to say also: 'Notwithstanding the establishment of the parliament of Northern Ireland . . . or anything contained in this Act, the supreme authority of the parliament of the United Kingdom shall remain unaffected and undiminished over all persons, matters and things in Ireland and every part thereof.' There is nothing in law to prevent the parliament of the United Kingdom from passing laws for Northern Ireland not merely on the specified reserved subjects, but on any subject whatever. Moreover, the parliament of Northern Ireland received its powers from the parliament of the United Kingdom, and the latter can reduce or increase or abolish these powers. Finally, laws passed by the parliament of Northern Ireland, even although they are within the powers of that parliament and have received the assent of the Governor, can be disallowed and rendered of no effect by the Home Secretary of the United Kingdom. Of these two governments in the United Kingdom, one only can be described as independent and that is the government at Westminster. The government at Stormont is a dependent government. There remains the fact that the government of the United Kingdom is also the government of Great Britain, whereas if the federal principle is to be strictly applied, the government of Great Britain should be separate and independent. And thus although great consideration is shown to Northern Ireland and no

---

[1] See R. Coupland, *The Indian Problem* and the *Report of East Indian Statutory Commission*, 1930 (Simon Report), Vol. I.

interference in provincial affairs occurs unless absolutely necessary, there is here no example of federal government.[1]

10

If it is agreed that these governments do not embody the federal principle but are organized on principles which are distinct from the federal principle, it is proper to ask what name should be given to these principles.

That form of association between states in which the general government is dependent upon the regional governments has often been described as a 'confederation' and the principle of its organization 'the confederate principle'. This is in many ways an unsatisfactory description. The terms resemble 'federation' and 'federal' too closely for the distinction to be obvious; there is no uniformity in political practice which would support it. It is true that the term 'confederation' has been used in constitutions which did embody the principle of subordination by a general government to regional governments. Thus it was used in the Articles of Confederation of 1777, in the Union of Utrecht, in the Constitutions of Switzerland from earliest times; of Germany from 1815 to 1867, of the North German Confederation of 1867 to 1871, and of the German Empire from 1871 to 1918. It was adopted by the seceding states in America in 1861 when they called themselves the Confederate States of America, and their use of it might give it authority, for they had deliberately rejected what we have called the federal principle in its favour. But on the other side it must be mentioned that immediately after calling themselves 'We, the people of the Confederate States', they declared that their object was 'to form a permanent federal government.' The terms are treated as interchangeable in the Swiss Constitution of 1874 which is headed 'Constitution fédérale de la Confédération Suisse'. The authors of *The Federalist* itself did not distinguish between the two terms,[2] although they distinguished between the two principles involved. A modern authority like Dicey uses the terms interchangeably in a single sentence.[3] To increase the confusion the Canadian Constitution which, when it is not federal, is unitary, describes the government it sets up as a 'Confederation'. Obviously if the distinction of principle is to be kept clear, the use of 'confederation' will not be very helpful. But it would appear that where 'league' or 'alliance' is not sufficient to describe an association, 'confederation' is the only suitable term left. Perhaps if its use is linked with the principles of the Articles of Confederation of 1777

---

[1] See F. H. Newark in *Ulster Under Home Rule* (ed. T. Wilson), and N. Mansergh, *The Government of Northern Ireland, a study in devolution.*

[2] For example, in No. XX Hamilton and Madison, after discussing the United Netherlands and calling it 'a confederacy of republics', end up by referring to it as 'a federal precedent'.

[3] *Law of the Constitution*, 9th ed., p. 603.

and of the Confederate States and of the German Confederations, its meaning may be kept distinct.[1]

The other form of association—that in which the regional governments are subordinate to the general government—is often described as 'devolution' and the principle of its organization as 'the devolutionary principle'. The term has been applied to the system in Northern Ireland and in South Africa; and the instrument by which the Government of India, under the constitution of 1919, gave legislative powers to the provinces in 1921 was called 'the Devolution Rules'.[2]

11

The test which I apply for federal government is then simply this. Does a system of government embody predominantly a division of powers between general and regional authorities, each of which, in its own sphere, is co-ordinate with the others and independent of them? If so, that government is federal. It is not enough that the federal principle should be embodied predominantly in the written constitution of a country. That is something, but it is no guarantee necessarily that a sytem of federal government will operate. What determines the issue is the working of the system. For this reason I have drawn a distinction between federal constitutions and federal governments. And finally I have thought it expedient to find a name for those constitutions or governments in which the federal principle, though not predominant, is none the less important, and these I have called quasi-federal constitutions and quasi-federal governments.

From this analysis of the federal principle and its application to constitutions and governments, there emerges the conclusion that the countries which provide us with the best examples of the working of federal government are the United States, Switzerland, Canada and Australia. It will be with these, therefore, that I shall be principally concerned in succeeding chapters. But they will not be studied to the complete exclusion of all others. On the contrary, whenever it is possible, the relevant experience of countries which have adopted quasi-federal or non-federal constitutions or governments will be considered, for it may happen often that the experience of a country which consciously rejected federalism, or which adopted federalism but with conscious modifications, may be even more instructive to the student of federal government than the experiences of a country which has normal federal government.

It seems important to emphasize a final point also. In these first two chapters I have defined the federal principle strictly and I have classified federal and non-federal constitutions and governments fairly strictly also. In later chapters, too, I shall be discussing very often the extent to which the federal principle is recognized in the

[1] The discussion by Kennedy in Chapter XXIII of his *Constitution of Canada* is valuable. *Simon Report*, Vol. I, p. 126.

various branches and activities of the federal governments. All this concentration on the federal principle may give the impression that I regard it as a kind of end or good in itself and that any deviation from it in law or in practice is a weakness or defect in a system of government. It seems necessary to say, therefore, that this is not my view. Federal government is not always and everywhere good government. It is only at the most a means to good government, not a good in itself. And therefore, while I have maintained that it is necessary to define the federal principle dogmatically, I do not maintain that it is necessary to apply it religiously. The choice before those who are framing a government for a group of states or communities must not be presumed to be one between completely federal government and completely non-federal government. They are at liberty to use the federal principle in such a manner and to such a degree as they think appropriate to the circumstances. Strict federalism in a few matters, or modified federalism in all matters or any other variation in the application of the federal principle may be the wise solution to a particular problem. Whether federal government should be adopted at all, and, if so, to what extent, are questions the answer to which depends on the circumstances of the case. In other words it depends on whether federal government is appropriate. And it is therefore time to consider this next question: When federal government is appropriate.

PART II

WHEN FEDERAL GOVERNMENT IS APPROPRIATE

Chapter III

SOME PREREQUISITES OF FEDERAL GOVERNMENT

1

WALTER BAGEHOT, in discussing the prerequisites of Cabinet government in his *English Constitution,* uses words which we may appropriately adopt for federal government. Federal government 'is rare because its prerequisites are many. It requires the co-existence of several national characteristics which are not often found together in the world, and which should be perceived more distinctly than they often are'.

In what circumstances is it appropriate to adopt a system of federal government? This is probably the most difficult question we have to consider in this book.[1] But it must be attempted because it is in many respects the most important. The best way in which to approach it seems to be through a study of the definition we have already given of the term 'federal government' itself. Federal government exists, it was suggested, when the powers of government for a community are divided substantially according to the principle that there is a single independent authority for the whole area in respect of some matters and that there are independent regional authorities for other matters, each set of authorities being co-ordinate with and not subordinate to the others within its own prescribed sphere. From a consideration of this definition it is possible to infer the sort of conditions which should exist before the federal principle is adopted.

To begin with, the communities or states concerned must desire to be under a single independent government for some purposes at any rate. That is essential. Unless they are prepared to go as far as this, the question of federal government does not arise. If they are not prepared to submit themselves to an independent government, but desire rather to retain a control over the general authority, then they

[1] I have not been able to discover any thorough discussion of the problem. Some suggestive hints are found in Mill, *Representative Government,* Chapter XVII; in Dicey, *The Law of the Constitution* (9th ed.), Chapter III and Appendix III, and, scattered here and there, in Freeman's *History of Federal Government in Greece and Italy.* A modern outline of the way in which the subject might profitably be treated is given by William P. Maddox in an article on 'The Political Basis of Federation' in *American Political Science Review,* Vol. XXXV, No. 6, Dec. 1941.

have not achieved the first prerequisite of federal government. A league, an alliance, a confederation may be appropriate for them, but not federal government. It is for this reason that the members of the British Commonwealth of Nations, for example, or the islands of the West Indies which joined the short-lived federation of 1957–62 are not ready for federal government. Indeed it was for this reason also that in Latin America, in the first half of the nineteenth century, the communities which composed, under Bolivar, the state of Great Columbia, soon disintegrated into the three states of Ecuador, Columbia and Venezuela, while the Confederation of the United Provinces of Central America, formed in 1823, had become by 1838 the five separate states of Central America—Guatemala, Salvador, Honduras, Costa Rica and Nicaragua.

But the desire to be under a single independent government is not enough. They must desire at the same time to retain or to establish independent regional governments in some matters at least. Without this desire to be separate in some things, the communities could form a unitary state with some appropriate degree of decentralization. There would be no reason why the federal principle should be invoked. The example of South Africa illustrates this position. The colonies desired to be united under a single independent government. But they did not desire to be under *independent* regional governments for some purposes. They were content with provincial authorities which, although powerful and distinct, were ultimately subordinate bodies.

So far, then, it would seem that federal government is appropriate for a group of states or communities if, at one and the same time, they desire to be united under a single independent general government for some purposes and to be organized under independent regional governments for others. Or, to put it shortly, they must desire to be united, but not to be unitary.

It seems necessary, however, to go further than this. It can be admitted that, if these two desires exist simultaneously, then there is good cause *prima facie* for saying that federal government is appropriate. But more is needed. To say that a thing is desired by a group of states is not to say that it is the right thing for them. They must not only desire it; they must also be able to operate it. They must have the capacities to work the system they desire. Federal government is not appropriate unless the communities concerned have the capacity as well as the desire to form an independent general government and to form independent regional governments. Some inquiry into the capacities of communities as well as into their desires or aspirations will be necessary before it can be decided whether federal government is the system which they ought to adopt.

2

The propositions so far stated are abstract and they do not appear to take us very far. If we pass now to more concrete matters, the answers become less concise, but they may be more helpful. The first inquiry which naturally comes to mind is this : What are the factors or circumstances which lead communities to desire union and at the same time to desire separation within the union? And, secondly, what produces in them the capacity to form an independent general government and, at the same time, independent regional governments? If we know the answers to these questions, we can begin to see what ingredients should be present before it can be asserted that federal government should be adopted for a given territory.

Communities have been led to desire union from a variety of reasons. But in the modern federations some factors seem always to have been present. A sense of military insecurity and of the consequent need for common defence ;[1] a desire to be independent of foreign powers, and a realization that only through union could independence be secured; a hope of economic advantage from union; some political association of the communities concerned prior to their federal union either in a loose confederation, as with the American states and the Swiss cantons, or as parts of the same Empire, as with the Canadian and Australian colonies; geographical neighbourhood; and similarity of political institutions—these half-dozen factors all operated in the United States, Switzerland, Canada and Australia, to produce a desire for union among the communities concerned. They operated in varying degree in each case, but they were all present. Some of them were present also in other examples of voluntary unions where the federal principle was not adopted. Thus, the need for common defence, the desire to be independent, geographical contiguity, and the hope of economic advantage all helped to produce a desire for union which was a force in leading England and Scotland to form the United Kingdom of Great Britain in 1707,[2] the Italian states to form the Kingdom of Italy in the years from 1856 to 1864,[3] the German states to form, first the North German Confederation of 1867, and then the German Empire of 1871,[4] and the South African Colonies—Transvaal, Orange River, the Cape and Natal—to form the Union of South Africa in 1909[5] And in all these cases, except the Italian states,

[1] It is significant that this factor was absent in the case of the West Indian territories in 1957 when they formed a federation. See on the whole question H. W. Springer, *Reflections on the Failure of the first West Indian Federation* (1962).

[2] See G. M. Trevelyan, *Ramillis and the Union with Scotland*; Dicey and Rait, *Thoughts on the Union of England and Scotland*.

[3] See Bolton King, *A History of Italian Unity* (2 vols.), and Bolton King and Thomas Okey, *Italy Today*.

[4] See C. Grant Robertson, *Bismarck*, and A. W. Ward, *Germany 1815–1890*.

[5] See Walker, *Lord de Villiers and his Times*; Walton, *The Inner History of the National Convention of South Africa*; *Cambridge History of the British Empire*, Vol. VIII., and L. M. Thompson, *The Unification of South Africa*.

there was some form of previous political association[1] and some substantial similarity of political institutions.

When we see that certain factors such as these have always been present in modern cases where the desire for union has been produced, we may feel tempted to conclude that this desire will not be produced unless all or most of these factors are present. That would be going further than is warranted. But it is justifiable to say, I think, that it is unlikely that states will desire union unless these factors—or most of them—are present. To that extent they may be classed as prerequisites of federal government.

I have mentioned certain factors which seem always or usually to have been needed before the desire for union could be produced. It is interesting to notice that some factors are unexpectedly absent. Thus community of language, of race,[2] of religion or of nationality[3] have not been listed as likely essential prerequisites of the desire for union. This is surprising, but the facts support it. Undoubtedly common language and common race assisted to produce the desire for union in the United States, in Australia, in Germany and in Italy. Common nationality operated strongly in Germany and in Italy. In Australia the desire for union remained long dormant until in the 1890's a campaign was undertaken by the advocates of union to awaken in the people of the colonies a feeling that they were all Australians as well as Victorians or Queenslanders or the like. The campaign had a striking success and the sense of common nationality thus produced made the desire for union effective. But in the United States the union was formed before any such sense of common nationality had come into being. In the words of Professor Morison, 'most citizens of the United States in 1790, if asked their country or nation, would not have answered "American" but Carolinian, Virginian, Pennsylvanian, New Yorker or New Englander'. 'The United States of 1788 were not a nation by any modern standard.'[4]

More striking still are the examples of Canada and Switzerland where the desire to unite arose in spite of differences of language

---

[1] Even in the Italian states there had been associations of some or all the states in the past, although not immediately prior to union.

[2] The notions of race and of racial differences have become so discredited in recent years as a result of a reaction against the theories of the German Nazis that it may seem necessary for me to justify my use of the term. But what is sufficient for my purpose is not whether differences of race exist in fact but the undoubted fact that the groups of people think that they differ from others in race. It is this belief which makes differences of race and community of race factors which must be included in any discussion on the prerequisites of federal government. For my part I may add that it seems to me that there are such things as differences of race. I would refer the reader to an interesting discussion of the subject by Dr. G. M. Morant in an article entitled 'Racial Theories and International Relations' in *The Journal of the Royal Anthropological Institute*, Vol. LXIX, Part II, 1939.

[3] 'Nationality' is defined in many ways. I have in mind here that sense which people have that they are bound together and marked off from others by common sympathies, common sympathies which arise usually from the possession of a common language, common race or common religion. This sense of being a distinct people may lead a community to demand a distinct and independent state, the national state, but in my view this is not an essential element in the notion of nationality. For a discussion of the question see C. A. Macartney, *National States and National Minorities*, pp. 1–18, and the report of a study group of the Royal Institute of International Affairs entitled *Nationalism*.

[4] S. E. Morison, *History of the United States*, Vol. I, p. 10.

and race—French and English in Canada; German, French, Italian and Romansch in Switzerland—of religion as between Catholic and Protestant, and of nationality. And the Union of South Africa occurred in spite of similar differences between Dutch and English.[1] It is clear that, strong as these forces of language, race, religion and nationality are in producing a desire for union—as the whole history of national movements shows—it has proved possible none the less to produce a desire for union among peoples who differ in all these important particulars. Community in these matters cannot therefore be described as an essential prerequisite of federal government.

Much the same may be said of another factor which has produced a desire for union among communities, namely similarity of social institutions. Such similarity existed in the Australian colonies for example, but it was modified in the American states notably by the fact that some states favoured the institution of slavery and others did not. In Canada and Switzerland there were differences of custom and of private law between the uniting regions. In the case of the union between England and Scotland, to take a non-federal example, there were differences in the law touching marriage and inheritance; there were distinct systems of judicial procedure. Yet these differences of social institutions did not prevent the desire for union from growing. But the example of the United States shows the limits that must be imposed upon this statement. For, although the difference of opinion about slavery did not prevent the growth of a desire for union and the establishment of the union, yet seventy years later that divergence had become so acute that it created in the Southern States a desire to break the union, a desire that issued in civil war. There is a limit to the degree of divergence that is compatible with the existence of a desire to unite.

It is well to add, perhaps, that the mere presence of all these factors in a given territory will not necessarily produce of itself a desire to unite, a desire of sufficient strength to prevail over contrary forces. A great deal will depend, for example, on leadership or statesmanship at the right time. It needed not only resistance to a common enemy and geographical contiguity and community of language and race and religion, and similarity of political institutions, for example, to produce a desire in the American colonies to unite. These factors had been present for a long time and had failed to produce much more than a desire to be loosely associated in a confederation. What was needed also was leadership and that came from Washington, from Hamilton, Jay and Madison, from Benjamin Franklin and James Wilson. In the same way the desire for union in Canada was made effective by the leadership of such men as John A. Macdonald, Alexander Galt and George Etienne Cartier; in South Africa of Smuts,

---

[1] H. C. Calpin, felt justified, even after thirty years of the union, in entitling his book *There are no South Africans*. After fifty years of the union, there is no reason for the title to be altered.

de Villiers, Merriman and Botha; in Australia of Parkes, Barton and Deakin; in Germany of Bismarck; in Italy of Victor Emmanuel, Garibaldi, Cavour and Ricasoli; in Great Britain of Godolphin on the English side and of Queensberry, Argyle and Seafield on the Scottish. This factor of leadership, of skill in negotiation and propaganda, can make all the difference between stagnation and an active desire for union.

3

If these are the sort of factors which produce in communities the desire to be united for some purposes, what are the factors which, operating at the same time, produce the desire to be separate for other purposes? It is not so easy in this case to generalize. One factor which was present in all the modern federations was that the regions which desired to unite had all had a previous existence as distinct colonies or states, although it is to be noted that none of them had had a long history as a truly sovereign, independent state. But the American states, the Swiss cantons, the Canadian provinces and the Australian states, although associated together prior to union in some way, enjoyed each a distinct history and a distinct government. Thus, although they came to desire union in some things, they still desired to remain separate in others.

Partly as a result of their previous history as independent states, these communities had developed a divergence of economic interests. Thus, although, as I have mentioned, the hope of economic advantage led them to desire union, divergence of economic interest made them anxious not to surrender more power over economic affairs than was absolutely necessary. For, though union might mean economic advantage for some, it meant economic loss, in the short run at least, for others. They desired therefore to remain independent for some economic purposes at any rate.

Geographical factors also assisted the desire to be separate. In the United States, Canada and Australia it was great distance which was most important. Distance isolated the communities and developed a regional consciousness which made them desire to keep to themselves. In Switzerland it was the barrier of mountains which divided up the country into isolated communities. In the West Indies there was the extreme example of each unit being separated by sea.

These seem to be the only factors for separation within union which are common to all modern federations. It is possible to detect their presence also—though in a modified form—in the process by which certain unitary states like Austria, Russia, Mexico, and some South American Republics—notably Brazil and Venezuela, for example—have adopted constitutions framed to some extent on federal lines. Here at first sight one would not expect to find these factors in operation. Since the countries concerned had been previously unitary states, the desire for separation could not come for example from a previous independent existence of their component parts. Yet it is to be noticed that in many cases where the federal principle was applied, the units chosen as regions of the federation had been the divisions of provincial or local administration under the previous system, which, though unitary, was often highly decentralized in practice. In Austria the provinces had had a previous history as divisions of the Empire and had had provincial diets of their own; in Russia, Mexico and South America the old lines of provincial administration were often followed. Moreover economic divergences had been there also, in spite of a unitary government. The federalism of Argentina, Brazil and Austria owed something to this. And the great size of the country, producing a revolt against centralized administration, was important also in creating a desire for local independence in all these countries with the exception of Austria. Is it permissible to assert, then, that a previous existence as a distinct governmental unit, economic divergence and a sense of isolation through geographical factors, are essential prerequisites of that desire for separation within union which goes to produce federal government?

It does not seem possible to accept this conclusion. There is one factor, at least, which itself alone quite certainly could produce the desire for separation among communities otherwise prepared to unite. This factor is divergence of nationality. It is surely quite conceivable that communities which had had no previous existence as distinct governmental units, no divergence of economic interest and no isolation through geographical factors, but which none the less differed in nationality from each other, would desire separation within union. This factor of difference of nationality did co-operate, of course, with other factors for separation in three of the four cases mentioned—in a moderate degree in the United States, and much more strongly in Switzerland and in Canada. In the last two cases it was assisted by differences of language, race and religion. These in their turn are very strong forces for separation; any one of them might alone produce a desire for separation within union. Indeed it is usually a matter of surprise that union is possible at all among communities which differ in language, race, religion or nationality. In Switzerland and Canada the desire for union grew in spite of these differences, but the desire for separation within the union, the desire, that is, for *federal* union, was directly produced by these differences. And it seems most likely that communities which were ready to unite but which differed in some one or all of these four particulars, might desire the federal form of union.

Another factor which might produce the desire for separation is dissimilarity of social (including political) institutions. This undoubtedly operated in Canada when Quebec desired to be separate in order that it might safeguard its own peculiar system of civil law. It had its effect in the United States where slave-states and free-states were anxious to keep within their own control decisions about the future of the institution of slavery within their own borders.

These are the kind of factors which, given the existence of a desire for union, are likely to produce a desire for federal union. It is not possible to pick on any one of them or any one combination of them and say that unless this or these are present, the desire for federal union will not arise. That desire may be produced by any one of them.

And here again, as with the desire for union itself, a great deal will depend on leadership. The factors which could produce a desire for federal union may be there but they may not come to the surface; or, if they do, they may be overcome by more effective leadership in favour of the unitary form of union. Thus in South Africa, where there existed all the factors which had produced the desire for federal union in Canada—separate existence as distinct colonies, divergence of economic interest, geographical isolation, difference of language, race, religion and nationality,[1] difference of social institutions, and where in addition to all this there had recently been a bitter civil war between the two peoples, none the less the desire for federal union was overcome by the desire for a unitary— albeit highly decentralized—state. And this was done largely by the force of leadership exercised by certain men—Smuts, Merriman and de Villiers in particular.[2] They had decided that there must be a union but that federal union was unsuitable. It was too expensive, too legalistic, too weak at the centre and too strong at the circumference. They urged their case with great effectiveness. The whole issue of federal versus unitary union was debated in the press[3] and on the platforms of the colonies and the desire for federal union, which Natal in particular felt strongly, was overcome.

A similar example is that of the union of England and Scotland where many of the same forces which produced a desire for federal union in Canada had been present—a distinct government, a different religious system, a divergence of economic interests, a different system of civil law and a distinct literature, as well as a common literature. Here also leadership had its effect. The English delegates firmly over-ruled any plan for the continued existence of a Scottish parliament in which they saw a centre of Stuart and French intrigue against England. Nor did the Scottish delegates press the suggestion very hard.[4]

---

[1] But it is right to stress that the communities which differed in these respects were not territorially concentrated and organized in South Africa in a single province or provinces as were the French Canadians in Quebec.

[2] See L. M. Thompson, op. cit.

[3] An interesting example of the way in which federalism and unitarianism were discussed is Olive Schreiner's *Closer Union*, a letter written in 1909 by the authoress of *The Story of an African Farm*. Lord Selborne's *Memorandum on the Mutual Relations of the South African Colonies* is the classic statement of the case for federation.

[4] See Trevelyan, op. cit.; Dicey and Rait, op. cit.

For there was another factor operative at that time. No example of federal government, as we understand it, was in existence when the plan for the union of England and Scotland was being discussed. There was no successful working model to which those who desired to be united but not unitary could point. There were and had been confederations. There was the United Netherlands. But the main lesson such associations taught was the weakness which beset general governments when they had to suffer the existence of regional governments.[1] The model of the United Netherlands could not commend itself to the English delegates and the Scottish delegates could not produce anything better. For this reason—and for other reasons of equal or greater importance—the desire to remain separate within union was overcome and Scotland accepted union with decentralization and autonomy, more particularly in matters of church government, private law and the judicial system.

The example of the union of England and Scotland thus illustrates one factor of importance which assists to produce the desire for federal union. England and Scotland had no model of federal government before them; they had nothing to imitate. Now, since the establishment of the United States, communities have had something to imitate. They can see a model of what they would like to do. This force of imitation can have great influence in producing the desire to form a federal union. There is no doubt that it influenced Switzerland, Canada and Australia.[2] They did not imitate the form of American government blindly, but they were influenced by it and led by its example to desire the federal form of union. The example of other federations clearly influenced also the constitution makers in India, Rhodesia and Nyasaland, Malaya, the West Indies and Nigeria in the years after the Second World War. In Central and South America the force of imitation is even more clearly seen.[3] For there, where many of the factors which might be expected to produce a desire for federal union were absent—difference of language, race, religion or nationality, and separate existence as independent states—a desire to introduce federalism did arise. And this was largely due to the imitation of the constitution of the United States. It was almost as if they said: 'We have attained our independence from European control just as did the American colonies. They adopted the federal form of government. So must we.'[4] And this imitation explains in some measure why federal government has not taken root in the Central and South American republics. The factors which might produce a desire for it were not rooted in the communities themselves. The force

[1] See above, Chapter II.
[2] See W. Menzies Whitelaw on 'American Influence on British Federal Systems' in *The Constitution Re-considered* (ed. Conyers Read).
[3] The subject is treated by several writers in Conyers Read, op. cit., Part III.
[4] This appears to have been true of Mexico in 1824 particularly, although the Spanish Constitution of 1812 had a strong influence there also. See J. Lloyd Mecham in Conyers Read, op. cit. pp. 359–64.

of imitation works well when it provides from outside a plan which
fits the circumstances inside the country.

4

So far we have dealt only with the factors which produce the *desire*
for union combined with the *desire* for independence within union
which we stated to be one of the prerequisites of federal union.
We have next to ask: Granted the existence of these desires, what
conditions are necessary before it is possible to say that the communities which desire the federal form of union have also the *capacity*
to work it? For unless they have this capacity, federal government is
not appropriate for them.

It goes almost without saying that the desires themselves provide
some guarantee of the capacity to form and work the system of
government desired. If states really desire to form an independent
general government for some purposes, then they have gone a long
way towards being able to work such a government. And the same is
true of the desire to remain as independent governments inside the
union. A desire for federal union among communities is a first and
obvious factor which produces in them the capacity to make and work
a federal union.

And again the forces which produce the desire for federal union
are in some cases—but by no means in all—forces which also produce a capacity to work federal union. Thus hostility to or fear of a
common enemy and the need for common defence produces the
desire to unite. It also provides cohesive forces which compel the
communities concerned to stand together and accustom them to
work together. They develop common external antagonisms which
override internal antagonisms. John Stuart Mill says: 'The federation
binds them always to fight on the same side; and if they have such
feelings towards one another, or such diversity of feeling towards
their neighbours, that they would generally prefer to fight on opposite sides, the federal tie is neither likely to be of long duration, nor to
be well-observed while it subsists.'[1] Switzerland is the classic example
of the way in which the need for common defence produced in communities which differed in language, race and nationality not only the
desire but also the capacity to form a federal union.

It will be obvious also that community of race, language, religion
and nationality would produce a capacity for union. With so much in
common, states could inevitably work easily together. Although, as I
have shown, such community has not always been present where
federal union has been chosen, it is important to stress the value any
such community of interest can give. The United States with its
factors for separation—difference of nationality, difference on the
cardinal issue of slavery, geographical isolation, previous independ-

[1] *Representative Government* (Everyman ed.), pp. 366–7.

ence of its component units, and the like—owed much of its capacity to form a union to the capacity for working together which community of race, religion and language helped to produce. And it is to be noted that even where differences in these points existed, as in Canada and Switzerland, there was community in some of the regions concerned. It is important to remember that Switzerland, for the first five hundred years of its existence as a confederation, was composed entirely of German cantons. It was only with the French invasion of 1798 followed by Napoleon's Act of Mediation in 1803 that French and Italian-speaking cantons were added. The Act of Mediation added six new cantons to the already existing thirteen, creating them chiefly out of territories which had been allied to or were considered subject to the German-speaking cantons. In 1815 three more French-speaking cantons were added. For centuries, therefore, the Swiss cantons were enabled to work together by the common race and language which distinguished them. It remains remarkable, nevertheless, that the Swiss cantons were able to form their closest union, the federal union of 1848, *after* the inclusion of the non-German cantons, when differences of language, race or nationality had come to play their part. In the initiation and working of this federal union it is clear, however, that community of language, race, religion and nationality helped the German-Swiss cantons to work together, and the French-Swiss similarly. In the same way this community brought the English-speaking provinces of Canada together.

But of all the factors which produce the desire for union, the one which at the same time produces best the capacity for union is similarity of social, and particularly political institutions. It has been remarked already that the desire for union has practically never been aroused unless similarity of political institutions was present either actually or potentially among those who envisaged the union. This factor is one of the strongest of the forces which help states to work together. So strongly is this felt that statesmen in framing federal constitutions have even insisted that all the units should adopt the same form of government. The Constitution of the United States and that of Switzerland requires that the state and cantonal governments respectively should be republican. In Canada and Australia the forms of constitutional monarchy are explicitly established in all the units. When the quasi-federal Weimar Constitution of Germany was drawn up in 1918 it was required that all the member states should be republican. It replaced a constitution in which all but three of the members were monarchies—a constitution which was confederate, not federal.

The example of Switzerland is most instructive. Before the federal form of union was established in 1848 there had been great divergence of political institutions in the cantons. There had been oligarchies, democracies, aristocracies and, in one case, Neuchâtel, a monarchy. Cantons with similar institutions had banded themselves together inside the Confederation from time to time and had damaged what unity it had. A condition of the closer union which federation required was similarity of political institutions and after a hard struggle the democratic and republican cantons prevailed and all were brought into line. There seems little doubt that just as the desire to form a federal union is unlikely to arise among states which differed in régime, the capacity to form and work such a union can hardly exist without substantial similarity.

It would not do to state absolutely that a union between states of different régimes is impossible to work. Much depends on the régime. American states and Canadian provinces differ in political institutions. The former have the non-parliamentary executive, the latter the parliamentary executive. Yet it is conceivable that the two systems could find a place in the same union. For they are fundamentally at one—they are founded on the democratic principles of free election, free criticism and representative institutions. What would be harder to combine are authoritarian or oligarchic institutions and democratic institutions. For this reason it would seem particularly difficult to operate a union between the states and provinces of India, as envisaged in the Government of India Act, 1935. At the Round Table Conference of 1930 the Indian princes offered to join a federation with the provinces of British India, although the princes governed their states autocratically and the provinces were on the way to representative and responsible government. It is clear that this dissimilarity would have added one more difficulty to the working of Indian government in a system of federal union. It is significant that Indian leaders, before inaugurating the union established by the Constitution of 1950, took steps to promote homogeneity in the political institutions of the component states in the union. What is more, the form of government in the States—cabinet government—is prescribed in some detail in the Constitution itself.

But I think one may go further on this matter of similarity of political institutions. Not only is it desirable that there should be similarity of political institutions in the majority, at any rate, of the federating units, but it is essential, I believe, that these institutions should not be autocratic or dictatorial. For autocracy or dictatorship, either in the general governments or in the regional governments, seems certain, sooner or later, to destroy that equality of status and that independence which these governments must enjoy, each in its own sphere, if federal government is to exist at all. Thus, suppose all the regional governments or a majority of them were dictatorships, what machinery could exist to choose a general government which would be independent of the regional governments? No free election by the people of the autocratic regions is to be expected. The general government would be composed of nominees of the autocrats in the regions. In the Indian Constitution of 1935, for example, it was assumed that the representatives of the Indian states in the general legislature would be nominees of their rulers and not elected representatives of the people of the states. Or suppose that the general government is a dictatorship, can it be expected that it will refrain from extending its control into the regions and so ensuring that the regional governments are its agents or representatives. This has been the experience in South American countries with federal constitutions. Dictatorial presidents have brought the regional governments under their control by thrusting their own supporters into the regional governments. So also at the outset of the Nazi régime in Germany, what elements of independent jurisdiction were left to the regions under the quasi-federal Weimar Constitution were immediately brought under the control of the central government.[1]

It may be possible in theory to conceive a federal government in which general and regional governments are dictatorships and yet each remains strictly within its own sphere, but it is difficult to imagine such a federal government coming into existence in the realm of practical politics or continuing to exist for any length of time. Dictatorship, with its one-party government and its denial of free election, is incompatible with the working of the federal principle. Federalism demands forms of government which have the characteristics usually associated with democracy or free government. There is a wide variety in the forms which such government may take, but the main essentials are free election and a party system, with its guarantee of a responsible opposition.[2]

What is said of similarity in political institutions can be said of the wider issue—similarity of social institutions generally. Here, as I have said, the desire to unite can be created in spite of dissimilarity of social institutions, as the examples of the United States, Canada and Great Britain alone show. But such differences do make government more difficult, and there is a limit to the degree of dissimilarity which can be permitted. The capacity to work together cannot survive an extreme divergence. That is the lesson of the slavery issue in the United States. For many years compromise had saved the union of the American people, but there came a point where the divergence became so acute that the capacity to work together could not live with it. That is one meaning of Abraham Lincoln's words of 1858: 'A house divided against itself cannot stand. I believe this government cannot endure permanently half slave and half free. . . . It will become all one thing or all the other.' And so it was that after the Civil War there were inserted in the Constitution of the United States amendments

[1] See R. H. Wells on 'The Liquidation of the German Länder' in *Amer. Pol. Sci. Rev.*, Vol. XXX, April 1936.
[2] This point is well made by William P. Maddox, loc. cit., *Amer. Pol. Sci. Rev.*, Vol. XXXV at p. 1125, and in Freeman, *History of Federal Government in Greece and Italy*, pp. 73–5.

designed to remove all traces in law of this particular divergence of social institution as between one state and another in the American union.[1]

So also in Canada, though some divergence is allowed, some uniformity is also required. Quebec has her own civil law; but there is one criminal law only for Canada. So Scotland has her distinct judicial system and private law, but the House of Lords is her final court of appeal and there is a common statute law on many matters for England and Scotland. This is not to say that the differences of social institutions in these countries are unimportant. They are important and it is remarkable that they are contained within a single government. But it must be emphasized that the capacity of states to form and work a federal union depends upon some agreement to differ but not to differ too much.

5

If these are some of the factors which give communities or states a capacity to unite, what are the factors which give them the capacity to remain distinct and separate inside a union? First of all it appears that, here again, some of the factors which cause states to desire to remain independent in some matters inside a union, also create in them the capacity to do so. Most important of these seems to be their previous existence as distinct governments. This means that the states joining to form a new general government, have at their disposal in their own regions a well-established system of government which will enable them to carry out their functions and maintain their integrity in the new system. More than that, it relieves the strain imposed upon the new system, by guaranteeing the stability of regional administration and leaving energies free for the one formidable task of establishing the new general government. This is a great gain. It means that the communities will be required to establish one new government and not a collection of half a dozen or more governments.

The value of this factor can be illustrated from the history of Italian unity. There was a party which advocated federal union for the Italian states. But the makers of Italian unity rejected it. When first it was put forward they rejected it because they did not believe that the despotic and usually alien rulers of most of the states—and particularly Naples and Sicily—would be prepared to surrender their independence in certain matters to an Italian government. They did not believe, that is, that these states desired union—the first essential of federal union. They decided, therefore, that the defeat of these despotisms was the first essential to union. But when this defeat was accomplished, nothing was left. There were no governments with authority rooted in the society they governed. It would have been

[1] Amendments XIII, XIV and XV.

a gigantic task to establish new and stable governments in these states, while at the same time establishing the new government for united Italy. And wisely, therefore, if only for this reason, the makers of Italian unity rejected the federal form.

The same can be said to a great extent of federal experiments in Central and South America and in particular of Mexico, Brazil, Argentina and Venezuela. The regions for which independent governments were established in these Latin American constitutions had had in most cases no history as distinct and established governments. They had been merely administrative divisions of an Empire. They had no deep-rooted political institutions of their own which could stand up to the pressure of central administration. And for this reason, among others, federal government did not become a reality in these republics.[1]

Thus this factor of a past history as an individual and established government which does so much to produce the desire for the federal form of union as opposed to the unitary form, is one which also produces the capacity in states to work the federal form. It gives the regions strength to stand upon their own feet; it also allows the energies of statesmen to be concentrated upon one task, the making of the general government. It helps to produce both the capacity to be separate and independent in some things and to be under a general government for others.

It will be apparent that this factor needs to be nicely balanced in the sum of forces at work in the union. People must have an established government to which they can be attached, but that attachment must not be too strong. Therein lies always a possible source of weakness in a federal government—that state loyalty may prevail over general loyalty. More particularly is this likely to be true where state boundaries coincide with racial, linguistic or national boundaries. It is obviously an advantage that the units in a federation should be homogeneous; nothing strengthens a regional government so much. But the danger is that the region may inspire a loyalty greater than that of the union and that in time of conflict the union will fall apart. It is the continual problem of statesmanship in a federation to avoid this clash of rival loyalties. That the two loyalties must be there is the prerequisite of federal government, but that the one should not overpower the other is also a prerequisite. The Italian example already quoted illustrates both dangers. So long as the despots ruled their states, there could be no certain loyalty to a general Italian government. Once they were swept away, there could be no stable system of institutions round which regional loyalty could establish itself.

It follows from what has been said, also, that although it is possible

---

[1] The fact that a few of the regions, such as São Paulo and Minas Geraes in Brazil and Buenos Aires in Argentina, did enjoy the strength that came from an independent existence in the past, only made the subordination of the weaker regions like Pará and Ceará more noticeable and indeed more expedient in the eyes of the general government.

for a state which differs in race, religion, language, nationality and the like to form a union and although such differences provide a good basis for a federal union, it is also desirable that some feeling of common attachment to the new general government should be developed. At the making of the United States, of Switzerland and of Canada there were differences of nationality, but as time went on a common nationality came to impose itself upon the differences. Citizens of these federal states came to feel a sense of double nationality. They are Swiss and German-Swiss; they are American and Virginian; they are Canadian and French-Canadian. Nationality in a federal state means something more complicated than it does in a unitary state. And one of the factors which produce in states the capacity to work a federal union is the growth of this sense of a new common nationality over and above but not instead of their sense of separate nationality.[1]

6

The capacity of states to work a federal union is also greatly influenced by their size. It is undesirable that one or two units should be so powerful that they can overrule the others and bend the will of the federal government to themselves. The example of Prussia in the German Empire shows how this factor can transform even a confederation into a unitary state. On the other hand, some divergence in size between the units is almost certain to be present before federal union is desired. It is this divergence which leads the poorer or less populous states to desire federal rather than unitary government for in it they see a safeguard for their independence. It is an important factor in the making and maintenance of federal systems today. The agricultural states of Western America with their smaller populations find in the federal form of union their safeguard against the wealth and population of the East and especially New York; the Canadian maritime provinces and the prairie provinces seek protection from Ontario and Quebec; the Australian states of Western Australia, Tasmania and South Australia with their small, predominantly agricultural, population seek protection from the more populous industrialized states of New South Wales and Victoria. A problem in the working of federal government is found to be therefore the harmonizing of the conflicting interests of these differing units. But the essential is, as John Stuart Mill says, 'that there should not be any one State so much more powerful than the rest as to be capable of vying in strength with many of them combined. If there be such a one, and only one, it will insist on being master of the joint deliberations: if

---

[1] James Wilson saw this clearly at the framing of the Constitution of the United States. He said: 'A Citizen of America may be considered in two points of view—as a citizen of the general government, and as a citizen of the particular state, in which he may reside. . . . I am both a citizen of Pennsylvania and of the United States.' Farrand, *Records of the Federal Convention*, Vol. I, p. 413.

there be two, they will be irresistible when they agree; and whenever they differ everything will be decided by a struggle for ascendancy between the rivals.'[1] The size of the units concerned—in wealth, area and population—is therefore of prime importance. There must be some sort of reasonable balance which will insure that all the units can maintain their independence within the sphere allotted to them and that no one can dominate the others. It must be the task of those who frame and work a federal government to see that no unit shall be too large, and, equally important, none too small.

And size reflects itself in one further aspect. If a federal government is to work there must be available a supply of men with capacity to govern, a supply sufficient not for one government only but for many. Federal government makes a big demand on a community's human resources. As a rule a small population cannot be expected to supply so many trained and capable men as a large population. In this sense a state's size will affect its capacity to form part of a federal union.

7

A discussion of the relative resources of the units in a federation leads to the consideration of a final factor which ensures the capacity of states to form a federal union. They must possess sufficient economic resources to support both an independent general government and independent regional governments. It is not enough that the general government should be able to finance itself; it is essential also that the regional governments should be able to do likewise. At the very outset, therefore, in considering whether federal government is appropriate, the question of adequate economic resources arises. If a general government is to be established and supported—and that is the first assumption of any union, federal or non-federal—will there be sufficient resources also to support independent regional governments? If there are not, then no matter how much states desire a federal union and no matter whether a federal constitution is drawn up, in practice federal government will not be possible. Soon the regional governments will be unable to perform their functions or they will be able to perform them only at the price of financial dependence upon the general government, that is, at the price of financial unification.

It was on economic grounds, among others, that federal union was rejected by the leaders in South Africa. They thought that the financial resources of the country would be unduly taxed if they were required to support not only a general government but also independent regional governments. For federalism is expensive and it is always a question whether the independence it gives is worth the price that must be paid for it. It has been alleged in the case of Australia, too, that federal government has not been appropriate

[1] *Representative Government* (Everyman ed.), pp. 367-8.

there because it imposes an undue financial burden on the people—
the provision of a full paraphernalia of government in six states as
well as for the Commonwealth as a whole.[1] It seems likely also that
one of the main reasons why federalism has not survived in the Latin
American republics has been the extreme poverty of so many of the
regions which have for long remained undeveloped economically.[2]
But the general principle here is clear. There must be sufficient economic resources available both to regions and to general governments to
make it possible for them to be financially independent.

It is not, however, a question merely of what resources are available
throughout the communities as a whole. A great deal will depend on
how these resources are divided between the general and regional
governments when the federal union is established. It may well be
proper that a region which desires independence in a federal union
but which lacks resources to make that independence real, after it has
surrendered certain of its revenues for the maintenance of the general
government, should be guaranteed certain incomes from the resources
of its wealthier neighbours. There arise, therefore, questions of allocating resources as between regions and general government and as
between one region and another. These allocations are most important in establishing a federal system. They raise questions not only
of what total resources are available, but also what is the right way—
granted or assuming that they are sufficient for the needs of all
governments—to allocate them, so that each government will get
what it needs.

We verge here on the problem not of when federal government
is appropriate but of how federal government shall be organized.
Once it is seen what conditions are necessary if states are to have not
merely the desire but also and more particularly the capacity to form a
federal union, it becomes necessary next to ask how it can be ensured
that, if these desires and capacities are there, they may be enabled to
express themselves effectively in a system of government. And it is to
this question, therefore, that we must turn.

[1] This question is considered below, Chapter VI.
[2] The point is made by R. A. Humphreys in his pamphlet *Latin American History* (Historical
Association, No. 127).

PART III

HOW FEDERAL GOVERNMENT SHOULD BE ORGANIZED

Chapter IV

THE CONSTITUTION, THE COURTS AND THE LAW

1

IF federal government is, as I have maintained, a distinct and peculiar form of government, appropriate to distinct and peculiar circumstances, it is natural to ask whether it has its own distinct and peculiar institutions, specially designed to enable it to perform its functions. There are indeed two questions. There is first the question whether there are any institutions which are essential to a federal government if it is to be federal. And there is secondly the question whether there are any institutions which are essential to a federal government if it is to work well. These two questions will not be considered in isolation in this chapter. Both will be considered together and some attempt will be made to provide an answer to them.

2

It is sometimes asserted that it is essential if a government is to be federal that it should be regulated by a written constitution. I think it is more accurate to say that if a government is to be federal, its constitution, whether it be written or unwritten, or partly written and partly unwritten, must be supreme. By this I mean that the terms of the agreement which establishes the general and regional governments and which distributes powers between them must be binding upon these general and regional governments. This is a logical necessity from the definition of federal government itself. If the general and regional governments are to be co-ordinate with each other, neither must be in a position to override the terms of their agreement about the powers and status which each is to enjoy. So far as this agreement regulates their relations with each other, it must be supreme. In other respects it may not be necessary for it to be supreme. It may regulate matters of governmental organization which do not bear directly or indirectly upon the mutual relations and status of the general and regional governments. Where that is so, the supremacy of the constitution in those respects is not essential for federalism, although it may be necessary for other reasons. But in all that concerns the division of authority between governments, the federal principle requires the supremacy of the constitution.

It is easy to see how the necessity for a supreme constitution in a federal government leads to the assertion of the necessity for a written constitution also. For where the terms of an agreement are so important, it is natural that it should be thought essential that they be committed to writing. So, while it could be asserted that a written constitution is not logically required by the federal principle, it must be admitted that it is practically necessary. The truth seems to be that while it is essential for federal government that its constitution be supreme, to the extent defined above, it is essential for good federal government that the supreme constitution be written. And in practice all modern federal and quasi-federal constitutions have, as we have seen, been put in writing.

So far as the supremacy of the constitution is concerned, it is interesting to notice how far this principle has been applied in the different cases.

The Constitution of the United States expresses the essential supremacy of a constitution in a federal government in the passage.[1] 'This Constitution and the Laws of the United States which shall be made in pursuance thereof . . . shall be the supreme law of the land; and the judges in every state shall be bound thereby, anything in the constitution or laws of any state to the contrary notwithstanding.'

There is no similar declaration in the Constitutions of Canada and Australia, but there is a similar recognition of the necessity that the constitution be supreme. Their constitutions—the British North America Act, 1867, and the Commonwealth of Australia Constitution Act, 1900—were acts of the United Kingdom Parliament and they were, for that reason, at the time of their enactment, supreme law in the Dominions concerned, for they prevailed over any laws of the general or regional legislatures which might be repugnant to them.[2] Nor was this position changed when in 1931 the United Kingdom Parliament passed the Statute of Westminster[3] which enacted that for the future the powers of the parliament of a Dominion should include the power to repeal or amend any act of the United Kingdom Parliament in so far as the same is part of the law of the Dominion. For it contained also an express reservation that this repeal of the former restriction did not extend to the acts containing the Constitution of Canada and of Australia. This reservation was inserted in the Statute at the request of Canada and Australia, and its object was to preserve intact the supremacy of the Constitutions in these federal Dominions. When, in 1949, the Canadian parliament obtained certain

[1] Art. VI (2).

[2] This rule was embodied in the Colonial Laws Validity Act, 1865 (28 & 29 Vict. c. 63).

[3] 22 & 23 Geo. v, c. 4. See my *Constitutional Structure of the Commonwealth*.

powers to amend the Constitution,[1] the supremacy of the Constitution, so far as the division of powers was concerned, remained intact and the principle was unquestioned by the Dominion government.

In Switzerland at first sight the supremacy of the Constitution seems less assured. Laws passed by the Federal Assembly are treated as valid by the court. But this must not be interpreted to mean that the Federal Assembly is regarded as possessing a legislative power superior to the Constitution. It cannot amend the Constitution. It is expected to keep within its powers, although no court is given power to declare when it transgresses its proper limits. As for the cantons, their constitutions must not conflict with the federal Constitution, and their laws may be declared void by the courts.

The principle of the supremacy of the Constitution is not asserted so thoroughly in some other states which are or claim to be federations, but it was of considerable significance in West Germany, India, Rhodesia and Nyasaland, Malaya, the West Indies and Nigeria.

3

These two institutions—the supreme constitution and the written constitution—are, then, essential institutions to a federal government. The supreme constitution is essential if government is to be federal; the written constitution is essential if federal government is to work well. From this there follows an obvious corollary. It is essential in a federal government that if there be a power of amending the constitution, that power, so far at least as concerns those provisions of the constitution which regulate the status and powers of the general and regional governments, should not be confided exclusively either to the general governments or to the regional governments.

Apart from this, it does not matter logically where the power is placed, but there can be no doubt that practically it is wise to associate both the general government and the regions, either their governments or their peoples, in the process. This is done in the United States, where amendments to the Constitution may be proposed either by two-thirds of both houses of Congress, or by a convention called together by Congress on the application of the legislatures of two-thirds of the states. These proposed amendments are valid when ratified by the legislatures of three-quarters of the states or by conventions in three-quarters of the states, according as one or other method of ratification may be proposed by Congress. In this way, although it would be possible for amendments to be initiated by the legislatures of two-thirds of the states, who ask for the calling of a convention, and to be ratified by the legislatures of three-fourths of the states when submitted to them by the convention, complete control by the state legislatures is avoided by the power which Congress has of choosing whether ratification shall be carried out by

[1] In the British North America Act. (No. 2), 1949. (12, 13 and 14, Geo. 6, c. 81).

the state legislatures or by conventions representative of the people of the states.[1] A further safeguard is found in the article that no new state shall be formed or erected within the jurisdiction of any other state, nor any state formed by the junction of two or more states, without the consent of the legislatures of the states concerned as well as of the Congress.[2]

In Australia the Constitution may be amended by a process[3] in which if the two houses of the parliament of the Commonwealth— or, in certain circumstances, one house—propose the amendment by an absolute majority, it must then be submitted to a referendum of the people. If in this referendum a majority of all the electors voting approve the proposed law, and if, in a majority of the states,[4] a majority of the electors voting also approve the proposed law, then it can be submitted for the royal assent. Further it is provided that no amendment diminishing the proportionate representation of any state in either house of the parliament or the minimum number of representatives of a state in the House of Representatives, or increasing, diminishing or otherwise altering the limits of the state, or in any manner affecting the provisions of the constitution in relation thereto, shall become law unless the majority of the electors voting in that state approve the proposed law.

This association of the people with the general legislature in the process of amending the constitution was borrowed from Switzerland. There the proposal to amend may be initiated by the general legislature, or, in some circumstances, by one house of the general legislature, or by 50,000 citizens. But however amendments have been initiated none can become effective until approved at a referendum by a majority of all the electors voting and by a majority of the electors voting in a majority of the cantons.

Canada provides an interesting example, for here the requirements of federalism are carried to an extreme conclusion. No authority in Canada—government or electorate—has power to alter the division of powers between Dominion and provincial governments. The power rests solely with the parliament of the United Kingdom. It explicitly amended the British North America Act, 1867, fourteen times up to 1962,[5] and two amendments only, those embodied in the British North America Acts of 1940, and of 1951, were concerned with the distribution of powers between Dominion and provincial governments. The power of amendment is never exercised except on a request from Canada. But the point of interest for us is whether

[1] Actually all twenty-two amendments to the constitution so far carried have been proposed by the Congress and all except the twenty-first were submitted for ratification to state legislatures, the twenty-first being submitted for ratification to conventions in the states.

[2] Art. IV, 3 (1).

[3] Art. 128.

[4] At present this means in at least four out of the six states.

[5] But see a note by F. R. Scott, *The Canadian Bar Review*, April 1942, on 'Forgotten Amendments to the British North America Act'.

action is taken on a request from the Dominion parliament and government alone, or from the provincial parliaments and governments alone, or through some co-operation of the two. The amendment of 1940 which gave exclusive power to the parliament of the Dominion to legislate upon unemployment insurance was passed at the request and with the consent of both Dominion and provincial authorities. But there is no clear convention on the subject. In seven out of the ten amendments passed up to 1947, action was taken by the United Kingdom parliament on requests from the Dominion government or parliament alone; there was no consultation with all the provinces nor was their consent asked. The amendments of 1871, 1886, 1915, 1943, 1946 and 1949 affected the provinces, but none was consulted. The amendment of 1930 affected some provinces, and these alone were consulted and their consent obtained. In one case where all the provinces were consulted and asked for their consent—that of 1907—the amendment was passed by the United Kingdom parliament at the request of the Dominion parliament in spite of the fact that one of the provinces concerned, British Columbia, did not give its consent to the proposed amendment.[1] There is clearly a danger, therefore, that if the United Kingdom parliament became content to look no further than the request of the Dominion parliament and to pass every amendment which the Dominion parliament requested, the principle of federalism might become endangered in Canada. The legal position would still be in conformity with federalism, for neither Dominion parliament alone nor provincial parliaments alone could alter the constitution. But if it came to be accepted that the United Kingdom parliament must act as the agent of the Dominion parliament acting alone, then by convention the federal principle of co-ordinate authorities would be modified. The question of an appropriate method of constitutional amendment is under discussion in Canada. It is recognized by Canadians that they must devise some method of making amendments which will be in conformity with federalism, since they wish to preserve the federal elements in their constitution, and that meanwhile the United Kingdom parliament should be careful not to permit itself to become the agent of the Dominion alone or of the Provinces alone.[2]

4

Since a division of powers is an essential part of any federal government, since any such division must be expressed in words whether written down or not, and since language is ambiguous, it is certain

---

[1] See evidence of Dr. O. D. Skelton, before the Special Committee of the Canadian House of Commons on the British North America Act, set up in 1935 (*Proceedings and Evidence and Report*, pp. 31–8).

[2] The whole topic is excellently treated by P. Gerin-Lajoie in *Constitutional Amendment in Canada* (1950). See also H. McD. Clokie in an article entitled 'Basic Problems of the Canadian Constitution' in *The Canadian Journal of Economics and Political Science*, Vol. VIII, No. 1, February 1942.

that in any federation there will be disputes about the terms of the division of powers. But since it is the criterion of a federal government not merely that there should be a division of powers, but also that this division should not be dependent upon the general government or the regional governments alone, it follows that the last word in settling disputes about the meaning of the division of powers must not rest either with the general government alone or with the regional governments alone.

This necessity has been recognized by the founders of most federal systems, but they have not always applied it with complete consistency. Moreover, when they have established some institution with power to decide disputes about the division of powers, they have not confined its jurisdiction merely to that part of the federal constitution; on the contrary they have given it power to decide the meaning of the whole constitution—an increase in authority which is not logically necessary for federalism.

Canada alone gave the last word in constitutional disputes, whether concerned with the division of powers or not, to a body which is completely independent of general and provincial governments—the Judicial Committee of the Privy Council[1] This position lasted for over eighty years. At the end of 1949, however, the Canadian parliament passed an act to make the Supreme Court of Canada the final court of appeal in all Canadian lawsuits. Now the last word in Canadian disputes about the division of powers rests with the Supreme Court of Canada, a body whose members are appointed by the Dominion executive and removable on an address by the two houses of the Dominion parliament.

In Australia, some disputes about the meaning of the constitution are decided in the last resort by the Judicial Committee, but the kind of dispute in which we are interested here—disputes 'as to the limits *inter se* of the constitutional powers of the Commonwealth and those of any state or states, or as to the limits *inter se* of the constitutional powers of any two or more states' can be decided finally by the High Court of Australia, a body whose members, like those of the Supreme Court of Canada, are appointed by the Commonwealth executive and removable on an address from the two houses of the Commonwealth parliament.[2] The High Court can, if it chooses, permit an appeal in such cases to the Judicial Committee, but so far it has done so in one case only.[3]

In the United States, similarly, the last word about the meaning of the constitution and consequently of the division of powers is with a body—the Supreme Court—whose members are appointed by the

---

[1] The same was true of India under the quasi-federal constitution in the Government of India Act, 1935.

[2] But on the ground only of 'proved misbehaviour or incapacity'. s. 72.

[3] *Colonial Sugar Refinery Co. v. Attorney General for the Commonwealth.* 15 C.L.R. 182 and [1914] A.C. 237.

chief executive of the United States, the President, with the consent of the upper house of the legislature, the Senate, and are removable on impeachment by the House of Representatives before the Senate, in which case a two-thirds majority of the senators present is necessary.

In Switzerland the last word does not appear to rest completely with the Federal Tribunal. It may declare cantonal laws invalid, but it must accept the laws of the general legislature as valid. This means that so far as the courts are concerned, any assertion of the general legislature that it has power to legislate on a particular disputed field, prevails and is accepted. It does not mean, however, that the general legislature has the last word in a dispute about the extent of its powers as against the cantons, for there remains the power, exercised upon the demand of 30,000 citizens or of 8 cantons that any law passed by the general legislature should be submitted to the people at a referendum. In a case of dispute, therefore, the electorate has the power, if it chooses to exercise it, to decide whether a law of the general government is to be valid or not.

It seems that in most federal governments the settlement of disputes about the meaning of the division of powers is confided to a body appointed and dismissable by the general government. The result has been that Supreme Courts or their equivalent have been accused from time to time of undue partiality to the general government. There have been charges laid, too, that appointments to the Supreme Court, have been made of persons who would look favourably on an interpretation of the division of powers which would increase the powers of the general government.[1] Inevitably when appointments to a Supreme Court are to be made, the appointing body, the other governments and the public are bound to consider the views of candidates on the division of powers. Are they, from their record, keen on states' rights, or are they centralizers? None the less in spite of many protests and of some possibly partisan appointments in some countries, the power of appointment has remained with the general government.

There are reasons for this. To begin with, the extent to which the Supreme Courts have been under the control of the general governments must not be exaggerated. It is true that in Canada and Australia it is possible for the executive of the general government to remove judges of the highest court in the country on an address from the general legislature, but in fact no such action has been taken—nor could it be taken in Australia except for proved misbehaviour or incapacity. In fact security of tenure is complete. In Switzerland judges of the Federal Tribunal are elected by the general legislature for six years at a time and this, in law, might seem to weaken their position. But we are told that although in Switzerland, as in the other

[1] An example was the nomination of Senator Hugo L. Black in 1936, by President Franklin D. Roosevelt.

three federations, 'their elections have come to be decisively influenced by political and regional conditions, it has always been customary to re-elect members of the Federal Tribunal as long as they live or care to serve'.[1] In the United States judges of the Supreme Court could be removed by the general legislature through the process of impeachment, if they were convicted of treason, bribery or other crimes and misdemeanours. In this process the House of Representatives impeaches and the Senate tries the impeachment. There has been one case only of an impeachment of a judge of the Supreme Court, that of Samuel Chase in 1804–5.[2] This was undoubtedly a case where the process of impeachment was being used for party ends; it was an attempt by the Republicans to curb the power of the Supreme Court and to punish their Federalist opponents. Had it succeeded, it is likely that a majority of the Supreme Court would have been removed from office by impeachment. Actually Justice Chase was acquitted.[3] Though his conduct had certainly been indiscreet and tactless, it was impossible to substantiate any charge of high crime or misdemeanour, and even the Republican majority in the Senate shrank from finding him guilty. Since that case and to some extent because of it, no attempt to impeach a justice of the Supreme Court on political grounds has been made.[4]

But in the United States one reason why this has not happened may be that the Senate there has an opportunity of preventing the appointment of any person whose views upon the constitution appear likely to be unsatisfactory. In 1930 the Senate rejected President Hoover's nomination of Judge Parker of North Carolina partly on the ground that his decisions in the inferior courts had shown that he was a strong conservative, hostile to organized labour, and that he would interpret the constitution accordingly. In the same year the Senate debated the nomination of Charles Evans Hughes for the Chief Justiceship and, although it confirmed the nomination, many senators criticized it on the ground that Mr. Hughes had been associated in his practice with powerful business corporations and that his outlook inevitably must favour their interests. As a rule presidential nominations have been accepted,[5] but the legal qualifications and views of the nominees are scrutinized critically, and seldom impartially.

In spite of the formal dependence of the supreme courts on the executive and legislature of the general government, they have exhibited a considerable impartiality in the exercise of their function

[1] Rappard, *The Government of Switzerland*, p. 91.

[2] See Albert J. Beveridge, *Life of John Marshall*, Vol. I.

[3] Morison and Commager, *The Growth of the American Republic*, Vol. I, p. 293.

[4] There have been seven cases of impeachment of judges of inferior federal courts in the United States, four of them successful.

[5] There had been nine outright rejections up to 1944, and twelve indirect rejections, that is by the Senate's failing to act or postponing the decision indefinitely. A list will be found in Ogg and Ray, *Introduction to American Government* (5th ed.), p. 436.

as interpreters of the division of powers. In Anglo-Saxon countries, the traditions of the bar and the bench tend strongly to safeguard the integrity and independence of the judges. In 1937 President Roosevelt proposed a reform of the judiciary of the United States which included a proposal aimed at altering the composition of the Supreme Court. His plan was rejected, largely as a result of the very strong opposition of the bar associations. It is commonly found also that judges, once on the bench, develop views on the constitution which are different from those which, from their record, people had expected them to form.[1]

It must not be assumed, however, that bias on the part of a supreme court will necessarily mean bad government. The most that is maintained here is that if the supreme court is dependent upon the general or regional governments, then the system of government is to that extent not federal. But it may work well none the less. The decisions it gives upon cases of dispute may fit in well with public opinion though they may not fit in so well with the letter of the constitution. Similarly independence in the supreme tribunal will not necessarily produce good government. In the extreme it can produce an irresponsible tyranny of the judges.

5

People sometimes ask why it is that the function of deciding the meaning of the division of powers and indeed of the whole constitution in a federal government comes to be performed by courts. Is it not a strange thing that one branch of the general government—the judiciary—should have the power to decide whether the other branches—the legislature and administration—are keeping within the limits of their powers?[2] This question has been discussed most keenly in the United States, where it has been argued by some writers that the framers of the constitution never intended the Supreme Court to exercise this power.[3] On this point it must be admitted that differences of opinion are to be found among those who framed the constitution, and that no explicit statement is to be found in the Constitution conferring upon the Supreme Court a power to decide upon the division of powers, nor in general to determine the meaning of the constitution.[4] But the conclusion one draws from reading what was said in the Convention is that a majority of the leading men among those who framed the Constitution expected the Supreme Court to act in this

[1] There are some interesting examples of this in Charles E. Hughes, *The Supreme Court of the United States*, pp. 45 ff. See also C. Warren, *The Supreme Court in United States History*.

[2] The best discussion of judicial review is Charles G. Haines, *The American Doctrine of Judicial Supremacy*. See also E. S. Corwin, *The Twilight of the Supreme Court*; Dean Alfange, *The Supreme Court and the National Will*.

[3] See Louis M. Boudin, *Government by Judiciary*, Vol. I, Chapter VI.

[4] See Farrand, *Records of the Federal Convention*, references under heading 'Constitutionality of Laws' in index. Mercer and Dickinson, e.g., were opposed to judicial review, Farrand, ibid., Vol. II, pp. 298–9.

way.[1] It is not possible to agree that the assumption of this power was a usurpation.

Indeed one may go further and say that unless the United States' constitution and other federal constitutions contain explicit provisions to the contrary it is difficult to see how the courts can avoid performing the function of deciding whether acts done by the legislature and executive are valid or not.[2] This follows logically from the nature of the constitution and was expressed in a classic form by Alexander Hamilton in *The Federalist* when he wrote: 'The interpretation of the laws is the proper and peculiar province of the courts. A constitution is, in fact, and must be regarded by the judges as, a fundamental law. It therefore belongs to them to ascertain its meaning, as well as the meaning of any particular act proceeding from the legislative body. If there should happen to be an irreconcilable variance between the two, that which has the superior obligation and validity ought, of course, to be preferred; or, in other words, the constitution ought to be preferred to the statute, the intention of the people to the intention of their agents.'[3] It was this argument, in fact, which was put forward by Chief Justice Marshall in the case of *Marbury* v. *Madison* in 1803 when the Supreme Court first nullified an act of Congress.[4] 'It is emphatically the province and duty of the judicial department to say what the law is,' he said. 'Those who apply the rule to particular cases, must of necessity expound and interpret that rule. If two laws conflict with each other, the courts must decide on the operation of each. So if a law be in opposition to the constitution: if both the law and the constitution apply to a particular case, so that the court must either decide that case conformably to the law, disregarding the constitution; or conformably to the constitution, disregarding the law; the court must determine which of these conflicting rules governs the case. This is of the very essence of judicial duty. If, then, the courts are to regard the constitution; and the constitution is superior to any ordinary act of the legislature; the constitution, and not such ordinary act, must govern the case to which they both apply.'[5]

The substance of the matter is that while it is the duty of every institution established under the authority of a constitution and exercising powers granted by a constitution to keep within the limits of these powers,[6] it is the duty of the courts, from the nature of their function, to say what these limits are. And that is why courts come to exercise this function in a federal government. It is significant that

---

[1] C. A. Beard, *The Supreme Court and the Constitution*, espec. Chap. II.
[2] The views I put forward in the following paragraphs are not universally accepted.
[3] No. LXXVIII.
[4] 1 Cranch, 137.
[5] See Albert J. Beveridge, *Life of John Marshall*, Vol. III, for a discussion of the case.
[6] Courts themselves can act unconstitutionally. It seems to have been the opinion of the majority of the Supreme Court of the United States in 1938 that that Court had been doing so for nearly a hundred years. But then, as the critics of judicial review may say, we have only their word for it. See *Erie Railroad Case*, overruling *Swift* v. *Tyson*, below, pp. 72, 74.

judicial review found a place in the constitutional systems of Western Germany, India, Rhodesia and Nyasaland, Malaya, the West Indies and Nigeria.

But it is necessary to make two qualifications. The first is that the exercise of this function by courts is not confined to countries with a federal government. It is found in a country like the United Kingdom, whose government is usually called unitary, for there the courts have the power—unless it has been expressly withdrawn from them by law—to say whether a governmental institution is acting within the limits of its power. In such unitary states as the Republic of Ireland also, the courts have a similar power. Where these countries differ from a federal government like the United States is in the limits imposed by the law of their constitution upon the various institutions of government, and thus upon the extent to which the courts are required to control other institutions. Thus in the United Kingdom the powers of the general legislature are not limited, so that the courts treat all acts of the general legislature as valid. In Ireland, on the other hand, some limitations are placed upon the powers of the legislature and the supreme court consequently may consider the validity of its acts. In a federal government the courts must go further because general and regional legislatures are limited in their powers and the degree of judicial control is correspondingly greater.

There is a second point. It must not be assumed that it is essential for federal government that the power to determine the meaning of the division of powers should be entrusted to the *courts* of the general government. All that has been demonstrated so far is that in the absence of provisions to the contrary, it is perfectly logical and necessary for courts to consider and pass an opinion upon these questions; they cannot avoid it. But it is not essential for federal government that they should have the last word upon them. What is essential for federal government is that some impartial body, independent of general and regional governments, should decide upon the meaning of the division of powers. It happens that in the United States and Australia the highest court of the land has had the last word in the matter and that, on the whole, it has proved independent of the rest of the general government. In Canada an independent court, the Judicial Committee of the Privy Council, has performed the function. But the example of Switzerland shows that federal government and good government do not inevitably require that the power should be exercised completely by the ordinary courts, nor that it should be exercised by lawyers at all.

This has led people to ask whether it would not be better to set up in the other federations some method of interpreting the division of powers which should remove it from the province of the judges. It is asserted that judges have proved too legalistic in their outlook, or that they have not been legalistic enough, but have introduced into judgements about the law their opinions about what it is desirable for the law to be. It is thought to be intolerable that the will of the people as expressed through the elected legislature should be thwarted in a supreme court sometimes by a bare majority of one.[1] Much of this criticism is sound. There is a great deal of inconvenience in the operation of the system of judicial review in the United States, Canada and Australia. In my opinion, however, no alternative scheme with less inconveniences seems possible, consistently with maintaining the federal principle.

It has been suggested that the inconvenience of judicial review could be avoided by the adoption of a rule that, if a law of the general government be declared void by a supreme court, it should be re-submitted to the legislature and if re-passed, say with a two-thirds majority, or after a general election, should be valid. No proposal of this kind really commands much support in the United States, nor in the other two federations where judicial review prevails. What must be faced is that by this suggestion an alternative method of altering the constitution is being proposed. Supreme courts are held to be too rigid; the ordinary method of altering the constitution is held to be too difficult to employ; some way round is sought. Here again it may well be that such a proposal if adopted would improve the government of these countries. The method of deciding the limits of powers confided to general and regional governments might be so devised that neither was subordinate to the other and yet change was made more easy; or the federal principle itself might be modified in this respect, with a result which was beneficial to the system of government. But it is important that when these alternatives to judicial review are discussed, it should be realized clearly that what is involved in the last resort is the method of altering the constitution.

And here the true significance of the Swiss system is brought to light. Switzerland has, in effect, two methods of amending its constitution. There is the method of explicit amendment already described where a majority is required in the two houses of the general legislature and thereafter a majority of all the electors voting, and a majority of electors in a majority of cantons. But there is also a method of amendment by implication. The general legislature may pass a law which conflicts with the constitution. That law may not be questioned at all, and in that case it comes into full effect and the constitution is to that extent amended. Or it may be submitted to a referendum of the people on the requests of 30,000 electors or of 8 cantons. In this case all it requires in order to be approved and to come into full effect is a simple majority of all the electors voting. There is no requirement here that a majority of cantons also is needed. This is apparently an easier method of altering the constitution. At the same

---

[1] In the United States up to 1944, about fifteen decisions adverse to Congress by a majority of one had been given by the Supreme Court.

time it may be asserted at once that it could be used to make small modifications only in the constitution. Any open and obvious amendment to the constitution would require in normal times in Switzerland the invocation of the ordinary method of constitutional amendment.

The Swiss example illustrates, however, a way in which disputes about the division of powers in a federation might be dealt with. It provides two methods of altering the constitution, and one is suited to those piecemeal and sometimes imperceptible changes which are held to be necessary in the division of powers when no larger explicit changes can be made. Whether such a system could be worked successfully in the United States, Canada and Australia is not easy to guess. It has been used with moderation in Switzerland, but the particular form which it has taken there—the referendum—might not work so easily in the other federations. On the other hand it might be possible to provide in the United States, for example, that any act of Congress invalidated by the Supreme Court and repassed by Congress should become law, unless the legislatures of twelve states demanded that it should be submitted to the legislatures of all the states, in which case it should become law if it was approved by the legislatures of a majority of the states. Many variations on this kind of procedure have been discussed from time to time as a method of overcoming alleged rigidities in the operation of judicial review by the Supreme Court of the United States and in the other two federations. There is no necessary inconsistency between such methods and the working of the federal principle, provided always, as I have said, that neither general nor regional governments acting alone is given the power of altering the division of powers. It seems unlikely, however, that any such scheme will be accepted in the near future in the United States, at any rate, nor for that matter in Canada and Australia. Judicial review, with all its admitted drawbacks, is strongly entrenched.

6

The organization of the courts themselves has some importance. If the federal principle were to be strictly applied one would expect a dual system to be established in a federation, one set of courts to apply and interpret the law of the general government, and another to apply and interpret the law of each state. In fact the United States alone of the four federations we are discussing comes near to applying this principle. There is a system of what are called 'federal' courts, ranging from District Courts up through a series of Circuit Courts of Appeals to the Supreme Court itself, and there is a system of state courts, terminating in each state in a state Supreme Court. This parallel system is sometimes spoken of as if each set of courts exercised a jurisdiction which was completely exclusive of the other. Bryce once wrote, for example, that 'in the United States there is a complete system of Federal Courts ramifying all over the Union and exercising exclusive jurisdiction in all cases arising under Federal Statutes, as well as in a number of the matters specified in Art. III, sect. 2 of the Constitution. But the state courts remain quite independent in all state matters, and determine the interpretation of the State Constitutions, and of all state statutes, nor does any appeal lie from them to the Federal Courts.'[1] This is an exaggeration of the position. There are indeed certain matters which Congress has provided shall be decided by the Federal Courts exclusively. Such matters as crimes against the United States, civil causes of admiralty and maritime jurisdiction, patent, copyright and bankruptcy cases, for example, come within the jurisdiction of the federal District Courts, to the exclusion of State Courts. But there are many matters falling within the judicial power of the United States in which state courts have a jurisdiction concurrent with that of the federal courts, and there are one or two matters within the judicial power of the United States which Congress has provided shall fall under the exclusive jurisdiction of the state courts. There are arrangements, however, in cases where the federal courts and state courts have a concurrent jurisdiction, that in certain circumstances regulated by act of Congress a case brought in a state court may thereafter be removed to a federal court. The details of jurisdiction are most complicated in the United States and no attempt will be made to enumerate them here.[2] What needs emphasis is that though there is a parallel system of courts in the United States, Congress has not made the jurisdiction of each system exclusive. What is true is that there is an opportunity for a litigant to choose a federal court in almost all matters where federal law is concerned, and to begin a case in a state court in most matters where a state law is concerned. The two systems interlock. One aspect of the interlocking is of the greatest importance for the working of the federal government. This is the provision that, broadly speaking, when in a case before a state court any question arises of the interpretation of the Constitution of the United States or of the validity of any act of Congress or treaty made thereunder, such questions fall to be decided by the federal courts or in the last resort by the Supreme Court, either because the case may be transferred from the state to the federal courts or because it can go on appeal to the Supreme Court of the United States from the highest court of the state.

The parallel system of courts in the United States is unique among the four federations. In Australia the constitution makes possible the establishment of a similar system but it has not so far been adopted. There is a High Court established by the constitution comparable to the Supreme Court of the United States, and the parliament of the Commonwealth is given power to establish courts inferior to the

[1] *Studies in History and Jurisprudence*, Vol. I, p. 416.
[2] There is a good short statement in, for example, Charles Fairman, *American Constitutional Decisions*.

High Court. It has used this power only to establish a Commonwealth Court of Conciliation and Arbitration, a Federal Bankruptcy Court and a Supreme Court of the Australian Capital Territory. For the rest it has made use of a power granted in the Constitution to invest other courts with jurisdiction in certain matters coming within the judicial power of the Commonwealth. As a result the state courts exercise much of this jurisdiction. They are both federal and state courts. But over them the High Court stands as a court of appeal in all types of case arising in state supreme courts. Its jurisdiction is thus much wider than that of the Supreme Court of the United States. When invoked, it can impose a uniform interpretation of the law—subject in certain cases to an appeal to the Judicial Committee of the Privy Council—upon the courts of the states.

The system in Switzerland resembles that in Australia to some extent. The cantonal courts exercise jurisdiction to apply both the law of the cantons and the law of the general government, subject to some reservations. The Federal Tribunal stands as a court of appeal over the cantonal courts; it has jurisdiction in all civil cases involving a sum of 4,000 francs or more, when they have been tried before a cantonal court of final appeal. This function of the Federal Tribunal is held to be its most important,[1] because 'in the absence of all inferior federal courts the unity of civil jurisprudence could not otherwise be assured in Switzerland'. The Federal Tribunal is not only a court of appeal. It has an original jurisdiction and some power of judicial review to which reference will be made later.

In Canada the system comes near to that of a single unified system of courts. Although there is power in the constitution for the legislatures of the Dominion and of the provinces to establish systems of courts for their own jurisdiction, and although both legislatures have made use of this power, all judges are appointed and paid by the government of the Dominion. The provinces have established their own courts and they regulate their procedure in civil matters. The Dominion has conferred upon provincial courts jurisdiction in most matters of Dominion law and it regulates procedure in criminal matters. The Supreme Court of the Dominion has an appellate jurisdiction in both civil and criminal matters from the provincial courts;[2] and, since the passing of the Supreme Court Act at the end of 1949, it has become the final court of appeal in all Canadian lawsuits.

It can be seen that there has been no uniformity among federations in organizing their courts. The general legislatures have been quite ready in Canada, Australia and Switzerland, and to a small extent even in the United States, to rely upon the regional courts to apply and interpret the law of the general government. In every case it is to

---

[1] Rappard, *The Government of Switzerland*, pp. 89–90.

[2] There is only one other Dominion court—the Court of Exchequer and Admiralty—which deals with patents, trade marks and the like, and has an original jurisdiction in revenue cases concurrent with the provincial courts.

be noticed that the general legislatures had power, if they chose to exercise it, to set up a complete system of federal courts with exclusive jurisdiction. But while there has been this practice of trusting the regional courts to apply the law of the general government in Canada, Australia and Switzerland, it is to be noted that there exists always some form of safeguard for the general government in the appellate jurisdiction and, in some matters, in the original jurisdiction, which has been conferred upon the supreme court of the general government. When any question arises concerning a federal law there is, as a general rule, the power for a supreme court of the general government in the last resort to hear and determine the appeal.

It seems true to say, therefore, that the method of organizing courts in a federal government need not be stereotyped. The principle of a co-ordinate status for the general and regional governments permits of some overlapping of jurisdiction, provided there is always some safeguard such as the power to establish a parallel system of courts or a right of appeal from regional courts of double jurisdiction to a supreme court of the general government, where matters affecting the law of the general government are concerned. On the other hand, the case of Canada, where the appointment of all judges is in the hands of the general government, is an example of a system which contradicts the federal principle. It is a further illustration of the modified or quasi-federal system which the Canadian Constitution established.

7

This is not the place in which to discuss the operation of the courts in the respective federations in any detail, nor will the effect of judicial review in particular be fully treated at this point. In the chapters of Part IV where the working of federal governments is discussed, the effects of judicial review will be illustrated frequently, and towards the end of the book where the whole record of federalism is reviewed, some attempt will be made in Chapter XI to discuss the importance of judicial review. But it is worth while at this point to say something of the influence which courts have had in the organization of federations. Under this head it is proper to discuss first the power given to the supreme courts to interpret the constitutions and, secondly, their power—varying in extent in the different countries—to interpret the ordinary law.

In all four federations the supreme court of the general government has some power to interpret the constitution and to determine disputes about its meaning, though the extent of this power varies from one to another. And this power carries with it, in all except Switzerland, some claim to consider the validity, not only of the statutes of the general legislature, but also of the statutes and the constitutions of the regions. There again the extent of the power varies from federation to federation. But it can be seen that there is confided to a single court the power to interpret a uniform constitutional structure for a variety of governmental organizations contained within a federal government. And it will be noticed at the same time that the last word upon these constitutional matters is made to rest not with the courts of the regions, but with the court of the general government.

It is in Australia and Canada perhaps that the widest powers of constitutional interpretation are conferred upon the highest court of the whole federation.[1] In Australia the High Court interprets the Constitution of the Commonwealth and can declare any act of a state legislature, or of the Commonwealth parliament, void to the extent to which it conflicts with the Constitution. It can have the last word, if it chooses, upon the extent of the powers conferred by the Constitution upon the states and the Commonwealth. Here it differed until 1950 from the Supreme Court of Canada, which had a similar jurisdiction, but exercised it subject to an appeal to the Judicial Committee of the Privy Council. Both the High Court of Australia and the Supreme Court of Canada have power to interpret the constitutions of the regional governments. This power extends not merely to deciding whether a state or provincial constitution is consistent with the constitution of the Commonwealth or the Dominion, but also to determining, on appeal from the regional courts, any disputed question about the regional constitution. It should be added that this jurisdiction is not exclusive. In Australia an appeal from a state supreme court on a matter which does not raise a question of the rights and powers *inter se* of the states and Commonwealth may be taken direct to the Privy Council or indirectly through the High Court. In Canada until the end of 1949 appeals from the appellate tribunals of the provinces might be taken direct to the Privy Council, or might go to the Supreme Court and thereafter to the Privy Council. The position in Canada now is that the Supreme Court exercises a final and exclusive power to determine all constitutional questions however arising.

The power of the highest court in Switzerland and in the United States is less. Switzerland requires judicial review only for the cantonal constitutions. The Federal Tribunal in Switzerland has the duty of maintaining the federal constitution against the cantonal constitutions, and the cantonal constitutions as against cantonal laws or administrative acts.

In the United States the power of the Supreme Court to control the constitutional law of the states can arise only from its power to interpret the Constitution of the United States. It lacks the powers of a general court of appeal with which the High Court of Australia and the Supreme Court of Canada have been endowed. None the less the Supreme Court of the United States is able, in constitutional matters, to extend its authority into the realm of state constitutional

[1] Until 1950 the Judicial Committee was Canada's highest court.

law. The reason for this is that the Constitution itself, and more particularly its Fourteenth Amendment, imposes certain restrictions upon the states, which it is the duty of the Supreme Court to apply and interpret.[1]

Broadly speaking, cases go on appeal to the Supreme Court, from state courts or from inferior federal courts, when they involve some question the decision of which depends on the interpretation of the Constitution, laws and treaties of the United States. Formerly if a state supreme court decided in favour of the validity of a statute or treaty of the United States or against the validity of a state statute on the ground of its repugnancy to the Constitution, laws or treaties of the United States, its decision was final. But as this involved conflicting interpretations, in various states, of the Constitution and laws of the United States, and sometimes restrictive and narrow interpretations, Congress, in 1914 and 1916, amended the provisions and made it possible for appeals to be heard by the Supreme Court of the United States even when the state court had upheld the claim of the general government.

Many of the cases dealt with raise questions of the division of powers between the general and state governments and may result in the invalidation of state statutes. But control goes much beyond this. Thus the Constitution says that 'all legislative powers herein granted shall be vested in a Congress of the United States'. When in 1933 Congress passed the National Industry Recovery Act, part of President Roosevelt's New Deal, under which extensive rule-making powers were granted to the President, it was objected that this was a case of Congress's attempting to delegate to the President some part of that legislative power which the Constitution vested in Congress alone. It was contended on the other side that this was no delegation of legislative power but merely of a sub-legislative or administrative rule-making power. The Supreme Court had to decide the point in 1935. It ruled unanimously that the Act attempted to delegate legislative power and that this was unconstitutional.[1] The Court was obliged to attempt some definition of 'legislative'. It was called upon to decide really whether 'delegated legislation' was possible under the American Constitution or not. Here is a matter not of federal government but of general governmental organization which the Supreme Court has had to deal with. The same questions have come before the High Court of Australia and the Supreme Court of Canada, though in cases of less importance, as a result of the form in which legislative power has been granted to the parliaments in their constitutions.

Another important provision in the Constitution of the United States is found in the Fifth and Fourteenth Amendments. The Fifth Amendment provides, *inter alia* that no person shall be 'deprived of

---

[1] See below, pp. 138, 148.

[2] *Schechter Poultry Corp.* v. *U.S.* (1935) 295 U.S. 495.

life, liberty or property, without due process of law'. It was directed exclusively to the general government. The Fourteenth Amendment imposes a similar restriction upon the state governments. When it was passed its main object was to protect the negro in his new status as a freeman. It has been the task of the Supreme Court to give a meaning to these vague terms, 'life', 'liberty', 'property', 'person', 'due process of law'. Its interpretation of them has restricted the activities of state and general governments to an astonishing extent. 'Person' becomes extended in meaning to cover a corporation or company. At one time, attempts by a state legislature or by the general legislature to fix minimum hours of labour for workers and rates of wages were declared invalid[1] as unjust interferences with the liberty of the subject contrary to due process of law. The general effects of the Supreme Court's rulings at that time are summarized by Professor Brogan in this passage: 'Great and new social problems were demanding legal remedies, and the degree of freedom or limitation to be given to or imposed on such monsters of private enterprise as the railways and the great trusts was the fundamental question of American politics. The policy decided on, that of general encouragement to these great enterprises, and general discouragement of social legislation, was the work of the Supreme Court. Not only did it cripple both state and federal governments, but when it did permit them to exercise some of the attributes of sovereignty, it did so under the disguise of special and exceptional grants. It utilized vague terms like 'the police power' to justify the exercise of normal governmental powers and created an atmosphere in which the burden of proof, in most fields of economic legislation, was imposed on the law-making bodies. Nor was it a matter of dividing authority between state and union, for powers denied by one decision to the states might be denied by another to the Union and the United States left impotent to legislate either in their separate or united capacity.'[2]

When in 1937 the Supreme Court began to reverse this trend of interpretation[3] it was exercising once more a tremendous influence upon the working of federal government, for it was removing from both general and regional governments shackles which had handicapped them both and created a situation in which the competition of each for power could enter upon new and important stages.[4]

8

In the sphere of ordinary law the supreme courts exercise an important influence. Here again the High Court of Australia and the

---

[1] See, for example, *Lochner v. New York* (1905), 198 U.S. 45 and *Adkins v. Children's Hospital* (1923), 261 U.S. 525.

[2] *Politics and Law in the United States*, p. 83.

[3] In 1937 it reversed *Adkins v. Children's Hospital* in the case of *West Coast Hotel v. Parrish*, 300 U.S. 379.

[4] For further discussion, see below, Chapter XI.

Supreme Court of Canada, the former subject to appeals to the
Judicial Committee of the Privy Council to some extent, have wide
power to interpret the law of the regions and of the general government upon uniform principles. The Swiss Federal Tribunal hears
appeals from all cantonal tribunals on important civil cases. But in the
United States no such general power is conferred upon the Supreme
Court. But here again the Supreme Court has come to exercise more
influence than might have been expected. The interpretation of the
'Due Process' Clause as applied to the States gave it a great opportunity for influence over ordinary law, as we have seen.

But quite apart from questions of constitutional validity, the
Court has tried to achieve some uniformity in the civil law. The most
interesting example of this kind arose from the clause in the constitution which placed within the judicial power of the general government the decision of cases between citizens of different states. Here
Congress has provided that cases involving less than $3,000 shall be
tried in state courts, but cases above that amount may be brought in
federal courts.

In such cases what law shall the federal courts apply? The Judiciary
Act of 1789 provided that the laws of the several states should be the
rules of decision. The Supreme Court follows the latest settled adjudi-
cations of the state courts concerned in cases of state statutes and the
law of real property, though there is of course room for some latitude
in deciding what the state courts have decided and in reconciling or
preferring conflicting views. But in one branch of the law, the law of
negotiable instruments, the Supreme Court decided in a famous case,
Swift v. *Tyson*, in 1842,[1] that it was, by the act of 1789, bound to
follow state statutes, but not the common law of the state and that it
was free to build up what amounted to a body of federal common
law. This decision stood until 1938. For about a century the Supreme
Court had influenced an important sphere of commercial law and it
had extended its influence to matters within such branches of the law
as contracts, torts and equity. Here was an attempt by the Supreme
Court to control state law and to produce some measure of uniformity. But it was not entirely successful. State courts persisted in their
own decisions and confusion and conflict of law arose. In 1938 the
Court explicitly reversed the decision of *Swift* v. *Tyson*. 'There is no
federal common law,' it said. It ruled that the law to be enforced in
cases of diverse citizenship must be that laid down by the Courts of
the state where the cause of action arose.[2]

There are one or two other provisions in the federal constitutions
which have made possible an increase in the influence of the supreme
courts. One problem which the formation of a federal government is
expected to solve is inter-state disputes. These disputes, it is usually

[1] 16 Pet. 1 (1842).
[2] *Erie Railroad Co.* v. *Tompkins* (1938) 304 U.S. 64. The effects of the decision in *Swift* v.
Tyson are fully set out in the judgement, and it was overruled by a majority of 6—2.

expected, will be settled chiefly perhaps through the new general legislature which is established by the federal constitution. But provision is made for adjudication and judicial settlement also. Thus in the Constitution of the United States, Australia and Switzerland, the supreme court is given an original jurisdiction to determine matters in dispute between the regions. A similar power can be exercised in Canada by a reference of a disputed question to the Supreme Court. The determination of these disputes is naturally of great interest to the student of federal government. It has been used most widely in the United States. The kinds of disputes that have arisen may be mentioned. There was a boundary dispute between Louisiana and Mississippi because of a change in the course of the Mississippi river; there was a dispute between Missouri and Illinois because Chicago emptied its sewage into a stream from which ultimately the city of St. Louis in Missouri obtained water; a dispute between New Jersey and New York State because New York City emptied its sewage into the Atlantic and it floated upon New Jersey beaches; and a dispute between Kansas and Colorado in which Kansas brought a suit in the Supreme Court to restrain Colorado from diverting water for irrigation from the Arkansas River which flowed through Kansas. In the course of its judgement in this last case the Supreme Court emphasized the importance of its function when it said that 'through these successive disputes and decisions this court is practically building up what may not improperly be called inter-state common law.'[1]

Another clause that has been of importance in the operation of courts in the United States is that requiring the states to give full faith and credit to the public acts, records and judicial proceedings of every state. A similar requirement is inserted in the Australian constitution. This clause, it may be noted, does not require a state to assist another state in enforcing its criminal law. It refers to civil matters only and it extends to the legislative acts, to records of deeds, wills, births, marriages, divorces and contracts, and to the decisions and judgements rendered by the courts of the states. It is obvious that difficulties can arise under this clause, through the difference of law in the various states. The Supreme Court of the United States, for example, has been required to say what is involved in full faith and credit, and how far the states have beeen fulfilling their obligations. The sphere of divorce provides an obvious illustration of the sort of difficulties that may arise and here the Supreme Court has held that the full faith and credit clause does not require a state to recognize all divorces granted by the courts of other states. Certain conditions must be fulfilled, and when these conditions are fulfilled a divorce must be recognized.[2] In this way the Supreme Court imposes some measure of uniformity in this field which, under the constitution, is left to be regulated by the states.

---

[1] *Kansas* v. *Colorado* (1907) 206 U.S. 46, at p. 98.

[2] See *Williams* v. *North Carolina* (No. 2), (1945), 325 U.S. 226.

9

The points which have been touched upon in this discussion of the courts in federal government will have emphasized one fact which is often overlooked. The courts, and especially the supreme courts, have a function which extends beyond the mere question of determining disputes about the division of powers between general and regional governments. And this wider function is of equal if not greater importance. Through their interpretation of the whole constitution of the federation and of the ordinary law, so far as they are permitted to do so, they may exercise an integrating influence which, because it is gradual and imperceptible, is of the greatest importance. Even in the United States where the power of adjudication is not so wide as in Australia and Canada, the influence of the federal courts and of the Supreme Court has been most striking. And if the Supreme Court has now resolved, as its decision in 1938 suggests,[1] to confine itself more and more to the decision of questions of constitutionality, that field alone, in view of the language and nature of the constitution, is wide enough, if not too wide.

[1] *The Erie Railroad Case*, overruling *Swift* v. *Tyson*, discussed above. Brandeis, J., giving the majority opinion of the Court, said that 'this Court and the lower courts have invaded rights which in our opinion are reserved by the Constitution to the several states', at p. 80.

Chapter V

CONCERNING, IN THE MAIN,
POWERS AND PARTIES

1

THE institutions so far discussed appear to me the only institutions which are essential to a government if it is to be federal. But it is necessary to consider some further topics because in the first place there are certain institutions which, while not essential to federal government, are essential to good federal government; and secondly there are some institutions which are commonly regarded as essential to federal government and it is proper that I should explain why I do not regard them as essential.

I propose to deal first with a question which arises from the problem of the division of powers. I have said from time to time that in a federal government some matters are placed under the exclusive jurisdiction of an independent general government, and other matters are given to the exclusive jurisdiction of independent regional governments. The use of the word 'exclusive' may be misleading. It may appear to rule out entirely the possibility that in some matters both sets of governments may be permitted to exercise authority. It is well to emphasize at once that the existence of a *concurrent* jurisdiction in some matters is not necessarily incompatible with the federal principle. But if there is a concurrent jurisdiction, there must exist also some provision to determine which authority, in case of conflict, is to prevail. That authority will possess, in my opinion, potential though not actual exclusive jurisdiction. It has the power to bring the subject in question under its exclusive control to the extent that it chooses to regulate it. It does not matter, so far as the federal principle is concerned, whether the overriding authority on subjects of concurrent jurisdiction is vested with the general government or the regional governments. But if there is to be federalism, one condition must be fulfilled. There must be some matter, even if only one matter, which comes under the exclusive control, actual or potential, of the general government and something likewise under the regional governments. If there were not, that would be the end of federalism.

A concurrent jurisdiction is found in all modern federal governments, and with it a provision that when the laws of the general government upon matters in the concurrent field conflict with the laws of the regional governments in that field, then the regional laws must give way to the general laws to the extent of their repugnancy. The extent of the concurrent jurisdiction varies greatly. In Canada it is small. It comprises immigration and agriculture only. All remaining subjects of legislation are exclusive either to the provinces or to the Dominion.

In the United States and Australia, on the other hand, the concurrent field is extensive. It contains even such subjects as the armed forces, and charges upon imports and exports. But there is an important difference between these and other topics in the concurrent field. The regions may legislate in respect of armed forces and import and export charges, but they do so only with the consent of the general government.[1] In all other matters in the concurrent field the regions may legislate without asking the consent of the general government, and their legislation is of full effect unless the general government not only decides to legislate upon such matters, but also legislates in conflict with regional legislation. Thus in the United States and Australia, general and regional governments may both legislate in respect of some aspects of inter-state and foreign commerce,[2] and in respect of bankruptcy, copyrights and patents, census and statistics, weights and measures—all of them subjects which in Canada are removed entirely from regional control, and given to the exclusive jurisdiction of the Dominion government. It is true that the general governments have legislated by now in most of these fields so comprehensively that regional governments are effectively excluded, but the fact remains that until and unless this is done, the regions have power to deal with such topics.

In Switzerland the concurrent field is smaller than in the United States and Australia, but it is wider than in Canada. It includes immigration, which is under concurrent jurisdiction not only in Canada, as I have said, but in the United States and Australia also. Quarantine and banking appear to be concurrent subjects in Switzerland; they are concurrent also in the United States and Australia,[3] but in Canada they are exclusive to the Dominion government. Agriculture—the other concurrent subject in Canada—is exclusive to the regional governments in the United States and Australia, but in Switzerland it is divided between the general and regional governments.[4] This device of dividing a subject between the governments is used frequently in Switzerland. It covers such topics as treaties and alliances, marriage, hydraulic resources, motor-cars and bicycles, and

---

[1] It is perhaps more accurate to call these legislative powers of the regions 'delegated' powers, not concurrent, for they are held by the regions at the pleasure of the general legislature.

[2] Subject, in the United States, to the reservation about import and export duties mentioned above, and in Australia to the reservation that, upon the imposition of uniform customs duties by the Commonwealth, the latter's power over customs, excise and export duties becomes exclusive.

[3] With the exception of 'state banking' operating intra-state in Australia, which is under the actual exclusive jurisdiction of the states.

[4] I mean that part of the subject is given to the general government and part to the regional governments.

the control of alcoholic liquors. This device is not employed to any great extent in other federations. The control of the militia and of commerce, for example, is divided in the United States, and the control of banking, commerce and railways, for example, in Australia.

The Constitution of the Republic of India is quasi-federal only, and I do not propose, as I have said already, to discuss it as an example of a federal constitution. But in one respect at least it is of interest and that is the way in which it dealt with the division of powers. The Constitution of 1950 contains three legislative lists.[1] The first enumerates, under ninety-seven heads, the subjects over which the union legislature has actual exclusive control; the second, under sixty-six heads, those under the actual exclusive control of the states; and the third, under forty-seven heads, the subjects upon which both union and state legislatures make laws. Here is an enumeration more complete than anything attempted in the four federations. The matters in the concurrent field are, on the whole, not unexpected. But it is interesting to notice that immigration, which appears in the concurrent list in all four federations, is under the exclusive jurisdiction of the general government in the Constitution of 1950. The provisions which deal with a conflict between general and regional laws are interesting.[2] In general they require that regional laws on concurrent subjects must give way to the laws of the general government to the extent of their repugnancy to such laws. But it is possible, if the President of India consents, for a regional law on a concurrent subject to prevail in spite of repugnancy. Thus there is room for flexibility in the exercise of the concurrent jurisdiction, and the general government is not inevitably supreme in case of conflict. Yet as it rests with the President to decide whether the general legislature is to be supreme, in this way a potentially exclusive control is vested with the general government.

It may be mentioned that the Constitution of Malaya also has three lists whereas the Constitutions of Rhodesia and Nyasaland, the West Indies, Western Germany and Nigeria are content with two, a general exclusive list and a concurrent list.

2

It is most important to decide whether a federal government should be organized with a concurrent jurisdiction or not. A concurrent jurisdiction, as I have said already, is not incompatible with federal government, but may it not be incompatible with a good federal government? It adds yet another series of disputes about jurisdiction to the already formidable list of possible conflicts which are inevitable in even the simplest federal system. The simplest way to organize a federal government, it might seem, is either to decide what matters are

---

[1] See Seventh schedule. Compare Government of India Act, 1935.
[2] Art. 254.

to be regulated by the general government and to place them under its actual exclusive control, leaving the rest to the actual exclusive control of the regional governments, or vice versa. There is then one list of subjects only and disputes can be confined to the meaning of the words in that list. If a concurrent list is added, there are not only disputes about the meaning of the words in the new list, but about the extent to which these words overlap or conflict with words in the exclusive list, and about the extent to which laws passed by the general and regional legislatures on concurrent subjects, conflict with each other and are void. Not merely lists but statutes also must be compared and in the result there may be piecemeal legislation and considerable uncertainty over a wide area. If to an exclusive list and a concurrent list, yet another exclusive list is added, as in Canada and India, then the problems of interpretation become even more varied. Three lists must be compared. It would be a supreme draughtsman who could so draw these lists that no charge of overlapping could be brought against them. A second exclusive list is a very great nuisance, as the experience of courts in interpreting the Canadian constitution testifies.[1] Undoubtedly the simplest form of division is obtained by having one list only and that actually exclusive.

But in practice it is not usually possible to organize a federal government quite so simply as this. When previously sovereign states decide to federate, it is possible to get them to agree upon a list of subjects upon which the general government is to legislate. But they are reluctant to surrender all control immediately over these subjects. Nor is it always convenient that they should do so, before the general government has organized a system of uniform legislation or efficient administration to cover these fields. For these reasons it is common to demand that some of them should be made concurrent, until the general government chooses to regulate them itself. Sometimes transitional arrangements are made for the exercise of concurrent power until the general government is ready to take over exclusive control. Thus in Australia it was provided that 'on the imposition of uniform duties of customs, the power of the parliament to impose duties of customs and excise, and to grant bounties on the production or export of goods shall become exclusive', and such uniform duties were required to be imposed within two years.[2] There are indeed many good reasons for providing a concurrent jurisdiction. The framers of the Constitution of India of 1935 stated them in this way: 'Experience has shown, both in India and elsewhere, that there are certain matters which cannot be allocated exclusively either to a Central or to a Provincial Legislature, and for which, though it is often desirable that provincial legislation should make provision, it is equally necessary that the Central Legislature should also have a legislative jurisdiction,

---

[1] See below, Chapters VII and XI, pp. 129–33, 216–19.
[2] *Australian Constitution*, ss. 88 & 90. See also s. 108.

to enable it in some cases to secure uniformity in the main principles of law throughout the country, in others to guide and encourage provincial effort, and in others again to provide remedies for mischiefs arising in the provincial sphere but extending or liable to extend beyond the boundaries of a single province.'[1] In the light of all these good reasons, it is better always, if possible, to admit concurrent jurisdiction, if only perhaps as a transitional measure. In most cases it will be unavoidable. But what is likely to work best is a short exclusive list and a rather longer concurrent list.

If a new federation of formerly sovereign states is to be formed, the simplest plan, then, would be to seek agreement on a list of subjects to be confided to the actual exclusive control of the new government. The constituent states see clearly to what they are committing themselves. But this involves the principle that all matters not given to the actual exclusive control of the general government remain with the states. Some people attach the greatest importance to the question where the residual power should be in a federation, and, as I have mentioned in a previous chapter, there are those who deny the name of a federation to a state which gives the residual power to the general government. There is no doubt that the question is important. There are objections to any method of allocating the residual powers. The principal objection to the method of allocating them to the states —the method adopted substantially in the United States, Switzerland and Australia and followed by Western Germany, Rhodesia and Nyasaland, Malaya, the West Indies and Nigeria—is that some new matter of general importance may emerge which was unforeseen at the time of the framing of the Constitution, and it falls automatically to the regional governments. Aviation is such a subject. In Switzerland this was dealt with in 1921 by an amendment to the Constitution which handed the power to legislate an aerial navigation to the general government.[2] But in the United States and Australia the powers of the general governments over aviation are only those which they have in virtue of their control over defence and inter-state commerce and from their powers to implement treaties.[3] Treaties apart, the rest of intra-state civil aviation is under state control. In Australia an attempt was made in 1937 and in 1944 to remedy this situation by a constitutional amendment, but on both occasions the amendment was rejected.

But it seems fairly certain that when sovereign states propose to federate they will be anxious not to give up an unlimited area of power to a new general government and they will be reluctant therefore to leave the residual power to the general government. If this is so, the fact must be accepted and with it the inconvenience that it entails.

[1] *Report of Joint Select Committee on Indian Constitutional Reform* 1934, para. 51.
[2] Swiss Constitution, Art. 37 ter.
[3] In Australia the matter was decided by the High Court in *The King* v. *Burgess*, ex parte *Henry* (1936), 55 C.L.R. 608.

The aim must be to get an exclusive list for the general government which contains as many as possible of the important subjects of general concern and to hope that if any new subject of general importance arises, the need for general control will ensure that it will be handed over to the general government. If, on the other hand, states are willing to enumerate the powers which they wish to retain exclusively, and to leave the residual power to the general government, objections of a different kind may be imagined. But the experience of Canada suggests that this need not mean that provincial powers will be by any means negligible or progressively whittled down.

3

So much for the division of powers in a federal government. But another question arises in connection with what is usually called 'the separation of powers'. It is unfortunate that this term should resemble so closely the term 'the division of powers', and it is necessary therefore to explain a little what is intended by it. The doctrine of the separation of powers holds that good government is ensured if the functions of legislation, administration and adjudication in a state are not placed in the hands of one body of persons but are distributed to a greater or less degree among distinct or separate bodies of persons. In its extreme form it would involve, presumably, the assignment of the legislative, executive and judicial functions of government each exclusively to a separate body of persons. In practice this absolute and exclusive separation has never been advocated. But, as explained in the last chapter, a modified application of it has occurred in the United States where Congress, the Courts, and the President and his officers, are each separated off from the other, and members of one group are forbidden by the constitution to be members of the other. The constitution then proceeds to allocate functions. All legislative powers are vested in Congress;[1] all executive power in the President;[2] all judicial power in one supreme court and in such inferior courts as Congress may from time to time ordain and establish.[3] Yet there are exceptions to this absolute separation even in the constitution itself. The President is associated with Congress in the exercise of the legislative function by his veto power; the Senate is associated with the President in his executive function in that its consent is necessary to his making treaties and to his making certain important appointments. But this partial adoption of the principle of the separation of powers in the United States has led some writers to argue that a separation of powers, to some degree at any rate, is essential to federal government.[4]

On the whole the right view seems to be that it is not essential,

---

[1] Art. I.   [2] Art. II, 1.   [3] Art. III, 1.
[4] It was argued in the Australian Convention of 1897, that responsible cabinet government and federal government could not live together. See *Official Report of the National Australasian Convention*, Adelaide, 1897, pp. 27–31.

if a state is to be federal, that its general government should be organized in accordance with the separation of powers, although it may prove that a federal government works better if it is so organized. The federal principle lays down no rules about how the general government itself is to be organized, provided it is organized in such a way that general and regional governments are co-ordinate, each supreme in its own sphere. The separation of legislature, executive and judiciary in the general government or their overlapping or complete fusion does not conflict with or connect with the federal principle. There is one exception to this. The separation of the judiciary in the general government from the other branches of the government is important if it is the tribunal which decides disputes about the meaning of the division of powers. As I have explained already this separation is almost complete in most federal systems, but there is a connection from the fact that members of the judiciary are appointed and removable by either the executive or the legislature or a combination of both.

For the rest it may be said that the separation of powers has a value in assisting the working of federal government in some cases. Its general effect is to weaken government, and a weak government is sometimes considered desirable by the units which form a federal union. Unless they have some assurance that there can be no swift decisive action by the general government in the matters committed to its exclusive care, the states which are to join a federation feel reluctant to hand over their powers. This was certainly true at the foundation of the United States. Professor Laski states it shortly in these words: 'The American system, in its ultimate foundations, is built upon a belief in weak government.'[1]

To those who live under and believe in the system of unitary government, it may seem suicidal to adopt the separation of powers in a federation. Surely federal government will be weak enough already from the division of powers, without adding to it yet another division within the bosom of the general government itself by adopting the separation of powers. The only justification that can be offered is this. In some circumstances there must be weak government, if there is to be government at all. In the American system, in my opinion, the separation of powers serves a useful federal purpose. It holds the federal union together because it provides so many obstacles to the carrying out of policies which are not strongly supported by a large body of organized political opinion. This obstructionism, this conservatism, this indecisiveness in the American general government, is a guarantee to all the units in it that nothing will be done to which they object very strongly. It means, of course, that in many cases nothing at all will be done. But that is the price of federal government and of any government at all for a heterogeneous continent.

[1] *The American Presidency*, p. 160; see also p. 240.

This is not to say that the separation of powers should certainly be adopted in a federal government. It would be unwise needlessly to weaken still further a government which from its nature is already likely to be weak. It would be wise where possible to attempt to strengthen the general government and particularly its executive. In this respect the cabinet system with its overlapping of personnel between executive and legislature, and its recognition of the principle that the heads of the executive should be those persons who can control the legislature, is likely to provide a stronger government than the separation of powers. It has been adopted in Australia and Canada and their example was followed by India, Rhodesia and Nyasaland, Malaya, the West Indies and Nigeria. Switzerland has a system midway between the two, for the executive there is chosen by the legislature, as in Australia and Canada. but holds office, as in the United States, for a fixed term of years. Yet it cannot be asserted that the cabinet system in a federation will inevitably produce a strong executive or a stronger executive than the American. Much depends on the party system.

4

Here is a factor in the organization of federal government which is of primary importance but which cannot be ensured or provided for in a constitution—a good party system. And a good party system is one in which sectional differences of interest and opinion have their opportunity and their due weight but where also an integrated organization can be created capable of effective political action on a nation wide scale. It is not easy to achieve these two objects. Sectional differences always threaten to break up the parties in a federal government and to paralyse legislative and executive action. Yet it is astonishing how well parties have worked and what strength and unity they have brought into the working of the general governments. The United States and Canada have been fortunate in possessing for most of their history substantially a two-party system, so far as political action in the sphere of the general government was concerned.[1] In both countries there have been times when the differences in the policies of these two parties—the Republicans and the Democrats in the United States, and the Conservatives and Liberals in Canada—have been fairly acute and obvious; but for most of the time it has not been easy to say what divides them, beyond the fact—and it is more important than is often realized—that one party was in office and the other party was out of office and seeking to discredit and criticize the work of the other.[2] It has often been true that the differences on policy

---

[1] Only from 1922–1926 did a third party hold the balance of power in Canada. This was the Progressive party, a product of discontent in the western provinces.

[2] The Conservatives like the Republicans have been identified with a high tariff or protectionist policy; the Liberals and Democrats with a low tariff-for-revenue policy; but in practice when in office both parties have come to believe in a tariff, and their policies when in office have differed little.

among members within any one of these parties were greater than the differences between members of different parties. The Liberals and Conservatives from Quebec have more in common than the Liberals of Quebec and Manitoba; the Democrats of New York State and of Georgia differ much more than the Democrats of Georgia do from the Republicans of New Jersey. And these differences inside the American parties have led to the adoption in some states of the system of primary elections—the 'primaries'—whereby each party holds a preliminary election among its own supporters to choose the candidate it will put forward later to oppose a candidate from the other party. In this way an attempt is made to permit freedom of opinion within a party and a united front against the opposite party.

It is not easy to explain why, in the United States particularly, where government is so divided under a federal system and where so much ground for difference of opinion exists, it should yet have been possible to create and maintain a two-party system.[1] That such a system is desirable in a federal government is, in my view, undoubted, but that it should have been achieved is always a matter for surprise and some admiration. Yet there appears one reason for it which is relevant to our present discussion of the executive in federal governments. In the United States the greatest prize of political struggle is the Presidency, which grants to the victorious party for four years the supreme control of the executive government.

When the Constitution was first drawn up it was intended that each state should choose a group of electors equal to the number of its senators and representative in Congress. These electors would then meet in each state and consider whom they should propose as President and send his name to the seat of government of the United States. But the rise of party soon modified this plan. Now the parties each nominate a candidate for the presidency and the people choose one of them by voting for electors pledged to support their particular candidate. Legally the president is still elected by the electoral colleges. Here is a qualification, however. The vote is taken by states, and if a candidate carries a state he obtains all the votes for the electoral college in that state. Similarly, if he lost the state even by a few votes, he would lose all the votes in the electoral college for that state. This system discourages small parties, which find it difficult to carry a whole state, whereas on a proportional system they might hope to win, here and there, a few votes in the electoral college. But they have to face a further handicap. The Constitution requires that to be elected to the Presidency a candidate must be supported by an absolute majority in the electoral colleges. He must capture more votes in the electoral colleges than all the other candidates put together. If no candidate does so then the choice of a President passes to the House of

[1] The best discussion of the American party system is V. O. Key, *Politics, Parties and Pressure Groups*.

Representatives.[1] This arrangement obviously discourages the growth of a multi-party contest. The result becomes uncertain and fluctuating if more than two or, at the most, three parties are engaged in the contest. Everything makes it more profitable to the parties to discourage new competitors in the field. However much the Republicans and the Democrats hate each other they must unite in hating much more any interloper who, by stealing votes from both, may steal the victory also from one of them. It has been the object of the American political parties, therefore, to assimilate new and competing movements: to steal their thunder, as President Franklin Roosevelt was seen, for example, to steal the thunder which the American Socialist Party or any possible Labour Party in the United States might hope to use some day.

The two Canadian political parties have much the same attitude to each other and to new opponents. The Conservatives have recently renamed themselves the Progressive Conservatives: they hope in this way to prevent the Canadian socialist party—the Co-operative Commonwealth Federation (C.C.F.)—from advancing far enough to keep the Conservatives out of office and perhaps to displace them as the second political party in Canada. The Liberals have to face the same possibility. The future of these manœuvres in Canada is uncertain.[2] An interesting struggle appears likely to develop among the three parties, but its result, though uncertain in some respects, is fairly certain in one—that two parties are likely to emerge in the end. For in Canada, as in the United States, the prize is power, power through winning a majority in the Canadian House of Commons, and the struggle is easier and the chance of success is greater if the competitors are two, instead of three or more. But in Canada the discouragements to a multi-party system are not so strong as in the United States. For a coalition cabinet is more intelligible and workable than a coalition president. The spoils of office can be shared in a cabinet among the leaders of two parties, but there can be only one president. Small parties are obliged to concentrate their support on one man in the United States, if they wish to have any certainty of success. Everything conspires to weld them into two main competing groups.

The Australian and the Swiss systems, though different from each other, both stress the points already made. In Australia a multi-party system has worked for some time, for here, as in Canada and unlike the United States, a coalition cabinet is a possibility, and where a third party cannot be excluded it must be accommodated. Australia has three parties—one, the Labour party, representing working-class especially urban working-class interests; another, under various names,[3] opposing the Labour Party: and the third representing rural

[1] This has happened once—in 1824.
[2] See R. McG. Dawson, *The Government of Canada*, cc. 21–23.
[3] Until 1917 the Liberal Party; from 1917–1932 the Nationalist Party; from 1932–1945 the United Australia Party; and from 1945, once more, the Liberal Party.

and agricultural interests, the Country Party. This last party represents a solid interest but one which could never, on its own, command a majority of seats in the House of Representatives. It could never expect to hold office alone. But it has been able to resist attempts by the other parties to absorb it or destroy it,[1] and it has held office jointly with the anti-labour party in several coalition governments. Australian experience illustrates by contrast the way in which the American federal system helps to produce that two-party system which has done so much to unify the United States. Switzerland emphasizes the same lesson. The Swiss executive is, like the Australian and Canadian, a committee not a single man. It may therefore be a coalition. On the other hand the Swiss executive may not be dismissed by the legislature, as may the Australian and Canadian executives, so that parties may act more freely in voting upon its proposals. These factors encourage a multi-party system in Switzerland,[2] and the executive—the Federal Council—has always been a coalition.[3]

This sketch of party organization in the federations is partial and inadequate. But it may serve to show the importance of a two-party system as an ideal, if not always a possibility, for the working of federal government. If there is one single factor which can be selected to explain why, as I believe, the government of the United States is the most successful federal government in the world, it is the existence of its two-party system which provides a unifying influence through the whole frame-work of government and makes possible as strong an executive as can be provided in Australia and Canada where the cabinet system prevails. Party overcomes in the United States those obstacles to executive efficiency which the separation of powers provides and which the cabinet system is held to avoid. Indeed, while it may be true that a weak American president is weaker than any Australian or Canadian prime minister could be, it is also true that the strongest American president is as strong as any Australian or Canadian prime minister could be. The Presidency has become essentially and pre-eminently the unique unitary and unifying institution in the general government of the United States.[4] And it is the party system which makes this possible.

5

It has often been asserted that an essential requirement of a federal government is that there should be no right of secession from the

---

[1] It provides an interesting contrast to the Progressive Party of Canada.

[2] It is not suggested that this factor alone explains the multi-party system of Switzerland. But it encourages what tendencies there are. For a discussion of Swiss parties see Rappard, *The Government of Switzerland*, Chapter VI, and Hughes, *The Parliament of Switzerland*, Chapter III.

[3] There was a Liberal-Radical Coalition from 1848–1891; a coalition of Liberals and Catholic Conservatives from 1891–1929; a coalition of Liberals, Catholic Conservatives and Farmers from 1929–1943; from 1943 to 1953 and again from 1959 a Social Democrat has been elected to the Council, making it a coalition of four parties.

[4] This is well illustrated in the sphere of the war power and, to a less extent in foreign relations. See below, pp. 182–3, 188.

federation on the part of the regional governments.[1] Put more narrowly, what is denied is often the right of a regional government acting alone to leave a federation or for the general government acting alone to expel a member government. The argument is that if such actions are permitted the general government is subordinated to the regional governments or vice versa and that is an end of federalism.

Some support for this view is found in the constitutions of our four federations, in all of which no place is found for a unilateral right of a region to secede or for the general government to expel. The only way in which states and provinces can secede or be expelled from the Australian and Canadian federations appears to be through an act of the United Kingdom Parliament. In 1934 the State of Western Australia petitioned the United Kingdom Parliament to pass an act for its secession from the Commonwealth of Australia, but the petition was not successful. A select committee of Lords and Commons decided that parliament was, by constitutional convention, not competent to deal with such a matter merely upon the petition of a single state of Australia. Their decision emphasized the fact that in practice as well as in law no right of secession rested with any state acting alone.[2]

In the United States, as is well known, there was a long controversy about the right of secession and it was by no means free from doubt as to what the constitution intended. It took the Civil War to settle the issue, and it is significant that the Supreme Court finally declared in 1868, when the war was over, that 'the Constitution in all its provisions looks to an indestructible union, composed of indestructible states'.[3] The only way in which states can secede or be expelled from the Union would seem to be by the process of constitutional amendment, and so far as expulsion is concerned, a state's own consent seems to be necessary, in view of the provision[4] that 'no state, without its consent, shall be deprived of its equal suffrage in the senate'. The same position appears to apply in the case of Switzerland. It seems indeed that no provision for unilateral secession or expulsion is found in any modern federal constitution. Among quasi-federal constitutions, that of the U.S.S.R. alone gives to the regions the right to secede.[5]

Yet I doubt whether it can be maintained that a right to secede unilaterally is inconsistent with the federal principle as a matter of logic. It must be distinguished from another right, the right to nullify the laws of the general government. The Southern States in the

---

[1] It was Freeman's view, for example, *History of Federal Government in Greece and Italy*, p. 90, that the right to secede was theoretically inconsistent with federalism, but probably desirable in practice.

[2] See *Report by the Joint Committee on the Petition of the State of Western Australia*, 1935, H.L. 62, 75; H.C. 88, paras. 8 and 9. The Committee appeared to think that a request from the general government alone would be more authoritative. But on this point their argument is often ambiguous.

[3] Chase, C. J., in *Texas* v. *White* (1868) 7 Wallace, 700 at p. 725.

[4] Art. V.   [5] Art. 35.

American Union, and particularly South Carolina, did assert a right to nullify the laws of Congress if they thought them unsatisfactory. John C. Calhoun, the most notable exponent of the doctrine of nullification, maintained that the general government was the agent of the states and that the states were therefore entitled to nullify any act of their agent of which they disapproved. Now this doctrine is contrary to federalism. It does place the general government, as a matter of law, in a subordinate position to the regional governments. The right of nullification claims that states may be at one and the same time members of the union and also entitled to decide which of the laws of the general government they will accept. The right of secession, on the other hand, claims that states may decide whether or not they will be members of the union. They can choose whether they will submit to the laws of the general government entirely and without exceptions, or whether they will reject the authority of the general government entirely. The right to secede does not make the general government the agent of the states as does the right to nullify; on the contrary it recognizes that the general government is to be either co-ordinate with a state government within the area of the state, or is to have no connection with it.

But while the existence of a right to secede unilaterally or a right to expel unilaterally may be quite consistent with federal government, it is not, I believe, consistent, as a rule, with good federal government. It is well not to exaggerate. There are cases where to grant the right to secede is to ensure that states will never exercise it. But as a rule it weakens government. It places a weapon of political coercion in the hands of governments which they may use in order to get their own way. A weak regional government may be threatened with expulsion by a strong general government if it does not conform to the general government's demands. And the general government itself may be weakened and coerced by the threats of secession from discontented regions. It will usually be true that a unilateral power to secede or to expel makes for bad federal government. It is indeed significant that the one modern government claiming to be federal which grants a right to secede, the U.S.S.R., is the one where the exercise of the right is least likely to be permitted.

6

There is a final question which must be considered. Many people regard it as essential to a government if it is to be federal that the regions should have equal representation in the upper house of the general legislature. In the United States, Switzerland and Australia this plan is adopted. The states and cantons are represented by two members each in the upper house of the United States and Switzerland; in Australia the states have ten representatives each. In Canada the principle of equal representation was not followed, though some small attempt was made to compensate the less populous provinces. The Senate is composed of 102 members, nominated for life by the Dominion government. Ontario is represented by 24, Quebec by 24, Nova Scotia and New Brunswick by 10 each, Prince Edward Island by 4, Newfoundland by 6, and Manitoba, Alberta, Saskatchewan and British Columbia by 6 each.

Here again, as in the case of some of the institutions already considered, the right answer seems to be that equal representation of the regions in the upper house is not essential logically for a government if it is to be federal, but at the same time it is often essential if federal government is to work well. States may be reluctant to enter a federal union unless they are guaranteed some safeguard in one house of the legislature against their being swamped by the more populous members of the union. This is especially true of agricultural states or states of small extent. Equal representation in the Senate gives some sort of security to the smaller states that the powers which have been handed over exclusively to the federal government will not be exercised as a general rule in the interests of a few states. Unless there is this feeling of security and unless there are the checks and obstructions which such a second chamber provides, it may be impossible to initiate a federation or to work it successfully. For these reasons it may be said that although equal representation is not essential to ensure that the system is federal government, it may be essential to ensure that it is effective federal government.

A few figures illustrate the problem. In Australia and Canada, for example, where the cabinet holds office because it has a majority in the lower house of the legislature, we find this situation. In the Canadian House of Commons of 265 members, Ontario and Quebec, the two most populous provinces, have 160 representatives; the remaining eight provinces have therefore less than half. In Australia, New South Wales and Victoria similarly have 79 representatives in a House of 124. In the United States, the industrial states of Illinois, Indiana, Michigan, New Jersey, New York, Ohio, Pennsylvania, have 174 representatives in a House of 437; while eight farming states—Iowa, Kansas, Minnesota, Nebraska, North Dakota, Oklahoma, South Dakota and Wisconsin, have only 47. In Switzerland two cantons, Berne and Zurich, had almost a third of the seats in the National Council—the lower house—of 196 in 1959. The seven cantons of Uri, Schwyz, Unterwalden, Glarus, Zug, Appenzell and Schaffhausen, had between them only fourteen seats—two less than the single canton of Vaud. One can see why the less populous regions feel overwhelmed. Majority rule, where it means a majority of people and not a majority of regions, may not be so satisfactory a method of obtaining political decisions in a federation as it can be in a unitary state. Some additional protection against the tyranny of such majorities may be needed, and it was for this reason that the method of equal representation in an upper house was adopted. It was one of the great compromises in the framing of the American Constitution at Philadelphia; it was carried by a narrow margin and was one of the most critical decisions taken in that assembly.

Yet with the exception of the Senate of the United States—and it is a most distinguished exception—the upper houses have not fulfilled this particular function with much success. It is not easy to explain this shortly. In the case of Canada, as I have indicated, not much could be expected, for the principle of equal representation was not adopted. Ontario and Quebec have almost half the seats in the Senate and are therefore in much the same position there as they are in the Lower House. Senators are appointed for life and their allegiance is usually to the party which was in power at the time of their appointment.[1] In Australia party divisions have usually proved stronger among Senators than state divisions. Votes in the Senate are cast more on strict party lines than upon a regional basis. Here perhaps the existence of a system of cabinet government where the executive requires the support of a party in the legislature makes party a more important matter than region. In any case since the government is primarily responsible to the House of Representatives, the Senate is less important from the outset. The Senate has not been powerless or voiceless, but it has been much less effective as a chamber to safeguard regional interests than had been hoped.[2] Party organization has largely accounted for this. In Switzerland the effectiveness of other institutions for safeguarding constitutional rights—particularly the referendum—has meant that the legislature as a whole is less important. Even so, the Swiss upper house, the Council of States, is more effective than either the Australian or Canadian senates.

The effectiveness of the American Senate is not easy to account for. Something is due to the additional powers in respect of foreign affairs and appointments, which are conferred upon it by the constitution and which give it a pre-eminence over the House of Representatives. Then again there is lacking in the United States a factor which tended to make the upper houses subordinate to the lower houses in Canada and Australia, and that is the system of cabinet government by which the cabinet is responsible to the lower house, which is consequently the more important. The President of the United States is responsible to neither house of Congress in this sense and the Senate does not therefore find itself subordinate to the lower house on this account. Here is one instance, indeed, where the separation of powers, already discussed, influences federal government. It is partly because the executive is separated from Congress in the United States that the

---

[1] See R. A. Mackay, *The Unreformed Senate of Canada.*

[2] It is significant that its chief influence has been exerted in the years 1913–1914, 1916–1917, 1929–1932, 1942–1943 and 1949–1951, when it contained a majority of opposition party members.

Senate is of at least equal importance with the House of Representatives. Again, party organization in the United States accounts to some extent for the effectiveness of the Senate. Both main parties, the Republicans and the Democrats, as I have said, reflect within themselves the differing regional interests of the United States and their members are free to express these differences in the Senate, as in the House of Representatives, because the action they take cannot dislodge the President and his cabinet from office.

These are some of the reasons which account for the fact that the Senate is not only as strong but probably stronger than the lower house of the United States Congress. The less populous states, therefore, gain an influence through their equal membership in this body. It has been emphasized, and rightly, that in modern times the Senate does not represent state rights so much as it used to. But inevitably it represents the views of groups of states, of regions in the United States, and it gives to less populous regions some compensation for the fact that they are outnumbered in the lower house by the more populous regions. Thus the eight farming states already referred to which were represented by only 47 members in the House of Representatives have 16 senators, while the seven industrial states with their 174 representatives have only 14 senators. The seven mountain states of Arizona, Idaho, Montana, Nevada, New Mexico, Utah and Wyoming have more senators than representatives (12). This arrangement has meant that in matters where regional interests conflict, like tariffs, foreign policy, economic planning and the like, the Senate has been able to afford to the smaller states a chance to express their views effectively.

This is not to say that federations in which the upper house has failed to safeguard state rights effectively have necessarily sacrificed the interests of their regional governments. Canada is an example to the contrary. Parties in Canada, both Conservative and Liberal, pay great heed to regional interests; the interpretation of the constitution by the Judicial Committee of the Privy Council has tended so far to maintain provincial powers and indeed to entrench them.[1] The method of having an upper house recruited on a basis of equal representation for the regions concerned is only one method of safeguarding regional interests. It is usually advisable to adopt such a system, but federal government does not necessarily work badly without it.

7

From the discussion in these last two chapters it will be seen that there are certain institutions which are essential to a government if it is to be federal and also that these same essential institutions do not inevitably guarantee that a federal government will work easily or well. The supremacy of the constitution, the necessity for a difficult

[1] See below, Chapter XI, pp. 215–19.

and rigid amending process, the existence of judicial review by which laws duly passed by elected representatives of the people may be declared void by judges, all these essentials of federal government suggest difficulties and problems of great complexity at any rate to the citizen of a unitary state, unaccustomed to thinking of governmental problems along such lines. Federal government not only produces peculiar institutions; it produces also peculiar problems in the working of these institutions.

It is with these peculiar federal problems that most of the following chapters are concerned. I have selected them to illustrate the way in which the federal aspects of the governments concerned affect the subjects chosen. They are subjects with which all governments deal and they produce problems common to all governments. But in federal states they produce in addition peculiar problems, problems arising from federalism, and it is with these problems that I am concerned.

PART IV
HOW FEDERAL GOVERNMENT WORKS

Chapter VI
FEDERAL GOVERNMENT AND ITS PUBLIC FINANCE

1

FINANCE is an essential prerequisite of government and for this reason it seems appropriate to begin our study of the working of federal government by an inquiry into some aspects of its public finance.[1] There are certain problems of public finance which are common to all governments, whether they are federal governments or not. We are familiar with them in the textbooks—the forms of direct and indirect taxation, the incidence and effects of certain taxes, the extent to which expenditure should be met from revenue and from borrowing, problems of currency control and central banking, of sinking funds, of appropriation and audit. I do not propose to deal with these problems in this chapter. What I am concerned with is the peculiar federal problem in public finance.

The peculiar federal problem is this. The federal principle requires that the general and regional governments of a country shall be independent each of the other within its sphere, shall be not subordinate one to another but co-ordinate with each other. Now if this principle is to operate not merely as a matter of strict law but also in practice, it follows that both general and regional governments must each have under its own independent control financial resources sufficient to perform its exclusive functions. Each must be financially co-ordinate with the other. To quote some words from *The Federalist*: 'It is, therefore, as necessary that the state governments should be able to command the means of supplying their wants, as that the national government should possess the like faculty in respect to the wants of the union.'[2] This is clearly an additional problem in public finance to those which confront all governments. And it is a very difficult problem. It is not easy to distribute functions, and when once

---

[1] The best short introduction to this subject is B. P. Adarkar, *Principles and Problems of Federal Finance* (1933) supplemented and brought up to date by G. F. Shirras, *Federal Finance in Peace and War* (1944). For more detailed treatment see, for Canada, the *Rowell-Sirois Report* and A. E. Buck, *Financing Canadian Government*; for Australia the *Third Report of the Commonwealth Grants Commission* and subsequent reports. The United States and Switzerland are less adequately treated. For the United States the best book is J. A. Maxwell, *The Fiscal Impact of Federalism in the United States*. There is much useful information also in the *Report of the Commission on Inter-governmental Relations* (1955) and in some of the published studies upon which that Report was based. For Switzerland, see the *Statistisches Jahrbuch der Schweiz* (*Annuaire Statistique de la Suisse*).

[2] No. XXXI, p. 149 (Everyman ed.).

they are distributed, it is even harder to allot resources with any confidence that future experience will show that resources and functions
expand or contract together, each adjusting itself harmoniously to the
other.

The best way in which to begin a study of this complicated problem
is to consider first, how far, in the constitutions of the federal systems
we are discussing, there has been allotted to the general and regional
governments respectively, independent powers of providing resources
from which to perform their allotted functions. What budgetary
autonomy, as a matter of law, was conferred upon them? Thereafter
it will be necessary to ask the further question: How far have these
independent powers proved adequate to the needs of the respective
governments? And on the answer to these questions we can base a
judgement upon the working of federal finance.

2

What independent financial resources have been allotted to the
general and regional governments respectively? A short general
answer to this question is that there is confided to both general and
regional governments in the four federations a sphere in which they
may exercise independent budgetary power, though the extent of this
sphere, as will be shown, varies from case to case. In the case of
Canada it is well to recall that the independence of the provinces in
financial affairs is limited always by the fact that, as a matter of law,
the Dominion government may disallow provincial acts dealing with
finance as with other matters. In practice this power has not been
exercised in regard to budget legislation[1] and it is legitimate therefore
to discuss Canada as an example of the working of federal finance.
But the power is there and could be exercised.

These federations may be contrasted with the system of the
U.S.S.R. where, by Article 14 of the Constitution of 1936, the powers
of the All-Union authorities are stated to include the 'confirmation
of the unified state budget of the U.S.S.R., as well as of the taxes and
revenues which go to form the All-Union, the republic and the local
budgets'.[2] This is the principle not of federal but of unified finance.
Provisions with a similar purpose in the Weimar Constitution[3] of
Germany were used to produce a similar result. The Weimar Republic
provides little evidence of the working of federal finance and it is not
treated with more than a passing reference in this chapter.[4]

If, then, there is a sphere of financial autonomy in the federations,
how extensive is it? There are, first of all, two matters where the general

---

[1] It was used in 1937 against currency legislation of the province of Alberta, but as this
legislation was in any case *ultra vires*, no restriction upon provincial autonomy really occurred.
See note on p. 95 below.
[2] Quoted from the Webbs' *Soviet Communism*, Vol. I, p. 528³.
[3] Espec. Arts. 8, 11, 48 and 84.
[4] See an article by Mabel Newcomer in *Political Science Quarterly*, Vol. LI, No. 2, entitled
'Fiscal Relations of Central and Local Governments in Germany under the Weimar Constitution'.

governments have a control which is not merely independent but also exclusive. The general governments in the federations have exclusive control, actual or potential, over currency and coinage. The power extends to the issue not only of metallic currency but also of paper currency. It is conferred on the general governments in Switzerland[1] and Canada[2] as an exclusive power; in the United States[3] and Australia[4] it is, in some degree, actually exclusive, in some degree potentially. The grant is not so wide in the United States, but in the course of judicial interpretation, culminating in the *Gold Clauses Cases* of 1935,[5] it has gained greatly in strength. It was described by the majority opinion of the Supreme Court in 1935 as a 'broad and comprehensive national authority over the subjects of revenue, finance and currency'.[6] There is authority also over banking, which, though it does not cover banks incorporated under state law in the United States, or state banking, not extending beyond the limits of the state concerned, in Australia, goes far to control banking institutions so far as their functions in the issue of credit are concerned. It is clear, therefore, that the financial autonomy of the regional governments is always conditional upon their working within the framework of currency and credit determined in the last resort by the general government[7]—so far as such matters are determined by governments at all.

It is the usual practice also, in most federal governments, that the general governments should be given exclusive control, actually or potentially, over revenue from customs and excise,[8] both as to the imposition of duties and the disposal of the proceeds.[9] Some exceptions have occurred. In Brazil,[10] for example, the states were given a power to lay export duties on goods of their own production, and import duties on foreign goods intended for their own consumption. In the latter case the revenue obtained was to go to the treasury of the general government. This appears to be the only case where a permanent division of authority as to imposing customs duties and disposing of the proceeds has been established in a federation. There

[1] Swiss Constitution, Arts. 38–9.
[2] Canadian Constitution, S. 91 (14), (15), (16) and (20).
[3] American Constitution, Art I (viii) and (x).
[4] Australian Constitution, S. 51 (xii) and (xiii) and S. 115.
[5] *Norman* v. *Baltimore and Ohio Railroad Co.* 294 U.S. 240; *United States* v. *Bankers Trust Co.*, ibid.; *Nortz* v. *United States*, 294 U.S. 317; *Perry* v. *United States*, 294 U.S. 330.
[6] *Norman* v. *Baltimore and Ohio Railroad Co.*, 294 U.S. 240 at p. 303.
[7] In 1937 the Social Credit Government of the Province of Alberta in Canada obtained the passage of 'An act to provide for the regulation of the administration of the credit of the province'. It was disallowed by the Dominion Government on the ground, among others, that the regulation of banking and credit was a matter exclusively within the power of the Dominion. The measure was repassed by the provincial legislature; but the Dominion government instructed the Lieutenant-Governor of Alberta to reserve the bill for the pleasure of the Governor-General of Canada, who, in due course, was advised to refuse his consent.
[8] In the United States the States are empowered to levy excises and use the power extensively.
[9] American Constitution, Art. I (8) and (10); Canadian Constitution, S. 91 (2) and (3); Australian Constitution, ss. 51 (i), (ii), (iii), and 90; Swiss Constitution, Arts. 28–32.
[10] Constitution of 1891, Art. 9.

were certain temporary provisions when the Commonwealth of Australia was first established. The State of Western Australia was permitted to exercise a limited power of imposing customs on a progressively decreasing scale for five years after the imposition of uniform duties by the Commonwealth parliament, in order that it might adjust itself to the new economy. Further it was provided that for ten years the Commonwealth should pay to the states three-quarters of the customs and excise revenue.[1] In this way the states were to be given time to develop new sources of revenue to replace those upon which they had relied so largely.

The first great independent source of revenue for the general government in the federations, then, is customs and excise, and it is a source which, generally speaking, is under its exclusive control. The other independent sources it shares with the regional governments. The chief of these are, firstly, receipts from property, commercial undertakings and monopolies; secondly, grants; thirdly, loans; and, finally, taxation. Each of these must be treated in turn.

3

Both general and regional governments derive revenue from property, commercial undertakings and monopolies. The postal service is an example of an undertaking conducted by the general government in all four federations. In some others the telephone and telegraphic service is a similar source of revenue. Switzerland has its powder and salt monopolies; there are undertakings like the Commonwealth of Australia's Transcontinental Railway, the United States' Panama Canal, the Canadian National Railways, the Swiss Federal Railways, and the like. And there is revenue from the ownership of lands and buildings. The regional governments have similar revenues. Most of them have public lands which produce an income. They receive fees for educational and other social services which they provide. The Australian states own railways. Indeed the income from business undertakings usually accounts for between one-third and one-half of the revenues of the Australian states. From sources of this kind, therefore, general and regional governments derive revenue under their own independent control.

Yet the extent of this independence must not be exaggerated. It is true that the Constitutions of Canada[2] and Australia[3] forbid the general governments from imposing taxes on the property of the regional government and vice versa. In the United States the Supreme Court has adopted a similar doctrine, although it was not explicitly declared in the Constitution.[4] Indeed the Supreme Court went further and

---

[1] Ss. 87 and 95.
[2] S. 125.
[3] S. 114. States may tax the property of the Commonwealth if the parliament of the Commonwealth consents.
[4] *McCulloch* v. *Maryland*, 4 Wheat. 316 (1819); *Collector* v. *Day*, 11 Wall. 113, at p. 127 (1870).

extended the immunity from taxation to persons in the employ of general and state governments, and in one case to the interest derived from state and local bonds.[1] But recent decisions have shown a tendency to apply the doctrine of immunity much more narrowly.[2] The High Court of Australia, after following the American example and extending the degree of immunity in its early years, adopted a much narrower doctrine in 1920.[3] And in any case it is open to general governments under their powers in inter-state commerce, for example, to fix the railway rates, say, of state-owned railways, so far as they operate in inter-state commerce. In ways like these the income of the regions from their properties and undertakings may be influenced by the general governments.

Grants, if they are to rank as independent sources of revenue, must not depend, of course, upon the good will of the contributing government. They must be obligatory contributions about which the contributing government has no discretion. General governments receive little by way of grants from the regional governments, whether compulsory or voluntary. There is a power in the Swiss Constitution by which the general government may levy contributions on the cantons, but it has not been exercised since 1849 and would seem to be a dead letter.[4] The general government was also entitled to half the gross yield of the military exemption tax levied by the cantons.[5] But such provisions as these were not important.

On the other hand obligatory grants from the general government to the regional governments form part of the financial arrangements of all four federal systems. Provisions for obligatory grants were found in three of the four constitutions—those of Switzerland, Canada and Australia. In Switzerland there were provisions in the Constitution of 1848 for compensation to be paid to the cantons for the loss of customs revenue consequent upon their surrender of the power to levy customs duties to the general government.[6] These payments were abolished in the revision of the Constitution in 1874. But other provisions remained or were added. For example, when a war tax on profits was introduced in 1915, it was provided in the Constitution that 10 per cent of the proceeds should go to the cantons; when a second war tax was imposed in 1919 the Constitution provided that 20 per cent went to the cantons.[7] When a stamp tax on securities, bills of exchange and the like was imposed in 1917, 20 per cent was

---

[1] *Pollock* v. *Farmers' Loan and Trust Co.*, (1895) 157 U.S. 429, (1895) 158 U.S. 601.
[2] *Helvering* v. *Gerhardt*, (1938) 304 U.S. 405, and *Graves* v. *New York* (1939) 306 U.S. 466, the latter case overruling *Collector* v. *Day supra*, in so far as it recognized an implied constitutional immunity from non-discriminating income taxation of the salaries of officers or employees of the national or state governments or their instrumentalities, at p. 486.
[3] *The Engineers Case*, (1920) 28 C.L.R. 129.
[4] Art. 42 (f).
[5] Art. 42 (e).
[6] Art. 30.
[7] These two amendments constitute in effect Art. 42 bis. And as each was temporary and lapsed as soon as the tax was imposed and collected, they are not formally incorporated in the Constitution.

required by the Constitution to go to the cantons.[1] Half the net receipts which the general government draws from the taxation of distilled beverages is to be distributed among the cantons proportionately to their population, on the stipulation that each canton must spend at least 10 per cent of its share to combat alcoholism.[2] These 'legal participations', as they are called, supply a distinct element in cantonal revenue, and they are distinguished in Switzerland from grants which are called 'subventions'. Finally, there is a more general provision which requires the general government to give subsidies to the cantons to assist them in the execution of their obligations in the field of primary instruction.[3] But here, though the right of the cantons to receive the grants is clear, the amount of the grant will depend on the good will of the general government. On the whole, however, it is clear that grants from the general government provide an independent source of revenue for the Swiss cantons.

In Canada the amount of certain grants was fixed in the constitution,[4] which neither general nor regional governments could alter, though it is important to remember that if the grants proved inadequate—and they did—any alteration in their amount required the consent of the Dominion. In Australia certain grants were guaranteed by the constitution for ten years only. The provision, already quoted,[5] stated that for a period of ten years after the imposition of uniform duties of customs and excise, three-quarters of the customs revenue was to be paid to the states. After the ten years it was left to the Commonwealth to decide what it should do. In fact when the ten years had elapsed the states still found themselves in need of grants, and the Commonwealth accordingly agreed to pay them subsidies at the rate of 25s. per head of population, a system which was continued until 1927. But these grants were clearly at the discretion of the Commonwealth. After 1927 the Commonwealth abolished the system of per head payments and undertook instead to make certain contributions towards the service of state debts. These last grants were given a constitutional guarantee and the states therefore had an independent claim to them.[6]

These are the main provisions for obligatory grants by the general governments to the regional governments and the latter are, therefore, not made dependent thereby upon the general government. But in all four cases—Switzerland,[7] Canada,[8] Australia[9] and the United States[10]—powers to make grants *at their discretion* are vested in the general governments and these powers have been used to a great extent to assist regional governments. All grants in the United States are voluntary grants of this kind; in Switzerland and Australia the

---

[1] Art. 41 bis. This participation in the proceeds of the stamp tax was repealed in a constitutional amendment of 1938.
[2] Art. 32 bis.   [3] Art. 27 bis.   [4] SS. 118–20.
[5] Section 87. See p. 96 above.   [6] Section 105A, see below, p. 99.
[7] e.g. Arts. 23, 27 bis., 35.   [8] Section 91 (3).   [9] Section 96.
[10] Principally the 'general welfare' clause, Art. 1, see below, pp. 101–2, 220–1.

greater proportion of the grants to the regions are given under voluntary arrangements and depend, therefore, on the good will of the general government. And even in Canada, where obligatory grants have been developed so much, there has been an increase, particularly since 1942, in the proportion of provincial revenue which comes by voluntary grants. More will be said of this aspect of grants at a later period in this chapter.[1] For the present it needs only to remark that so far as they exist, such grants involve some degree of dependence by the regional government upon the general government.

The power to raise revenue by borrowing was conferred both on general and on regional governments in the original constitutions of all four federations. This has subsisted unaltered in all cases except in that of Australia. There, by an agreement between the Commonwealth and the States in 1927, borrowing (except for defence purposes) is controlled by a Loan Council composed of representatives of the Commonwealth and state governments. The establishment of this Loan Council was part of a wide re-organization of Commonwealth and state financial relations. For present purposes it is enough to say that, largely on the initiative of the Commonwealth government, the independent powers of borrowing of both state and Commonwealth governments were given up and in their place came control by the Loan Council. The objects of the change were, chiefly, to avoid competition between the various Australian governments in the loan market and thus to enable them to secure better terms; and the control of the states' expenditure which had been lavish for some years and which in the end imposed a burden on the Commonwealth which was expected to make up deficits by grants. By the terms of the Agreement which established the Loan Council, the Commonwealth took over the existing public debts of the states and agreed to make substantial contributions towards their service and liquidation. Future borrowing was to be controlled by the Loan Council. On this Council there was one representative each of the Commonwealth and of the six states, but the representative of the Commonwealth had two votes and a casting vote, so that if the Commonwealth had the support of two states, it could obtain a majority on the Council. Since many important matters could be decided by a majority vote, the Commonwealth had a large share of power on the Council. The whole agreement was made legally binding upon all the Australian governments by virtue of an amendment to the constitution which was carried in 1928.[2] It empowered the Commonwealth to enter into such agreements, and conferred on the parliament of the Commonwealth powers to make laws for the carrying out by the parties of any such agreement—a power to coerce any state which attempted to evade any of its obligations under the agreement. And, most important of all,

[1] See below, pp. 110 -11.
Section 105A.

it made any such agreement binding upon the Commonwealth and states, notwithstanding anything in the constitution of the Commonwealth or the constitutions of the states.

The establishment of the Loan Council in Australia, an institution for compulsory co-operation between general and regional governments, super-imposed upon the federal system, is a unique event in the history of the financial relations of general and regional governments in a federation.

4

The final source of revenue for general and regional governments is taxation and here we come to complicated problems. If the federal principle is applied in this matter it would follow that each government in a federation would be able to exercise its power to tax unfettered by the control of any other government. The taxing powers would be independent. Yet in practice not all federal governments appear to have applied the federal principle to this extent. Let us look first at the terms in which the taxing power has been conferred in the different systems.

In Canada the words seem clear. The Dominion parliament is empowered to raise money by any mode or system of taxation; the provinces may impose 'direct taxation within the province in order to the raising of a revenue for provincial purposes', and they may grant 'shop, saloon, tavern, auctioneer and other licences in order to the raising of a revenue for provincial, local or municipal purposes'.[1] The provincial power is thus restricted. It covers direct taxation and certain licences only, and it must be taxation for provincial or local purposes only.

In Australia the taxing power of the general government is more restricted than in Canada. The parliament of the Commonwealth may make laws with respect to taxation—but so as not to discriminate between states or parts of states. Subject to this grant of power to the Commonwealth the powers of the states to tax remain as before the federation.[2] But, as I have mentioned, both Commonwealth and states are expressly forbidden to impose taxation upon the property of the other, though the states may impose such a tax upon Commonwealth property if the parliament of the Commonwealth consents.[3]

In the United States the power of Congress to tax was even more restricted than in Australia. The Constitution empowered Congress 'to lay and collect taxes, duties, imposts, and excises, to pay the debts and provide for the common defence and general welfare of the United States'. That was a wide grant, but it was immediately qualified. First of all there was a qualification like that in Australia—'All

---

[1] S. 92 (2) and (9).
[2] The power to impose duties of customs and excise was, of course, surrendered exclusively to the Commonwealth, as already mentioned.
[3] S. 114.

duties, imposts and excises shall be uniform throughout the United States.'[1] Secondly there was the restriction that 'no capitation or other direct tax shall be laid unless in proportion to the census or enumeration hereinbefore directed to be taken.'[2] This introduced a distinction between direct and indirect taxes as sources of the general government's revenue and it imposed an obstacle upon its freedom to impose direct taxes. It involved from time to time a reference to the Supreme Court to decide whether a given tax was a direct tax or not. The Supreme Court appears to have given conflicting decisions.[3] One decision in particular hampered Congress. The Supreme Court decided[4] that income tax was a direct tax, and must be levied therefore according to population. This made it practically impossible for Congress to levy income tax effectively at all. In 1913, by the Sixteenth Amendment to the constitution, the restriction was removed and Congress was empowered 'to lay and collect taxes on incomes, from whatever source derived without apportionment among the several states, and without regard to any census or enumeration'. Outside the income tax, the restriction upon the power of direct taxation remains, and in this relatively unimportant respect the powers of Congress are less than those of the parliaments of Canada and Australia. The taxing powers of the states in America subsist, subject to the grant made to Congress in the Constitution.

In these three federations consideration has been given to the question whether the governments can use financial powers to carry out objects which they are not permitted to achieve by the process of ordinary legislation. Can a general government raise and spend money on matters concerning which it cannot make laws? On a strictly federal view, perhaps, it would seem that financial power should be confined in its objects to the same ambit as the legislative powers. Yet this has not been the view of the supreme courts in all the federations. In the United States the Supreme Court had to decide in 1935 whether the power of Congress to tax or provide for the general welfare of the United States involved the power to raise and spend money upon agriculture, a matter almost entirely within the legislative powers of the states. The Court decided that Congress did possess such a power, though by a majority of one it declared the act in question void, on the ground that it was not in truth a taxing and appropriating act but in truth an act to regulate agriculture.[5] In 1937 the Social Security Act was declared valid, also by a majority of one, the majority of the Court holding that this was a taxing act primarily,

[1] Art. I, Section 8 (i).

[2] Art. I, Section 9 (iv).

[3] *Hylton* v. *U.S.* (1796) 3 Dallas 171; *Scholey* v. *Rew* (1874) 23 Wallace 331; *Springer* v. *U.S.* (1880) 102 U.S. 586; *Pollock* v. *Farmers' Loan and Trust Co.* (1895) 157 U.S. 429 and (1895) 158 U.S. 601.

[4] *Pollock* v. *Farmers' Loan and Trust Co.*, cited above.

[5] *U.S.* v. *Butler*, (1936) 297 U.S. 1. Compare *Carter* v. *Carter Coal Co.* (1936) 298 U.S. 238 Compare the *Child Labour Case* (1922) 259 U.S. 20.

although the purpose for which the tax was imposed—the relief of unemployment—was capable of legislative regulation for the most part by the states alone.[1]

The Constitution of Australia authorizes a similar line of approach, illustrated in 1942, when the making of grants by the Commonwealth to the states to induce them not to impose an income tax was held valid.[2] It was held that such grants were an inducement, not coercion, although it was admitted that by such methods all state powers could be controlled by the Commonwealth, a result which would mean the end of the political independence of the states.[3]

But in Canada a decision of the Judicial Committee of the Privy Council in 1937[4] followed another line of interpretation. Legislation had been passed by the Dominion providing for unemployment and social insurance and it had been attempted to justify this legislation by arguing that it was in essence a taxing and appropriating act and therefore within the competence of the Dominion, whereas an act which was in essence an insurance act admittedly lay outside the powers of the Dominion. The Judicial Committee said: '. . . Assuming that the Dominion has collected by means of taxation a fund, it by no means follows that any legislation which disposes of it is necessarily within Dominion competence. . . . Dominion legislation, even though it deals with Dominion property, may yet be so framed as to invade civil rights within the Province, or encroach upon the classes of subjects which are reserved to provincial competence. . . . If on the true view of the legislation it is found that in reality in pith and substance the legislation invades civil rights within the Province, or in respect of other classes of subjects otherwise encroaches upon the provincial field, the legislation will be invalid. To hold otherwise would afford the Dominion an easy passage into the Provincial domain.'[5]

It is not correct to conclude that the Judicial Committee has adopted a completely different principle from the supreme tribunals of the United States and Australia. It doubtless recognizes, as they do, that the taxing and appropriating power can be used to affect a wider field of activity than that strictly confined within the legislative area of the general government. But where it may differ from the other two is in the degree of latitude which it permits. Its decision in the case just mentioned is comparable with that of the majority of the Supreme Court of the United States in the Agricultural Adjustment Act Case of 1936.[6]

[1] *Steward Machine Co.* v. *Davis,* (1937) 301 U.S. 548. Compare *Massachusetts* v. *Mellon* (1923) 262 U.S. 447.

[2] *South Australia* v. *The Commonwealth* (1942) 65 C.L.R. 373. See below, pp. 106–8. Here the power to make grants was the decisive thing. s. 96. This decision was affirmed in the Second Uniform Tax Case in 1957, *Victoria* v. *the Commonwealth,* 99 C.L.R. 575.

[3] Per Latham, C. J., at p. 429.

[4] *Attorney-General for Canada* v. *Attorney-General for Ontario* [1937] A.C. 355.

[5] At pp. 366–7.

[6] *U.S.* v. *Butler,* cited above.

5

In Switzerland the original division of taxing powers in the Constitution of 1848 allotted customs duties to the general government and practically no other taxing power. The remaining powers of indirect taxation and the whole power of direct taxation seems to have been left to the cantons. This distribution came to be modified when Switzerland felt the effect of an event which probably affected federal public finance more than any other single factor—the First World War. Switzerland was not a belligerent but she felt the effects of the war none the less. Her army was completely or partially mobilized for over fifty months; her customs revenue fell sharply with the decline of international trade; and the revenue from the federal railways declined. To meet these increases in expenditure and decreases in revenue constitutional amendments were passed to authorize the general government to enter the field of direct taxation. Taxation of incomes, property and profits was imposed by amendments of 1915 and 1919 and a tax on securities, insurance premiums and the like, by an amendment of 1917. In all three cases, as I have mentioned earlier, an arrangement was made that the cantons should obtain some share in the proceeds of the tax.[1] In 1925 a tax on tobacco was authorized by constitutional amendment.[2] In 1938, largely to meet increased defence expenditure, an amendment of the Constitution authorized taxes on war profits, income and capital, a tax on beer, and repealed the arrangement of 1917 by which the cantons shared in the yield of the stamp taxes.[3]

What happened in Switzerland as a result of the First World War, happened also in the other three federations—the entrance of the general government into the sphere of direct taxation which, until that time, the regions had been left practically free to exploit. In Australia, the Commonwealth had not imposed an income tax before the war of 1914–1918. But as soon as the strain of war expenditure was felt an estate duty was imposed in 1914 and an income tax in 1915. The states had already entered these fields of taxation and it was the war, therefore, which brought the Commonwealth into competition with them. That competition continued and in 1941 there were 23 separate state and Commonwealth income taxes in operation. Greatly increased and unexpected war expenditure led the Commonwealth in 1942 to determine that it must somehow prevail upon the states to retire from the income tax field for the duration of the war. The states were unwilling to do this, and the Commonwealth therefore passed legislation, of which I shall say more in the next section, to induce and indeed to compel the states to give up the income tax and receive in return compensatory grants.

[1] See p. 97–98 above.
[2] Art. 41 ter.
[3] The effects of the Second World War were equally drastic. See *The World To-day*, December 1949.

In Canada the same result has been achieved by agreement. In the war of 1914–1918 the Dominion entered the income tax field in 1917 and remained there in competition with the provinces. In the war of 1939 the strain on the Dominion's resources was greater than ever, and after much discussion and persuasion, the provinces were induced in 1942 to agree to vacate the field of income tax for the duration of the war and twelve months thereafter, receiving in return annual grants calculated either on the basis of their receipts from income tax and taking account in some cases also of special needs, or on the basis of the burden of their debt service.[1] In 1947 all the provinces except Ontario and Quebec entered into further agreements with the Dominion government. Thereafter at roughly five-year intervals new agreements were negotiated, Ontario joining in to a limited extent from 1952. It seems clear that the system has come to stay, though there is room for much argument about the proper terms for the bargain, on each occasion of its negotiation.

In the United States a similar process has occurred. Seligman wrote in 1927: 'Most of the fiscal changes which we find in this country up to recent years have been due to war or the fear of war.'[2] Experience since that date confirms the truth of what he said. Until the United States entered the war in 1917, it had relied, apart from the period of the Civil War and the years around the Spanish War, almost entirely upon customs and excise for its revenue. In 1856 the customs produced 97 per cent of the revenue; in 1890, just before the Spanish War, customs and excise produced 99 per cent. From 1909 a tax of 1 per cent on corporation incomes introduced an element of revenue from direct taxation, and the outbreak of war in Europe in 1914, by reducing customs revenue, made further direct taxation necessary. The entry of the United States into the war in 1917 led to increased income taxes, war profits taxes and excess profits taxes. In 1919 customs provided only 4 per cent of the total tax revenue. This was an exceptionally low figure owing to war restrictions. In 1930 customs produced 16 per cent and the tobacco duty 12 per cent of the revenue, but direct income taxes still accounted for 66 per cent. The great increases in armament expenditure by the United States from 1940, followed by her participation in the war from 1941, raised the level of direct taxation to unprecedented heights. Personal and corporation income taxes were raised; personal income tax was made subject to surtax and to a special victory tax; corporation income taxes to a surtax and an excess profits tax. It was estimated in 1943 that 20 per cent of the national income of the United States was being taken in taxation—a sum of between $24,000,000,000 to $26,000,000,000—whereas in the First World War less than 10 per

---

[1] See *Statutes of Canada*, 6–7 Geo, 6, Chapter 13. Corporation taxes were also similarly surrendered.

[2] Quoted in B. P. Adarkar, op. cit.

cent of the national income was taken—$5,000,000,000 at that time.[1] In 1945, the receipts of the United States Treasury from taxation amounted to nearly $48,000,000,000. Of that total, income tax produced 74 per cent and customs duties hardly 1 per cent.[2] In 1961 the proportions were 80 per cent and 1 per cent respectively.

Meanwhile the states which, until recently, had relied on a general property tax, had been forced by rising expenditure to enter new fields of taxation. The income tax has been adopted in about three-quarters of the states and it produced in 1949 about 17 per cent of the states' revenue. The chief source of state revenue is, however, sales taxation, which, excluding the unemployment compensation tax, produced 59 per cent of the revenue in 1949.[3] In 1961 sales taxes produced 60 per cent of the states' revenue; income tax produced 19 per cent.[4] It can be seen that in the field of direct taxation, the states are greatly restricted by the extent to which the general government has developed its taxing powers.

6

These are the terms in which the power to tax has been conferred upon general and regional governments in the federal systems we consider. Though the powers are restricted in certain cases, the restrictions do not appear at first sight to make the power of a general government dependent upon that of the regional government or vice versa.[5] Yet in practice complete independence would not seem to be secured in all cases. An example may be given to illustrate the point.

The power to tax involves, it may be assumed, the power to lay taxes and also the power to collect these taxes. If the federal principle is applied strictly this should mean that both general and regional governments have an independent power to lay and collect taxes. Suppose a case where both governments impose an income tax at rates so high that a tax payer is unable to pay both taxes in full. What is the status of each government in relation to the tax payer's resources? If the federal principle is to be applied, both general and regional governments are on the same footing. Neither can claim priority over the other. The tax payer's resources must be distributed proportionately to the debt owing to each government. Yet in Australia[6] and Canada[7] it has been decided judicially that the general government can give priority to its debt over the debt to the regions.

[1] I take these figures from *A Handbook of the United States of America*, produced by the U.S. Office of War Information, 1944, pp. 120–22.
[2] There is an interesting chart in H. Zink, *Survey of American Government*, p. 438.
[3] See *Book of the States, 1950–51*, p. 231.
[4] Ibid., 1962–3, p. 235.
[5] There is of course the qualification in respect of the Canadian provinces already mentioned, viz. disallowance or veto by the Dominion government of provincial taxing proposals. See above, p. 94
[6] *South Australia* v. *The Commonwealth*, (1942) 65 C.L.R. 373.
[7] *In re Silver Bros. Ltd.* [1932] A.C. 514.

In 1942 the Commonwealth of Australia needed greater revenue to pay for war expenditure. It had imposed an income tax but the state governments also had imposed taxes at levels varying from state to state. The Commonwealth proposed to the states that they should vacate the income tax field for the duration of the war in return for grants from the Commonwealth. The states refused. The Commonwealth then passed a series of four acts, the first of which imposed a uniform Commonwealth income tax at rates high enough to bring in as much revenue as the former Commonwealth and state taxes combined; the second act offered to pay to any state which did not collect income tax a grant equal to the average amount of its own income tax collections during the first two financial years of the war; and the fourth entitled the Commonwealth to take over the state income tax organizations. But it was the third which seems to have most compulsion in it. It gave priority to the Commonwealth in the payment of income tax over debts due to the states for income tax. In this way a state which decided to resist the temptation of the grant offered by the Commonwealth and to continue to finance itself by imposing income tax would find itself unable to collect any more income tax, as a matter of law, not merely as a matter of political expediency, than the Commonwealth chose to leave to it. The High Court of Australia was unanimous in holding that the act which gave this priority to the Commonwealth was valid.[1]

The argument by which this act was justified may be shortly stated. The constitution, it was said, gives the Commonwealth a power to make laws in respect of taxation. Subject to this grant the states also have power to make laws in respect of taxation. But if a Commonwealth law in respect of taxation conflicts with a state law in respect of taxation, what is to happen? The answer is found, said the Court, in section 109 of the constitution which says: 'When a law of a state is inconsistent with a law of the Commonwealth the latter shall prevail, and the former shall, to the extent of the inconsistency, be invalid.' It was conceded that the mere fact that Commonwealth and states make laws on income tax does not of itself necessarily produce inconsistency between Commonwealth and state laws. Both may be allowed to stand, but if a conflict does arise—and it does when a Commonwealth act gives priority to Commonwealth debts in respect of income tax over state debts in respect of income tax—then the Commonwealth act prevails. The argument followed the same lines as that which was used in the case of Canada in 1932 by the Judicial Committee of the Privy Council where a similar conflict of debts had arisen. Some words from that judgement summarize the decision: 'The two taxations, Dominion and provincial, can stand side by side without interfering with each other, but as soon as you come to the

---

[1] This decision was disapproved in 1957 by the High Court by a majority of four to three in the Second Uniform Tax Case. 99 C.L.R. 575. *Victoria* v. *the Commonwealth*.

concomitant privileges of absolute priority they cannot stand side by side and must clash; consequently the Dominion must prevail.'[1]

It is not for the layman to say whether these judgements on the meaning of the Australian and Canadian constitutions are good law or not. What the student of federal government can say, however, is that if they are good law, then the federal principle does not appear to find a place in these constitutions so far as the taxing power is concerned. For on the basis of these judgements it is open to the general governments to nullify in law the power of taxation conferred on the regional governments.[2] It is permissible also for the student of federal government to put forward another possible interpretation of these two constitutions against that which the High Court of Australia and the Judicial Committee have adopted.[3]

A careful reading of the Australian Constitution leads one to conclude that one of its objects was to establish general and regional governments each, within a sphere, independent of the other. That characteristic seems predominant in the system of government which the constitution prescribes.[4] Now is it consistent with this fundamental fact that the power of taxation, the power of providing the very resources upon which government action depends, can have been bestowed on Commonwealth and states in such a way that the Commonwealth can take effective steps for the performance of its functions, but that the states cannot, because the Commonwealth can exclude the states from all fields of taxation? The answer to this is that such a thing is possible, but that one should be slow to interpret a constitution in this way; that any possible interpretation which supports the states' equality with the Commonwealth should be chosen rather than that which subordinates the states to the Commonwealth or vice versa.

It is necessary to distinguish the taxing power from other legislative powers.[5] Its nature is different. It is a power to raise means, it is not a power to regulate specific fields. It may be used to provide the means by which the Commonwealth may carry out the functions which are committed to it in the constitution, but however widely it is used it must not be used so as to deny to the states the like power to provide the means by which they are to carry out the functions which are left

---

[1] *In re Silver Bros.* [1932] A.C. 514 at p. 521.
[2] It is proper to say that this view of the effect of the judgements is regarded by some judicious critics as extreme.
[3] The view I put forward seems to obtain some support from passages in the judgement of Dixon J. in an earlier Australian case, *Federal Commissioner of Taxation* v. *Farley*, 63 C.L.R. 278 at pp. 314 ff.
[4] I would apply a passage in the judgement of Starke J. in *South Australia* v. *The Commonwealth*, already cited (1942) 65 C.L.R. 373, where he says: 'The government of Australia is a dual system based upon a separation of organs and of powers. The maintenance of the states and their powers is as much the object of the Constitution as the maintenance of the Commonwealth and its powers. Therefore, it is beyond the power of either to abolish or destroy the other. The limited grants of powers to the Commonwealth cannot be exercised for ends inconsistent with the separate existence and self-government of the states, nor for ends inconsistent with its limited grants.' At p. 442. In spite of this view Starke J. held the 'priority' act valid though he held the 'grants' act invalid.
[5] e.g. Dixon J. at p. 316 in the case mentioned in note 3.

to them in the constitution. The taxing powers of each should not be thought of as concurrent, as are their powers over bankruptcy, copyright and the like. They are separate and independent taxing powers. When the constitution granted the Commonwealth powers to make laws in respect of taxation, it did not intend, surely, that in that small sub-head of a section it should provide the means legally to render a great part of the constitution superfluous. Yet, on the interpretation which the High Court has chosen, this seems to be the result. And in Canada, likewise, the interpretation of the Judicial Committee seems to render superfluous the careful enumeration of provincial and Dominion powers. Herein lies the essence of the dispute. Is the distribution of powers to legislate on other topics to be subordinate to the power to legislate on taxation, or is the power to legislate upon taxation to be subordinate to the distribution of power to legislate on other topics? If the power of the Commonwealth and of the Dominion to tax includes a power to nullify the powers of the states and the provinces to collect their taxes, then it is a power to destroy the independence of these regional governments. In my opinion this was not the intention of the constitution. But, as I have shown, there was a strong argument to the contrary, and it prevailed with the highest judicial authorities for Australia and Canada.

These decisions can be expected to exert an enormous influence on the future of federal government in Australia and Canada. The whole distribution of powers in the constitution is made subordinate to the taxing power of the general government. This does not eliminate the federal principle entirely from the constitution, but it does eliminate it so far as this aspect of public finance is concerned, and it does tend to eliminate it in the practical working of the governments. It becomes interesting to speculate whether the Supreme Court of the United States will adopt such an interpretation of the meaning of the taxing power conferred upon Congress. The Supreme Court has until recently set rigid limits to the use of the taxing power in any way which might permit the general government to interfere with the operation of the state governments within their own allotted sphere. The great principle laid down by Chief Justice Marshall in the case of *McCulloch* v. *Maryland* in 1819 that 'the power to tax involves the power to destroy' and that 'the only security against the abuse of this power is found in the structure of the government itself'[1] has operated to limit the exercise of the taxing power by subordinating it to the distribution of powers laid down by the constitution and not vice versa. Recently some modifications have been permitted by the Supreme Court in the rigid application of Marshall's principle.[2] One member of the Court has gone so far as to permit himself to call it a 'seductive *cliché*'.[3] But it is still too early to say that the Supreme Court would agree to a

[1] (1819) 4 Wheat. 316 at pp. 431, 428.
[2] *Helvering* v. *Gerhardt*, (1938) 304 U.S. 405; *Graves* v. *New York* (1939) 306 U.S. 466.
[3] Frankfurter, J., in *Graves* v. *New York*, cited above, at p. 489.

use of the federal taxing power which would prevent a state from collecting the debts due to it under its taxing laws.

7

Some idea has been given of the resources available to general and regional governments in the four federations, and of the extent to which these governments have independent control over their share of these resources. It has become clear that, so far as taxation is concerned, only the general governments have any important method of taxation confided exclusively to them, either actually or potentially. In all four federations the raising and spending of revenue from customs duties has come to be given to the general governments alone. And in two out of the four federations—Canada and Australia —the general governments seem to be empowered to make the methods of direct taxation also exclusive to themselves. In Switzerland the general government has entered the field of direct taxation and has excluded the regional governments increasingly from that field. In the United States the general government similarly competes with the regional governments, but so far it has asserted no power to exclude them or take priority over them. In all four cases there remains to the regional governments no important taxing power which is not either shared with the general government, or liable to be taken over by the general government. Apart from this, the general and regional governments have independent resources, subject to qualifications already mentioned, from grants—negligible for the general governments—from revenue arising out of undertakings and property, and from loans—controlled in Australia jointly by general and regional governments in the Loan Council.

From this analysis it is apparent that in all four countries the general governments have become incomparably the most powerful financial authorities in their federal systems, and the regional governments have been reduced to a restricted, if not subordinate position. It is interesting to inquire, therefore, how far the general and the regional governments have been able to perform the functions allotted to them upon this basis of division in their financial resources. Do general and regional governments 'live of their own' or do they depend upon each other? The short answer to this question is that the general governments have been able to acquire sufficient resources under their own control to perform their functions, but the regional governments have come to rely upon grants from the general government. They have accepted, in varying degree, some measure of financial subordination to the general government.[1]

---

[1] Reference may be made to V. O. Key, *The Administration of Federal Grants to States*; the Report of the Commission on Inter-governmental Relations (U.S.), 1955, especially chapter 5. L. Gettys, *The Administration of Canadian Conditional Grants*; J. A. Maxwell, *Federal Subsidies to the Provincial Governments in Canada*; Austin F. Macdonald, *Federal Aid*; *Third Report of the Commonwealth Grants Commission*, Australia, 1936, and succeeding reports.

In 1939, for example, in the United States, the states were receiving in voluntary grants from the general government the sum of $580,000,000 or about 15 per cent of their income;[1] in Canada the provinces were receiving about $22,000,000, or 10 per cent of their income;[2] in Australia the states were receiving about £15,000,000, or 12 per cent of their income;[3] and in Switzerland the cantons were receiving 231,000,000 Swiss francs, or 25 per cent of their income.[4] These figures all represented increases if not in the proportion which the grants of the general governments bore to the total income of the regions, at any rate in the absolute amount which the general government contributed. Thus in the United States the proportion which the general government had contributed in 1921 was 10 per cent. In Canada the total grant had increased steadily, but its proportion to provincial revenues had decreased. In 1874 it was only $3,800,000 but it represented about two-thirds of the provincial revenue; in 1913 it was about $12,000,000 or 25 per cent; and in 1921 it was the same sum but now represented only about 12 per cent.[5] In Australia similarly, although the amount of the grants increased up to 1939, the proportion it bore to the total revenue decreased. In the first ten years of the Commonwealth, subsidies from the general government accounted for about 25 per cent of the states' revenue, whereas in 1939 they were 12 per cent.[6] In Switzerland there had been a steady increase both in absolute amount and in proportions. In 1913 the cantons received about 25,000,000 Swiss francs or 7 per cent of their revenue; in 1930 about 100,000,000 or 14 per cent; and in 1936 a great increase, largely as a result of grants for unemployment relief, bringing the total to about 261,000,000 or 25 per cent.

These figures for 1939 give an indication of peace-time trends. But the ensuing war carried the process much further, and its effects cannot yet be gauged adequately. It is enough to say, however, that the income tax arrangements in Australia and in Canada[7] in 1942 whereby the regions were to be induced to vacate the field of income tax in return for compensatory grants by the general government, meant that in Australia the Commonwealth provided by voluntary grants a further 25 per cent of the income of the states and in Canada

[1] My figures for the United States are taken from an article by Austin F. Macdonald in the *American Political Science Review*, Vol. 24, 1940, No. 3.

[2] Based upon *Rowell-Sirois Report*, Book I, p. 246. It is to be noted that the greater part of the grants in Canada consisted of subsidies guaranteed by the Constitution, so that although the provinces did not 'live of their own' they were not correspondingly dependent merely upon the good will of the Dominion.

[3] Based upon the *Finance Bulletin, No. 32* (1940–41) issued by the Commonwealth Bureau of Census and Statistics, p. 14. About half of this amount was an obligatory payment towards interest on state debts under the Financial agreement in Section 105A of the Constitution.

[4] Based upon *Statistisches Jahrbuch der Schweiz*, 1940, pp. 339–40, 344–5. This figure does not include the amount of 47,000,000 francs which came to the cantons as their 'participations' in taxes levied by the general government. The figure is shown in *Statistisches Jahrbuch*, p. 341.

[5] *Rowell-Sirois Report*, Book III, pp. 32 ff.

[6] See *Third Report of the Commonwealth Grants Commission*, already cited.

[7] See above, pp. 103–4.

the Dominion provided similarly a further 25 per cent of the income of the provinces. In the United States the increase was not so great, but the total grant in 1948 was nearly $1,400,000,000 and the proportion it bore to state revenue was about 14 per cent.[1]

In Australia, in the financial year 1959–60 grants from the Commonwealth accounted for 37·5 per cent of the states' revenues; it was the largest single source. The next largest was income from business undertakings, which provided 31·9 per cent. State taxation provided only 16·7 per cent. In Canada, for the year 1958, grants from the government at Ottawa accounted for about 22 per cent of the revenue of the provinces. In the United States federal grants accounted for 20·5 per cent of the states' revenue in 1958 and for 23·3 per cent in 1960. In Switzerland the grants from the general government to the cantons have increased steadily each year in absolute amount; in 1960 they constituted about 10 per cent of the income of the cantons.

It is not easy to explain why this situation has arisen. But some hints are suggested in the following paragraphs.

It is necessary to emphasize at the outset the nature of the functions originally allocated to the regional governments. They included almost all of what it is now usual to call the social services—education, police, public health, old age and disability pensions, poor relief, unemployment assistance, social insurance, the care of the blind, maternity and child welfare.[2] From the point of view of public finance, these services have one important characteristic—they are expensive. And they are expensive not only in themselves—the provision of schools, hospitals, houses, clinics and the payment of a large wages or salaries bill—but also because few people who need them can afford to pay for them in full, and those people who need them most are usually those who can least afford to pay for them. Governments charged with the provision of these services have therefore an expensive task to perform. And if this is true in normal times it is intensified and multiplied in times of economic depression. For then the demand for the services increases and at the same time the capacity to pay of those who need the services decreases.

With this preliminary point in mind we may turn to consider why it is that the regional governments accept grants from the general governments. The first reason is that some of the regions at any rate have not been able to afford to provide the services which were demanded of them. In all the federations there are regions, like the Australian states of Western Australia, South Australia and Tasmania, or the prairie provinces of Canada, or states of the American Far West like South Dakota or Oklahoma, or of the South-East like South Carolina, which either through sparsity of population or

[1] *Book of the States, 1950–51,* p. 251.

[2] Australia was an exception to some extent. Invalid and old age pensions were placed within the power of the Commonwealth parliament.

poverty are unable even in normal times to maintain their services at the same level as that of their more prosperous associates in the federation. Such regions are compelled to ask for assistance from the general government or to allow their standard of services to decline or stagnate. Many states in the United States, for example, chose this latter alternative in the years before 1930. But in other federations some regions have asked for assistance and the best example of assistance on these grounds are the grants made by the Commonwealth of Australia to the poorer states of Western Australia, South Australia[1] and Tasmania.

But if these regions could not afford to provide their services in normal times through an inequality of financial resources, in times of economic depression, such as those of the 1930s, there was scarcely a region which could afford to bear the whole burden alone. In the United States, Switzerland, Australia and Canada the assistance of the general governments was needed in almost all cases, and such services as unemployment assistance and poor relief in particular were financed by grants. Economic depression reveals indeed a great weakness in the financial resources of many regional governments for they rely to a great extent for their revenue upon the receipts of certain industrial undertakings and from the rents of agricultural lands. An economic depression produces an immediate drop in this source of revenue. In Australia, for example, during the depression of 1929–1932 revenue from this source fell by 25 per cent. And when the regions turn to the field of direct taxation to make up for their losses, they find, as I have shown, that the encroachments by the general government in this field, chiefly by reason of war, have reduced the area available for exploitation. It is in circumstances of this kind that regions find themselves unable to perform their functions and obliged to ask for grants from the general governments.

The general governments in their turn, though faced with demands for increasing expenditure, especially in the sphere of defence, are able to render assistance. For they have available to them, as I have shown, the whole of the resources of the country and all the most powerful engines of taxation. They can exploit the richer areas for the benefit of the poorer. What wealth there is, they can seek out. Whereas the government of a depressed region, with great demands for social services, and correspondingly small resources to meet them, is confined within the area of its own territory for the resources it may tap, the general government can range over the whole field. One function which the general government of a federation is coming increasingly to perform, rightly or wrongly, is the redistribution of the wealth of the whole country, taking it from the more prosperous regions and giving it to the poorer.

And here one is brought into contact with a new factor—the

Since 1959 South Australia has not been a claimant state.

initiative which general governments have come to take in these matters. Although it is true that some regional governments have always been unable to afford to provide services at the same level as their neighbours because their financial resources are inadequate by nature, and although there have been times, such as the depression of the 1930s, when all regions felt this poverty to some extent, yet it is true also that many regional governments could have done much more than they did. Some of them could have afforded to provide the whole of their social services at a high standard; others could have gone a part of the way. A few did what they could, but most argued, naturally, that they did not desire to impose additional burdens upon their tax payers unless other regional governments were going to do the same. And how could they be sure that if they provided these services, people from other states would not come and make use of them.[1] In these circumstances only the initiative of the general government could solve the problem.

The most striking example of this initiative was the New Deal of President Franklin D. Roosevelt in the years from 1933 onwards. There the general government produced a social service programme, which by offering financial inducements to the states if they adopted the programme and financial penalties if they did not, gave the states sufficient resources to perform their functions and encouraged them also to carry them out. Nor was this initiative confined to social services. Agriculture is a matter which is in the hands of the states in the United States. Without the initiative of the general government the states acting singly could not have produced a plan to deal with the depression in farming which was upon them. The general government offered grants to the states upon conditions and the states were eager to accept. Although the original act—the Agricultural Adjustment Act—was declared invalid by the Supreme Court in 1936, a new act, the Soil Conservation Act, was passed soon afterwards by which the general government still provided the greater part of the funds, while the state governments enacted the necessary legislation.

Some idea of the effect of the New Deal upon state finance can be obtained from a few figures.[2] In 1930, when the general government granted about $135,000,000 to the states, 50 per cent of this amount went to the expenditure on highways, and another 22 per cent to the National Guard, the successor to the State militia. By 1940 the grants had increased by 300 per cent; they were made for twenty-one separate objects, as against eleven in 1930, and among these objects services grouped under the head of social security now comprised

---

[1] A good example of this was the attitude of the State of Massachusetts to unemployment insurance. It passed an act in 1935 but prescribed that it should not become operative unless the Social Security Act was passed by Congress or unless eleven other states, which it named, imposed substantially equivalent burdens on its employers. See Cardozo, J. giving the opinion of the court in *Steward Machine Co.* v. *Davis*, (1937) 301 U.S. 548, at pp. 587–8.

[2] Based on the article by Austin F. Macdonald already cited.

53 per cent of the total.[1] In other words, social security occupied in 1940 the position occupied by highways in 1930. The grants for old age assistance, which did not appear in the list until 1936, accounted in 1940 for 35 per cent of the total grants. These figures are based on regular grants-in-aid and do not take into account emergency grants and loans, which were substantial in the worst years of the economic depression of the thirties. Nor have the sums allocated to states by the Works Progress Administration or the Public Works Authority, two important agencies in the Roosevelt Recovery Programme, been included. If these latter are added, the total of assistance would come near to $800,000,000 for any one of a number of years before 1940. In the United States the great period of development in respect of grants by the general government came therefore in the thirties and particularly through the Roosevelt Recovery plan. Every state activity which had been aided by the general government in 1930 continued to be aided in 1940 but on a more generous scale, while, in addition, new and more important services had come into existence as aided activities by 1940. Of these the social services are most important. On a rough calculation the 48 states spent about $3,000,000,000 on the social services[2] in 1940;[3] they received from the general government in grants for such purposes about $360,000,000,[4] or 12 per cent. More significant are the proportions in respect of certain services. The general government undertook to pay 50 per cent of the amount which states spent on old age assistance; in regard to aid for the blind the grants from the general government have worked out to be about equal to the appropriations from state and local government treasuries.

[1] This is the list:

		$
1.	Highways	161,730,958
2.	National Guard	42,053,582
3.	Vocational Education	19,616,000
4.	Vocational Rehabilitation	1,820,000
5.	Agricultural Extension Work	17,821,531
6.	Agricultural Experimental Studies	6,541,250
7.	Support of Agricultural Colleges	5,030,000
8.	Forest Fire Protections	1,972,968
9.	Distribution of Nursery Stock	88,212
10.	Restriction of Wild Life	1,000,000
11.	Old Age Assistance	210,159,949
12.	Unemployment Compensation Administration	58,812,390
13.	Dependent Children	31,466,619
14.	Crippled Children	2,997,915
15.	Child Welfare	1,520,894
16.	Maternal and Child Hygiene	3,724,362
17.	Aid to the Blind	5,271,609
18.	Public Health Services	7,985,119
19.	Employment Offices	1,950,000
20.	Houses for Drilled Veterans	709,296
*21.	State Marine Schools	246,665
		$582,529,319

* Made to 4 states only.

[2] Including in this category protection to persons and property, health and sanitation charities, hospitals for the handicapped, correction schools, libraries, recreation, unemployment compensation and services.
[3] The figure is calculated from *Statistical Abstract of the United States*, 1941.
[4] Taking the figures given in the table of note 1 above.

What has happened in the United States is more striking than in Australia and Canada. But in these federations also there has been the same initiative by the general government in the sphere of social services. Although they have been debarred in most cases from legislating upon this field, they have entered into it by the offer of grants. Thus the Dominion government of Canada contributed 75 per cent of the old age pensions fund which the provinces administered from 1930. It was responsible for about 33 per cent of provincial and municipal expenditure on the relief of the poor in 1937.[1] The Commonwealth government of Australia has made grants to the states for unemployment relief and for the provision of roads and the encouragement of agriculture.[2] The general government of Switzerland has made grants to the cantons for such services as education, public health, sickness and unemployment insurance, and unemployment relief works, as well as for other purposes such as the assistance of agriculture and commerce, and the provision of roads and bridges.[3] But in Switzerland also some attempt has been made to deal with the inadequacy of cantonal revenues to provide the social services by the method of transferring the services to the general government. By constitutional amendment, accident and sickness insurance, for example, old age and widows' pensions, and the counteracting of certain contagious diseases were handed over to the general government. Canada made a similar transfer of unemployment insurance in 1940 and of old age pensions in 1951. In Australia in 1946 power was granted to the Commonwealth parliament to legislate upon certain social services including unemployment and sickness benefits and childrens' allowances.

But if what is often called 'welfare politics' has led the general governments to take the initiative in the federations and almost to force grants upon the regions, they have been driven on also by a force which is far stronger, at any rate in its immediate effects—war. Under the stress of two great wars the general governments of the federations have been forced, as I have shown, to enter the field of direct taxation of which, before 1914, the regions were generally speaking in sole possession, and in Australia and Canada they have been able to exclude the regions from this field in return for the payment of grants. Nothing less than the overriding necessities of war could have permitted initiative by the general governments on such a scale as this. No economic depression had ever been held to demand such extreme centralization of finance. And when the war ceased there was no sign that the general governments would withdraw from the field. On the contrary, repeating the experience after the first of the great wars, the general governments used their increased financial strength to take the initiative once again in the fields of social services,

[1] *Rowell-Sirois Report*, Book I, pp. 208–9.
[2] See *Finance Bulletins* issued by the Commonwealth Bureau of Census and Statistics.
[3] See *Statistisches Jahrbuch*, already cited.

social reconstruction and economic reconstruction, where the regions still possess the legislative powers but lack the financial resources. In Australia and Canada some legislative powers have actually been transferred. In the United States itself, however, the general government has occupied the field of taxation, by agreement with the states, to an unprecedented degree. Grants have not been used as in Canada and Australia to persuade the states to withdraw, but there has been, as in Canada, a voluntary withdrawal of the states from many fields of taxation hitherto occupied.

It is most important that the extent of financial dependence by regional upon general governments in the federations should not be exaggerated and that a generalization should not be allowed to give a false impression. In the United States the degree of dependence has grown considerably in recent years, but it is too early yet to conclude what the tendency will be. In Switzerland, Canada and Australia dependence has gone further, and the most striking development in subordinating the regions in the latter two has come first by judicial decisions giving priority to the taxes of the general governments, and second, by war-time arrangements about income tax. But in spite of all this it must be remembered that not only are the different federations affected to a different degree, but also different regions in the same federation are affected differently. While South Carolina received assistance from the general government of the United States up to 100 per cent in providing for the relief of unemployment in 1934, Connecticut received between 10 per cent and 12 per cent. In Canada the province of Quebec received only a small proportion of its revenue by grant from the Dominion government; Ontario had a similar independence.[1] New South Wales, Queensland and Victoria were less dependent upon federal aid than Tasmania, Western Australia and South Australia. With the adoption in 1942 of grants in place of income tax the position has been altered, of course, because the wealthier regions had collected a larger sum in income tax than the poorer regions and they consequently receive a greater grant. Though the generalizations which I have offered in these sections are true, they apply in varying degree in the different cases.

8

This analysis of the working of public finance in federal governments has made one thing clear. The allocation of financial resources to the general and regional governments in the original constitutions has not corresponded with the allocation of functions to these governments. This is not surprising. Conditions in a variety of communities joined together in a federation differ too much from time to time and from place to place for a fixed division of financial resources to be laid

---

[1] In 1937 the proportions were, for example, Quebec and Ontario about 1·4 per cent; Saskatchewan 13 per cent; Prince Edward Island 32 per cent; Nova Scotia and New Brunswick about 10 per cent. *Rowell-Sirois Report*. Book III, pp. 46–7.

down finally in a constitution. There is and can be no final solution to the allocation of financial resources in a federal system. There can only be adjustments and re-allocations in the light of changing conditions. What a federal government needs, therefore, is machinery adequate to make these adjustments and to make them also in such a way that the financial independence of the general and regional governments is preserved so far as possible. And here the experience of the working of federal government can give us some answers.

Switzerland provides an example of one method of adjustment. That is the method of constitutional amendment whereby functions are redistributed, and financial resources to assist in the performance of these functions are also redistributed. By a steady process of amendment the cantons have handed over functions to the general government and with them financial resources. Moreover when, as in the case of defence, the general government found that it needed more money to perform its own task, the cantons handed over further financial resources. They claimed some share in the revenues which they surrendered, and they often obtained a constitutional guarantee of such a share. Thus some independence was retained though resources and functions were re-allocated. Yet this is not the complete picture, as I have shown. The Swiss cantons do depend on grants from the general government fixed at the discretion of that government, and the amount of these grants far outweighs the 'legal participations' guaranteed to the cantons. What is interesting in Switzerland, however, is the extent of readjustment and reallocation which has been possible by constitutional amendment.

With the exception of the XVIth amendment to the Constitution of the United States—and it is an important exception—this method of readjustment has not been used to any considerable extent in the other federations. In the United States the method of grants by the general government has been used, but no machinery has yet been devised for settling the principles on which these grants should be allocated. There is no system. It is a matter of politics.[1] Nor has it been much different in Canada. The grants were guaranteed in the constitution, but when they have proved inadequate and an increase is desired, bargaining between governments, with the Dominion government in the strongest position, is the only method so far found possible.

In Australia, however, some experiments have been tried which indicate the basis upon which institutions for readjustment may be devised. There is, first, the Loan Council, to which reference has already been made, where borrowings by Commonwealth and state governments are regulated by these governments acting jointly. This has modified federalism but it has not by itself destroyed it. There is, secondly, the experiment of the Commonwealth Grants Commission,

---

[1] See the article already referred to by Austin F. Macdonald in *American Political Science Review*, XXXIV, 1940, No. 3.

an independent expert body established to consider applications by states for grants from the Commonwealth, and to make recommendations to the Commonwealth government. In every case these recommendations were adopted. In a series of reports from 1934 onwards the Grants Commission laid down principles upon which it was prepared to recommend the Commonwealth government to make grants to the states. It considered that special grants were justified when a state, through financial stress from any cause, was unable efficiently to discharge its functions as a member of the federation, and that these grants should be determined by the amount of help found necessary to make it possible for that state by reasonable effort to function at a standard not appreciably below that of the other states.[1] The determination of grants was of course a matter of great difficulty, and any calculation, as the Commission recognized, was open to criticism. But it undertook a calculation each year; it was ready to modify its principles and practice in the light of experience; and it was careful to refrain from inventing mathematical formulae which would automatically be applied year by year. So far as it has gone, the Commission, in my opinion, has justified its existence. Some body of this kind working on these principles could prove a valuable part of the machinery of readjustment in federal finance.

It would seem that the Royal Commission on Dominion-Provincial Relations in Canada had the experience of this Australian institution in mind when it recommended the establishment in Canada of a system of National Adjustment Grants, supplemented by emergency grants in abnormal conditions, in order that all provincial governments could provide services up to the Canadian average, without exceeding the national average in taxation, and along with this the establishment of a Finance Commission to advise the Dominion Government on such grants and their review and adjustment from time to time.[2]

It may be added that the Indian Constitution provided for a Finance Commission[3] and the Malayan Constitution for a National Finance Council,[4] both of which included among their functions advice to the general government on making grants to the states. A Loans Council, on the Australian model, found a place in the Constitution of Rhodesia and Nyasaland.[5] In all three constitutions, and in that of Nigeria, the general government is empowered to make grants to the constituent units.

Yet if grants are to be a permanent feature of federal finance, it seems essential that their amount should not depend upon the

[1] *Third Report* of the Commission, pp. 75 and 85.
[2] *Rowell-Sirois Report*, Book II, pp. 83–5.
[3] Arts. 280–81. The Commission's Reports of 1952 and 1957 are particularly interesting and valuable.
[4] Art. 108.
[5] Secs. 88–91.

good will of the granting government, for if they do so depend, the federal principle is thereby modified. From this point of view, while it seems right that an expert body should recommend the amount of the grants, it does not seem in accordance with federalism that the general government should decide whether it will accept the recommendation. Some body representative of general and regional governments, organized on the lines of the Australian Loan Council, would seem more suitable for this purpose. It must be admitted, I think, that a political body is needed to take these decisions, although there is a strong case for the view that an independent body like the Grants Commission should have the final decision of the whole question.

But the final test of the system of public finance in these federations is not, it must be emphasized: Does it produce or preserve federal government? but, Does it produce good government? It will be seen that the object before the members of the Australian Grants Commission was just that. They proposed to recommend grants which would ensure a minimum of good government in all the states; if strict financial federalism could not ensure it, then a measure of dependence upon the general government would be necessary. That is not the only way. Constitutional amendment, as Switzerland shows, can bring some adjustment. But the test in the end is: Does the observance of the federal principle in finance produce the result that is desired? Is it worth preserving in spite of all the difficulties involved in any attempt at readjustment? That question is one which citizens of federal governments have got to answer. They have not dealt with it so far in more than piecemeal fashion. And meanwhile the federal principle is being modified increasingly in the public finance of all four federal governments.

Chapter VII

FEDERAL GOVERNMENT AND THE
CONTROL OF ECONOMIC AFFAIRS

1

WE may begin with the control of trade between the federal country and foreign countries, considering in particular the problem of the customs tariff. This is a question which in all countries provokes sharp controversy, for the interests of those who depend for their prosperity upon imports from abroad or upon exports conflict obviously and, at first sight, irreconcilably with the interests of those who depend upon home-produced resources or a home market. In federal countries it is even more difficult as a political problem, for it often happens that these interests are regionalized and are found concentrated in one state or in a group of states, and thus the hostility of economic interest groups is intensified by becoming translated into the hostility of well-organized, loyally supported state governments. In federal countries, too, the problem has a special importance at the very outset of the federal union, because the states which propose to form the union have usually themselves regulated independently their trade relations with foreign countries and have established in their midst economic interests which rely upon their support. What is to be the future of these protected interests under a federal union? How is the difficult transition stage from a plurality of tariff systems to a single tariff system to be organized? Indeed should it be attempted at all? All modern federal systems have faced these problems and it is clear that they have not yet solved them.

All the federations which we have discussed grant to the general government a power to regulate trade and commerce with foreign countries. In Canada[1] and Switzerland[2] the power is actually exclusive.[3] In the United States and Australia, the states can impose inspection charges on imports and exports, but this power cannot be exercised without the consent of the general legislature. In the United States the provision runs : 'No state shall, without the consent of Congress, lay any imposts or duties on imports or exports, except what may be absolutely necessary for executing its inspection laws ; and the net produce of all duties and imposts laid by any state on imports or exports, shall be for the use of the Treasury of the United States ; and all such laws shall be subject to the revision and control of the Congress.' 'No state shall, without the consent of Congress, lay any

[1] British North America Act, 1867, s. 91 (2).
[2] Swiss Constitution, Art. 28.
[3] It includes the powers to impose duties on imports and exports and bounties on production.

duty of tonnage.'[1] It will be seen that the states have little inducement or opportunity to impose such duties. In Australia the power to impose duties is even more restricted, for it is confined to 'such charges as may be necessary for executing the inspection laws of the states'.[2] These may be passed without receiving the prior consent of the Commonwealth parliament, but they are liable to be subsequently annulled by it, and in both cases it is clear that the power of the general government to control foreign commerce is exclusive, but potentially exclusive, not actually, as in Canada and Switzerland. In practice there has been no difference.

The fact that exclusive powers have been conferred upon the general governments in a matter where such acute differences of opinion are possible should not lead one to conclude that there was and is no conflict. The power was not conceded without conflict and it is not exercised without conflict.

An indication of the fears of the separate American states when they formed the union is seen in the requirements in the Constitution that any duties imposed by Congress should be uniform throughout the United States[3] and that they should not give preference to the ports of one state over those of another.[4] In Australia the fears of an agricultural state which relied on an export market, Western Australia, that its peculiar economy would suffer under the industrial and agricultural protectionism of the Eastern states of Australia—Victoria, New South Wales and Queensland—is illustrated by the provision in the Constitution that the parliament of Western Australia might, during the first five years after the imposition of uniform customs duties by the Commonwealth, impose customs duties on goods passing into that state and not originally imported from beyond the limits of the Commonwealth. These duties were to be progressively reduced year by year and were to expire at the end of the five-year period.[5] In this way an attempt—though, as will be seen, an unsuccessful attempt—was made to assist Western Australia to adjust itself to a uniform tariff system. There were in the Australian Constitution also provisions similar to those in the American Constitution forbidding the general government from exercising its powers to impose duties and grant bounties in such a way as to discriminate between the states.[6]

The Swiss cantons were slow to surrender their tariff power and the Constitution of 1848, even after its thorough revision of 1874, still permitted to the cantons a small right of imposing import duties. These were the duties on wines and other alcoholic beverages which certain cantons had levied. They were continued for such cantons but not extended to others, and it was provided further that 'all import duties at present levied by the cantons, as well as similar duties levied by the communes, shall be abolished without compensation at the end of the year 1890'.[1] This was, therefore, a small and temporary exception to the general power of actual exclusive control over foreign commerce which was conferred on the general government.

The chief interest of this topic lies, then, in seeing how far the conferring of this wide power of customs regulation upon the general governments in these federal systems is reconciled with the admitted differences in economic interest of different regions in the federation. It may be said at once that, with the possible exception of Switzerland, the exercise of this power has been regarded in all the federations, at some time or another, as producing unsatisfactory results, and in particular as operating unequally and unjustly as between the different regions in the federation.

In the United States the most severe strain placed upon the federation in its early days arose from a difference of opinion about the tariff. It led to the assertion in South Carolina of the doctrine of 'nullification'.[2] In virtue of this doctrine South Carolina maintained that while the Congress had power to impose a customs tariff, the states were entitled if, in their opinion, the Congress abused its power, to declare the customs law null and void in the state. Up to 1816 the United States tariff had been largely intended for revenue rather than protective purposes. After 1816 the protective policy came forward and it reached a peak in the tariff of 1828. The Act of 1816 had not affected the South adversely to any great extent, but with successive increases it began to feel that it was destined to suffer almost in direct proportion as other regions were to benefit. South Carolina in particular felt the burden of the tariff and was therefore the natural spokesman of the dissidents. Its view of the effects of the tariff power as exercised by the general legislature was expressed by its leader, John C. Calhoun, Vice-President of the United States under President Andrew Jackson, in these words: '. . . . the tariff, however disguised, is but a tax on our process, to be given as a bounty, to the process used by the other sections. It compels us to take less in our exchanges with the rest of the world (an essential portion of our process of manufacturing our supplies)—in order that the other sections may secure more in their exchanges with us; to compel us (to be more specific) to give more rice, cotton and tobacco for every pound of iron, or yard of cloth we get from abroad, in order that they may secure more rice, cotton and tobacco for every pound of iron, or yard of cloth they sell to us, while at the same time they take to themselves our loss, in our foreign exchanges, exacted in the shape of duties on imports— by appropriating the proceeds, through the action of Congress, in various ways, to their almost exclusive use. It is thus our industry is

[1] Art. 32.

[2] See Chapter V above, at p. 87.

discouraged, that theirs may be encouraged—ours dispoiled that theirs may be protected.'[1]

This is the substance of the complaint against the tariff in the other federations. The tariff is imposed in the interest of the industrialists and it is paid at the expense of the exporting agriculturists. The same protest was made in Australia one hundred years later when the Government of Western Australia declared 'East is east and west is west'.[2] 'Western Australia has a natural aptitude for unprotected industries; she is essentially a primary producing country, her staple products for many years having been wheat and wool. . . . So long as she continues within Federation, Western Australia will ever present the picture of a community obliged to earn in the unprotected world market, the credits with which to pay for the goods purchased in the highly protected Australian market. . . .'[3] The States of South Australia and Tasmania, both primarily agricultural, would support this view. In Canada the Maritime Provinces of Nova Scotia, New Brunswick and Prince Edward Island with their dependence on agriculture, forest industries and fishing; the Prairie Provinces of Manitoba, Alberta and Saskatchewan, relying on the export of wheat; and British Columbia with its timber and shipping industries, all regard themselves as suffering from a tariff designed to protect the industrial interests concentrated largely in Quebec and Ontario. All these Provinces brought evidence to this effect before the Canadian Royal Commission on Dominion-Provincial Relations which reported in 1940.[4] The divergence of economic interest is there and the effect of the tariff policies appears to have made it more acute.

The conflict has issued in different forms in each country. In Canada the Provinces have protested, have demanded compensation, have bargained. The Dominion Government has given them grants.[5] The problem is not solved, but no desperate remedies have been invoked. In the United States more extreme courses have been taken. The tariff of 1828 made South Carolina, under the leadership of Calhoun, proceed to the nullification of the customs law. At a convention of the people of the state on November 24,1832, the tariff act of 1828 and a modifying Act of 1832 were declared null and void within the jurisdiction of the state. In Calhoun's view the terms of the tariff act of 1828 were an abuse of power and it was competent for the State of South Carolina to nullify. Thus the divergence of interest in the United States had brought up the whole question of the nature of the union. Was it a federation or a confederation? As it happened the issue was avoided. No other states followed the lead of South Carolina. Calhoun himself was for compromise and not for conflict,

---

[1] Address to the People of South Carolina, 1831, Calhoun, *Works* (ed. Grallé), Vol. VI, pp. 129–30.
[2] *The Case of the People of Western Australia* (Perth, Western Australia, 1934), p. 335
[3] Ibid., pp. 484–5.
[4] See *Rowell-Sirois Report*, Book II, p. 230.
[5] See previous chapter.

and in the end, after a firm proclamation from President Jackson asserting that the laws of the United States must be enforced, a new tariff was adopted, providing for a return by stages to the position of 1816, and the nullification ordinance was repealed in South Carolina.

Calhoun had not advocated secession but the protesting people and government of Western Australia did go so far a century later. They asserted that the divergence of interest between the Western and Eastern states was so acute that it could not be adjusted under a single tariff system. 'Western Australia,' it was asserted, 'does not object to Eastern Australia building up its body economic by such means as that unit may prefer; what Western Australia does object to is that she should be compelled to submit to the means so preferred by Eastern Australia when those means are to Western Australia so deleterious.'[1] And she petitioned the parliament at Westminster to dissolve her partnership with the other states in the Australian Commonwealth. No action was taken, the matter was referred back to Australia and by compromise and concession the crisis was passed. Whether it will recur cannot be prophesied.

The divergence of interest is there. It remains to. be considered how its more disintegrating results may be avoided. In the first place it is clear that the power of the federal government must be moderately exercised, and it may be that such movements as those for nullification in South Carolina and for secession in Western Australia are necessary and valuable because they recall the protectionist states to a sense of moderation in pursuing their interests. Secondly, it must not always be assumed that the conflict grows out of what Calhoun called 'circumstances of a fixed and durable character'.[2] Changes in the organization of industry and agriculture, increase of population, and the development of new territories may alter the balance of power in a federation.

These moderating factors operated in the United States after the tariff compromise of 1833. By successive stages tariff reductions were made and in 1846 the country was accustomed—both sections of it— to moderate duties. At the same time the opening up and establishment of new states, while it sometimes involved the increase in the number of free as against slave states—and this was feared by the South—always meant the setting up of agricultural, and that meant low tariff or free trade, states and this was to the advantage of the South. So effective were these forces that 'at the beginning of the Civil War the tariff could in no sense be termed a Southern grievance. South and West had joined against New England in lowering the tariffs of 1846 and 1857; indeed tariff policy for nearly three decades prior to the Civil War had been shaped with an eye to Southern interests'.[3]

[1] *Case of the People of Western Australia*, p. 342.
[2] Op. cit., p. 134.
[3] J. G. Randall, *The Civil War and Reconstruction*, p. 375.

The great safeguard of the less populated, agricultural, low-tariff states was, of course, their representation in the Senate in equal numbers with the more populous high-tariff states. In the United States it has undoubtedly safeguarded the interests of the less populous regions. In Australia, as I mentioned in Chapter V,[1] the Senate has not been so effective. The reason appears to be that party organization in Australia has cut across state boundaries. Both the Labour Party and the anti-Labour Party[2] have been in favour of high tariffs and their representatives in the Senate are party men first and state representatives second. The Country Party is avowedly out to protect the ordinary producers and undoubtedly has done so, but it has never obtained more than a few seats in the Senate. The existence of a third party of this kind ought to act as a moderating influence in producing the tariff policy of a federation. In Australia it has preferred to obtain protection for primary producers by such methods as subsidies, fixed home prices, and even tariffs.

Another method of compensating the states which suffer most from the tariff is that of making grants from the general government either out of the customs revenue or from general funds. This has been advocated in Canada and Australia, and certain of the regions there have sought to justify special grants to themselves on the ground of actual inequality in the working of the tariff. But although they have received grants, the general government has not usually been prepared to say that these grants are given as a direct compensation for tariff injuries. It has been maintained by the general government that although certain regions do suffer from the tariff, they gain much more than other regions by certain other policies of the general government, so that on balance they are not less favourably placed, when all factors are taken into account, than are regions which the tariff benefits. The Australian Grants Commission has stressed this point in dealing with complaints from Western Australia, South Australia and Tasmania.[3] It may be remarked, however, that even if grants are not given because of the ill effects of tariff policy, the fact that they are given at all will help to soften the hostility which is aroused by the unequal incidences of certain aspects of the tariff.[4]

That there is inequality seems undoubted, however difficult it is to get a precise and accurate account of its extent. It is founded upon a fundamental diversity. 'It is the part of wisdom,' in Calhoun's words, 'to see and admit a fact so important, and to take it into the estimate of measures, and not to expect to prevent its natural consequences by overlooking its existence.'

[1] See p. 89 above.

[2] Known under various names, see note 2, p. 84 above.

[3] See, for example, the *Third Report* of the Commission (1934), pp. 64–69. A similar attitude was adopted by the *Rowell-Sirois Report*, Book II, pp. 230–33.

[4] This seems to have happened in Western Australia.

2

So far as the control of external trade and commerce is concerned
it seems clear that the general governments in these federal systems
have in law full powers, although in practice these powers must be
exercised moderately if the unity of the federation is not to be submitted to an excessive strain. When we turn to consider economic life
within the boundaries of the federation a more complicated situation
is found. Powers are divided between general and regional governments in such a way that it is difficult to find any useful principle of
comparison between the countries or, more bewildering still, to state
with precision just where within any federation authority over a given
topic may be said to lie. An attempt will be made here, however, to
give some general guiding lines which, if they succeed in providing a
simple account of the complications, may perhaps be more enlighten-
ing than any attempt at unravelling the complications themselves.

If we look at the Constitutions of Switzerland, the United States,
Canada and Australia, we can find that the general governments in all
four federations possess powers of exclusive control, actual or
potential, over certain aspects of economic life. Among these may be
mentioned currency, coinage and legal tender;[1] weights and measures; copyrights and patents; bankruptcy and insolvency; immigration and emigration from and to countries outside the federation;
and the raising of loans on the credit of the general government.
Beyond this list, it is difficult to find any important topic in economic
affairs which is granted without some qualifications to the general
governments in *all* federations.

Take the important question of banking. This subject is under the
exclusive control of the general government in Canada and Switzerland; in the United States and Australia it is divided between the
general and state governments subject, as I have indicated, to the
supremacy of the general government in matters of currency and
legal tender. In the United States the Constitution forbade the states
to coin money or emit bills of credit; but it did not forbid them to
charter banks with the power to issue notes. Thus two kinds of banks
exist in the United States, those holding charters under the general
government and those chartered by state governments. But the issue
of paper money is now confined to notes issued directly by the general
government of the United States and notes issued through the Federal
Reserve Banking System which is established by the general government. In Australia the constitution empowers the Commonwealth
parliament to legislate upon: 'Banking, other than state banking; also
state banking extending beyond the limits of the state concerned,
the incorporation of banks, and the issue of paper money.'

[1] This power has been finally assigned to the general government of the United States only
after a long series of judicial decisions, culminating and summarized in 1935 in the *Gold Clauses
Cases*. See above, Chapter VI, p. 95.

Navigation and shipping is similarly divided. The Dominion Government in Canada has control of all navigation and shipping except intra-provincial navigation and shipping; the power of the Australian Commonwealth extends to deal with navigation and shipping, but only so far as it is relevant to inter-state and foreign trade and commerce. There is thus both Commonwealth and state shipping legislation, the latter dealing with intra-state shipping exclusively. Similarly the power of the United States Congress to regulate shipping and navigation is derived from and extends no further than its power to regulate inter-state and foreign commerce. In Switzerland the subject of navigation is under the control of the general government.

The control of railways is similarly conferred in all four federations. In Canada, Australia and the United States it is divided between general and regional governments, in Switzerland it is in the hands of the general government alone. Civil aviation is in Canada and Switzerland in the control of the general government; in the United States and Australia it is divided between the general and regional governments. Insurance and marketing are divided between the two sets of authorities in all four systems. The regulation of the hours and conditions of labour and rates of wages is in the hands of the general government in Switzerland, it is shared between general and regional governments in the United States and Australia, and it is in the hands of the Provinces exclusively in Canada.

More examples could be given, but the main point is established. Apart from certain limited, though important, topics, the control of economic affairs in the federal systems is not unitary but multiple. It may be true that economic life is one, but in the federal countries this fact is not recognized so far as the allocation of governmental powers is concerned. The legal and political pluralism of the federations is imposed upon the alleged unity of economic affairs.

This makes a confusing picture. However, it is possible to clarify the picture a little, if instead of being content with displaying the divided authority over economic affairs in federal countries, we attempt to discover whether there are any principles of governmental organization which account for this division. For this purpose it seems preferable to take Switzerland and Canada separately, and to consider the United States and Australia together, before attempting any general statement.

3

The position in Switzerland may be simply stated. By the Constitution the cantons are sovereign in so far as their sovereignty has not been limited by the federal constitution, and, as such, they exercise all the rights which have not been handed over to the general government. To discover the powers of the general government in economic affairs, we have therefore merely to look at the terms of the Constitution and see what topics are expressly given to it.

What has happened in Switzerland is that the Constitution of 1848, as amended in 1874, conferred certain important but limited topics in economic affairs on the general government. Since 1874, principally by the process of constitutional amendment, certain further economic topics have been added to the powers of the general government, and they have been sufficiently numerous and important to justify one in saying that there has been a steady and substantial increase in the economic powers of the general government. The powers granted in 1848 were those over weights and measures,[1] coinage,[2] the postal service[3] and the customs,[4] with the proviso that trade and commerce throughout the country were to be free. There was, in addition, the power to order at its own expense or encourage by means of subsidies public works which interest Switzerland or a considerable part of the country, such public works to be carried out by the cantons.[5] This was used principally to subsidize road works undertaken by the cantons. With the revision of 1874 certain further powers, which had long been considered necessary by many cantons, but opposed by a strong minority, were conceded. The general government was given power over banks,[6] the construction and working of railways (under this power the railways were taken over by the state in 1898),[7] and over insurance companies not established by the state.[8] An important new power was that to enact uniform provisions concerning child labour in factories, the hours of labour which may be imposed upon adults, and on the protection to be afforded in unhealthy and dangerous industries.[9] This topic had been previously within the powers of the cantons and some of them had legislated upon it. But their legislation was only a beginning and it was difficult to expect a canton to penalize its own industries as against those of another canton which had no such regulations.

Since 1874 important extensions of the general government's powers of economic control have occurred. A few may be mentioned. In 1885 (subject to amendment in 1930) the general government was given control over distilled and alcoholic liquors;[10] in 1891 its powers over banking were extended;[11] in 1897 it was given powers over forests and rivers, though it shared its control of these topics with the cantons;[12] in 1908 it was given control (again shared to a small degree with the cantons) over hydraulic resources;[13] in 1917 it was authorized to tax securities, insurance premium receipts, bills of exchange

[1] Art. 40
[2] Art. 38.
[3] Art. 36.
[4] Arts. 28–29.
[5] Art. 23.
[6] Arts. 38–39.
[7] Art. 26

[8] Art. 34.
[9] Art. 34.
[10] Art. 32 bis.
[11] Art. 39.
[12] Art. 24.
[13] Art. 24 bis.

and other commercial documents, and the cantons were not permitted to tax documents which the general government taxed or had excluded from tax.[1] This power was primarily, of course, intended as a revenue producing power, but like all taxing powers it contains within itself the power to regulate or even to destroy. In 1919 the general government was given power over navigation;[2] in 1922 it obtained power, shared with the cantons, to regulate motor vehicles and bicycles;[3] in the same year aerial navigation was very naturally given to it;[4] and in 1925 another taxing power, that upon tobacco.[5] In 1929 comprehensive powers, primarily for defence purposes, over grain, flour and bread in order to ensure adequate supplies of these commodities and their proper distribution, were granted to the general government.[6] In 1947 a further grant, in rather general terms, of powers over economic affairs was made to the general government, so that it might be free to deal with economic crises arising from unemployment, threat of war and the like.[7]

It seems correct to conclude that so far as the control of economic affairs is concerned, the Swiss Constitution has proved adequate to the demands of its people. This appears to be due to the fact that it has been found sufficiently flexible to be adapted to the needs of the times. The Swiss people, who are really the inventors of the referendum as a modern political institution, do not hesitate to use it, and by its use, as has been shown above, they have extended the powers of the general government in economic affairs. This is not to say that all proposed amendments get through easily. The Swiss are conservative, but if one compares the frequency with which, in economic matters, they have been willing to amend their constitution with the infrequency with which Australia or the United States or Canada have been willing to act, it seems clear that a greater degree of flexibility exists in Switzerland.

4

At a first glance the provisions in the Canadian Constitution conferring legislative powers on the Dominion government in economic affairs seem generously comprehensive. The Dominion parliament is empowered in the words of s. 91 of the British North America Act, 1867, 'to make laws for the peace, order and good government of Canada in relation to all matters not coming within the classes of subjects by this Act assigned exclusively to the legislatures of the Provinces, and for greater certainty, but not so as to restrict the generality of the foregoing terms of this Section, it is hereby declared that (notwithstanding anything in this Act) the exclusive legislative

---

[1] Art. 41 bis.   [2] Art. 24 ter.
[3] Art. 37 bis.   [4] Art. 37 ter.
[5] Art. 41 ter.   [6] Art. 23 bis.
[7] Art. 31 bis—quinquies. A feature of the change was that it envisaged co-operation with the cantons in the administration of such legislation.

authority of the Parliament of Canada extends to all matters coming
within . . .
2. The Regulation of trade and commerce.'
There is a wide grant of power. It is not restricted, as in the United
States and Australia, by such phrases as 'with foreign nations and
among the several states'. Yet it has proved to be much less comprehensive in its operation than have the seemingly more restricted
powers conferred in the United States and Australia.

The only restriction mentioned in Canada was, as shown above,
matters coming within the classes of subjects by this Act assigned
exclusively to the legislatures of the provinces. Suppose there is some
class of subject enumerated on the provincial list which conflicts with
or overlaps with a subject enumerated on the Dominion list and in
particular with trade and commerce, which is to prevail? The Judicial
Committee of the Privy Council decided that, if such cases arise, the
enumerated Dominion powers prevail over the enumerated provincial
powers.[1] The particular provincial power which seems relevant here is
that of legislating upon property and civil rights in the province.[2]
One would expect, therefore, that the Dominion's power to legislate
for trade and commerce would often overlap and conflict with this
provincial power, but that it would prevail over it, and that as a result
the Dominion would exercise a fairly wide control from this source.
In fact the Judicial Committee has not construed the words in that
way.[3] It asserted that, taken literally, the phrase trade and commerce
would extend over the whole range of economic life but that such a
construction would ignore and render meaningless many of the other
heads of legislation specifically enumerated in the Dominion and
provincial lists.[4] It decided that the phrase ought to be construed so
as not to conflict, if at all possible, with these other heads, and in the
result it adopted a construction which, to the layman, seems to
amount to 'trade and commerce, except where it conflicts with property and civil rights in a province'. This latter phrase has been given a
wide interpretation at the same time, so that the scope of 'trade and
commerce' has been greatly narrowed.

The exact scope of the phrase 'regulation of trade and commerce'
is not yet clear. But it is so far settled that it does not extend to the
regulation of purely provincial trades, businesses and business
transactions. Power to establish such regulation belongs exclusively to
the Provinces. The Dominion power is confined to the inter-provincial
and international aspects of trade. Thus, as a result of Judicial Committee decisions,[5] the Dominion did not, through its power to regulate

---

[1] *Attorney-General of Ontario* v. *Attorney-General of Canada* (1896) A.C., 348. It is known as
the *Local Prohibition Case*. See *Rowell-Sirois Report*; Book I, pp. 58–59.
[2] s. 92 (13).
[3] See *Citizens Insurance Co.* v. *Parsons* (1881), 7 A.C. 96, at pp. 112–13. *Bank of Toronto* v.
Lamb (1887), 12 A.C. 575.
[4] *Bank of Toronto* v. *Lamb, supra*, at p. 586.
[5] These decisions are referred to in the *Rowell-Sirois Report*, Book I, p. 250.

trade and commerce, have authority to regulate the financial practices of insurance companies;[1] nor to undertake a general regulation of the grain trade through a system of licences;[2] nor to prohibit trade combinations; nor to regulate the supply and price of the necessities of life;[3] nor to enact compulsory provisions for investigating industrial disputes.[4] In 1937 the Dominion's Natural Products Marketing Act, a part of Mr Bennett's New Deal legislation, was declared invalid on the ground that the power to regulate trade and commerce did not extend to the regulation of trading transactions completed within a single province.[5] In each of these attempts by the Dominion to regulate economic affairs, the defect was that each involved an interference with trade and business carried on within a single province and was not applicable merely to inter-provincial aspects of trade and commerce. 'Trade and commerce' was interpreted narrowly; 'property and civil rights in the province' was interpreted widely.

The result of this judicial interpretation from about 1882 to 1937 has been to make what appears a comprehensive phrase come to be of little value. Indeed in 1925 the Privy Council went so far as to doubt whether the phrase could be relied upon as an independent source of power.[6] Its value chiefly lay in supporting some other more definite conferring of power in other parts of section 91 which might, with its assistance, be construed to prevail over the provincial power to regulate property and civil rights. It is to such heads as banking, currency and coinage, navigation and shipping and the like that the Dominion must turn to obtain overriding powers to regulate economic affairs.

Under such heads as these, it is worth while emphasizing, the Dominion has important powers. It has some control over companies incorporated under its own charters;[7] by the use of its power to declare local works to be for the general advantage of Canada, it has been able to exercise effective control over the grain trade;[8] under its power to enact the criminal law, it can prohibit certain economic practices, e.g. certain kinds of trade combinations, provided the Courts agree that such practices are in truth 'criminal';[9] and it has extensive powers over monetary policy, banks, bankruptcy, railway

---

[1] *Attorney-General of Canada* v. *Attorney-General of Alberta* [1916] I A.C. 588. In re *The Insurance Act of Canada* [1932] A.C. 41.
[2] *Rex* v. *Manitoba Grain Co.* (1922) 2 W.R.R. 113; *The King* v. *Eastern Terminal Elevator Co.* (1925) S.C.R. 434.
[3] *In re* Board of Commerce Act [1922] I A.C. 191.
[4] *Toronto Electric Commissioners* v. *Snider* [1925] A.C. 396.
[5] *Attorney-General of British Columbia* v. *Attorney-General of Canada* [1937] A.C. 377.
[6] *Toronto Electric Commissioners* v. *Snider* [1925] A.C. 396 at p. 410.
[7] This paragraph is based on *Rowell-Sirois Report*, Book, I, p. 250.
[8] The Dominion declared all grain elevators used in the western grain trade to be works for general advantage of Canada. Its power to do this is derived from an exception to section 92 (10) of the British North America Act. The action was upheld by the Supreme Court of Canada in *The King* v. *Eastern Terminal Elevator Co.* referred to above.
[9] The law is not easy to state shortly. See *Proprietory Articles Trade Association* v. *Attorney-General of Canada* [1931] A. C. 310.

and air transportation, shipping and inter-provincial communications.

These are considerable powers. But they are, practically speaking, all there are, since 'trade and commerce' is so narrowly construed. Attempts have been made to claim more extended powers for the Dominion but they have failed. One line of argument was to assert that the general words at the beginning of section 91 (quoted on p. 129): 'Peace, order and good government of Canada in relation to all matters not coming within the classes of subjects by this Act assigned exclusively to the legislations of the Provinces' ought to be construed as permitting some degree of encroachment on the powers of the Provinces. But the Privy Council did not accept this view.[1] While it laid down that in case of conflict between the *enumerated* heads given to the Dominion in section 91 and those given to the Provinces in section 92, the powers conferred in the enumerated heads of section 91 should prevail over those of section 92, it was not prepared to give the same authority to the general words 'peace, order and good government'. They must therefore give way in normal times to the enumerated heads of section 92. The only exception that is permitted is the occurrence of a grave emergency, such as that of the war of 1914–1918,[2] but as soon as the crisis is over, the power disappears.[3] The economic crisis of the 1930s was not regarded by the Privy Council as sufficiently grave to support the overriding by the Dominion of provincial enumerated powers. An attempt was made to justify much of the Bennett New Deal legislation on this emergency argument. The Weekly Day of Rest in Industrial Undertakings Act, the Minimum Wages Act, the Limitation of Hours of Work Act and the Employment and Social Insurance Act all affected, it was admitted, property and civil rights in the Provinces, but they were all defended on the ground that they were intended to deal with a grave emergency. But the Privy Council in 1937 did not accept this view and declared them invalid.[4] The position thus was that 'temporary evils of great magnitude may be grappled with by Dominion legislation under the general clause of section 91 but an enduring and deep-rooted social malaise, which requires the mobilizing of efforts on a nation-wide scale to deal with it, is beyond the power of the Dominion unless it is comprised in the enumerated heads of section 91. Generally, therefore, the power to deal with these pressing social questions rests with the provinces'.[5] Under normal conditions only a few matters of minor importance, which are not relevant to the present topic,

---

[1] *The Local Prohibition Case* already referred to above [1896] A.C. 348 at p. 361.

[2] *Fort Frances Pulp and Paper Company* v. *Manitoba Free Press* [1923] A.C. 696.

[3] *In re Board of Commerce Act* [1922] I A.C. 191.

[4] The first three acts were dealt with in *Attorney-General of Canada* v. *Attorney-General of Ontario* [1937] A.C. 326, and the fourth act in a case with the same title reported in [1937] A.C. 355.

[5] *Rowell-Sirois Report*, Book I, p. 249.

have been held to come within the scope of the general power in section 91.

Another method by which it was sought to establish an over-riding Dominion control in certain economic matters was by the assertion of a power in the Dominion parliament to implement treaties. This matter is treated more fully in a subsequent chapter on foreign affairs. It is enough to say here that some of the Bennett New Deal legislation—the first three of the acts referred to above—was defended on the ground that it was legislation to put into effect conventions which Canada had made through the International Labour Organization and that the Dominion parliament had power to legislate to give effect to such treaties and that this power overrode the enumerated provincial powers if and when it conflicted with them. The Judicial Committee held that by virtue of the peculiar terms of the Canadian Constitution, unless[1] the treaties in question were treaties made by the imperial executive and the treaty obligations involved were assumed by Canada as part of the British Empire, the power of the Dominion to implement treaties by legislation depends entirely on whether the subject matter of the treaty falls within section 91 or section 92. The treaties concerned in these cases were not such 'British Empire' treaties; they had been negotiated by Canada alone. The Dominion's power to implement them must be sought in section 91. As stated above, when section 91 was studied, the only argument it could provide to justify the legislation was that it was designed for an emergency and thus overrode the provincial powers in property and civil rights, and this argument was not accepted as valid by the Judicial Committee.[2]

In the outcome, therefore, the control of economic affairs is divided in Canada between the Dominion and provincial legislatures and it is clear that the powers of the Dominion are not very extensive. The position has arisen first because of the surprisingly wide inter-pretation of the 'property and civil rights' clause; secondly, because of the surprisingly narrow interpretation given to 'trade and com-merce'; thirdly, from the narrow interpretation of the general words about 'peace, order and good government' in section 91; and finally, from the peculiar provisions of the Constitution itself in regard to the implementing of treaties by legislation which, it seems reasonable to argue, made it difficult for any court to give the Dominion parliament full power to implement treaties.

The interesting contrast between Canada and Switzerland is, of course, that judicial interpretation has done so much in Canada to restrict the Dominion powers, while in Switzerland it does not oper-ate at all to bind the powers of the general legislature. But, it may be asked, what of the people of Canada? Have they not been able or

---

[1] The reasons for the decision are explained in Chapter X, see pp. 174–6.
[2] *Attorney-General for Canada* v. *Attorney-General for Ontario* [1937] A.C. 326.

willing to do what the Swiss people have done—confer wider powers upon the Dominion parliament? The answer is that they have not always been willing to do so. There is strong opposition to increased Dominion control over economic affairs, as is illustrated by the defeat of Mr. Bennett's government in the election of 1935, which followed closely upon the enactment of this 'New Deal' and was really a referendum on it. But there are sections of the people who would support such extensions of power if they had the opportunities which the Swiss people or the Australian people have to alter their Constitution. But the division of powers is alterable only by the Parliament of the United Kingdom. That Parliament acts only on the request of the Canadian Dominion parliament, and the latter is naturally unwilling to put forward proposals for its own aggrandizement unless it can obtain the consent of all the important provinces. So far it has not had that support. Quebec and Ontario, in particular, the two most industrialized provinces, are each, for different reasons, intent upon preserving their control over property and civil rights and upon resisting Dominion encroachment.

It is true that one amendment in this sphere has been passed. In 1940 a unanimous request from the Dominion and provinces asked that unemployment insurance should be placed in the hands of the Dominion parliament and this was done by the British North America Act, 1940. But all other attempts by Dominion-Provincial Conferences to obtain some agreed method of amending the Constitution or to agree upon amendments which would increase the control of the Dominion government over economic affairs have so far failed. Whatever sections of the people may feel, the interests of the provincial governments are strongly opposed to it. At present nothing short of unanimous consent from the provinces will suffice before any alteration in the distribution of economic powers is requested at Westminster.

5

The United States and Australia resemble each other in that the power of their general government to control trade and commerce is restricted by the phrase 'with foreign nations and among the several states', in the case of the United States, and 'with other countries and among the States', in the case of Australia. Put shortly, their control is confined to inter-state and foreign commerce; such commerce as remains lies within the exclusive control of the state legislatures. There at first sight is a restriction from which the general government in Canada was free. But, as was indicated earlier, it may be doubted whether in the end the general government's powers in Canada are as great as that of the United States or of Australia.

In the course of its interpretation of the 'commerce clause' the Supreme Court of the United States has upheld a steady extension of the powers of Congress.[1] For the first hundred years of the Constitution, Congress did little to regulate commerce, but since 1887, when it passed the Inter-State Commerce Act, it has undertaken a large and important amount of such regulation. That Act required the rates of carriers engaged in inter-state commerce to be reasonable, that there should be no discrimination in rates or service, that the receipts of different railways should not be pooled and divided, and that rates should be published. It created the Inter-State Commerce Commission to enforce its provisions. Since 1887 the Act has been extended and strengthened. The Commission has been given power to fix rates and regulations. The powers given under the Act have been extended to cover express companies, sleeping-car companies, telegraph, telephone and cable companies, and pipe lines, air communications, radio and stock exchanges, though in 1934 the control of telegraphs, telephones, cables and radio was given to Federal Communications Commission.[2] In 1890 Congress used its powers over inter-state commerce to pass the Sherman Anti-Trust Act, which made it a criminal offence to enter into a contract, combination or conspiracy in restraint of trade or commerce among the states, or with foreign nations, or to monopolize or conspire to monopolize any part of such trade. In 1914 the Federal Trade Commission was established to prevent unfair business practices in inter-state commerce. It has investigated alleged violations of the anti-trust laws.[3]

It is necessary to emphasize the liberal interpretation which has been accorded to the phrase 'inter-state commerce' by the Supreme Court, because this is easily overlooked. The decision of the Court in one case[4] under the New Deal legislation in 1935 has given the impression that the Supreme Court has always restricted the powers of Congress in regulating economic affairs. In that case it is true that the Court declared a large part of the New Deal machinery unconstitutional on the ground, among others, that it dealt with matters in intra-state commerce. It is worth recalling that this was a unanimous decision of the Court, the so-called 'liberal' members, Justices Brandeis, Cardozo and Stone, being in agreement with their conservative or neutral colleagues. It can hardly be doubted that it was the correct decision. The phrase 'inter-state commerce' can be generously interpreted, but it cannot be interpreted so generously that 'intra-state' disappears altogether. It may be true that all commerce is one. 'There is a view of causation,' said Justices Cardozo and Stone,[5] 'that would obliterate the distinction between what is national and what is local in the activities of commerce. Motion at the outer rim is communicated perceptibly, though minutely, to recording

---

[1] 'Commerce is a term of the largest import,' said Field, J. in *Welton v. Missouri* (1875), 91 U.S. 275 at p. 280.
[2] Radio, for a time, was under a Federal Radio Commission.
[3] See Sharfman, I. L., *The Inter-state Commerce Commission*, G. C. Henderson, *The Federal Trade Commission*, and Blaisdell, T. C., *The Federal Trade Commission*.
[4] *Schechter Poultry Corporation* v. *United States* (1935) 295 U.S. 495.   [5] At. p. 554.

instruments at the centre.' It is therefore difficult to decide, in some cases, what is inter-state and what is intra-state commerce. It is a matter of degree. The Constitution is so framed that the Supreme Court must decide this question of degree and it undertakes to do so. The principles which it attempts to follow were stated by the Court in this case in these words: 'In determining how far the federal government may go in controlling intra-state transactions upon the ground that they "affect" inter-state commerce, there is a necessary and well established distinction between direct and indirect effects. The precise line can be drawn only as individual cases arise, but the distinction is clear in principle.'[1] By 1942 the Court had gone further. It was no longer a question of 'direct' effects but of 'substantial' effects. The Court said: 'Even if an activity be local and though it may not be regarded as commerce, it may still, whatever its nature, be reached by Congress if it exerts a substantial economic effect on inter-state commerce, and this irrespective of whether such effect is what might at some earlier time have been defined as "direct" or "indirect".'[2]

The National Industrial Recovery Act of 1933, whose principal provisions were invalidated by this decision of the Supreme Court in 1935, had established a National Recovery Administration to draw up codes of fair competition for different industries. These codes were to eliminate child labour, shorten hours of work, raise minimum wages, eliminate price cutting and the like. About 600 codes, covering about 22 million workers were drawn up. It was obvious that they covered aspects of economic life which could fairly be called intrastate. To say that these aspects were inseparable from inter-state aspects was to abolish the distinction altogether. In the words of Justices Brandeis and Stone: 'To find immediacy or directness here is to find it almost everywhere. If centripetal forces are to be isolated to the exclusion of the forces that oppose and counteract them, there will be an end to our federal system.'[3]

In spite of this and other reverses in the Supreme Court, President Roosevelt was able to get a large measure of economic regulation effectively imposed through the existing powers of Congress. The N.I.R. Act itself was in effect repassed and its operations confined to inter-state commerce in the wages and hours act of 1938 (entitled the 'Fair Labour Standards Act') which provides for minimum wages and maximum hours with overtime rates. The Act was upheld by the Supreme Court in 1941, and in that year it regulated fifteen and a half million workers. That part of the original N.I.R. Act which granted labour the statutory right of collective bargaining and legalized the right to strike was re-enacted in a revised form in the National Labour Relations Act of 1935 (usually called the Wagner Act). The Act was

[1] Hughes, C. J., at p. 546.
[2] *Wickard* v. *Filburn* (1942) 317 U.S. 111 at p. 125; *U.S.* v. *Darby* (1941) 312 U.S. 100 at p. 119.
[3] At p. 554.

upheld by the Supreme Court in 1937.[1] It has done much through the National Labour Relations Board to protect workers against intimidation and has put their right not merely to organize but also to strike and picket beyond legal question. Agriculture has been regulated through the Agricultural Adjustment Act and the Administration it set up, and although this Act was declared unconstitutional in January 1936,[2] it was replaced by a Soil Conservation and Domestic Allotment Act which by a different method achieved practically the same end. It was supplemented by another Agricultural Adjustment Act in 1938, devoted particularly to marketing.[3] Financial reform was carried out through the Securities Act of 1933, designed to prevent frauds on investors; the Securities and Exchange Act of 1934 which supplemented and strengthened it; the Banking Acts of 1933 and 1935 which strengthened and extended the control of the general government, through the Federal Reserve Board, over banking and credit; and the Holding Companies Act of 1935 which, among other things, attempted to suppress public utility holding companies which existed purely for financial purposes. Much of this legislation owed its validity, as will be obvious, not so much to Congress's power to regulate inter-state commerce but to its specific powers to deal with banking and currency. But it illustrates how, in spite of restrictions, Congress can exercise a very extensive control over economic affairs. This conclusion is supported by a recital of some of the other organizations established to conserve the natural resources or to promote the economic welfare of the United States—the Taylor Grazing Act of 1934; the Re-Settlement Administration of 1935, established to remove from cultivation sub-marginal land and to rehabilitate rural areas; the Farm Security Administration of 1937 which succeeded it and which provided aid to tenants, farm labourers and the destitute; the Soil Conservation Service; the Public Works Administration of 1933 designed to assist economic recovery by public works; the Works Progress Administration of 1935, which was established to co-ordinate and provide governmental relief and relief works; and the Tennessee Valley Authority, established in 1933, to develop the whole of the Tennessee River Valley for electric power, navigation, reafforestation and agriculture.

The powers of the general government over economic affairs in the United States are great. That they are not greater or great enough is not due entirely to the division of powers between general and state governments, that is to say to the federal system. It is due in equal

[1] *National Labour Relations Board* v. *Jones & Laughlin Steel Corporation*, 301 U.S. 1. This decision, which was made by a majority of 5 to 4, went a good way towards reversing some of the effects of the decision in the *Schechter Case*.

[2] *United States* v. *Butler*, 297 U.S.1. From this decision the three liberal members, Justices Brandeis, Cardozo and Stone dissented. Their opinion was delivered in strong terms by Stone, J. The case is often referred to as the *Hoosac Mills Case*.

[3] It was upheld in *Mulford* v. *Smith* (1939) 307 U.S. 38; see also *U.S.* v. *Rock Royal Corp.* 307 U.S. 533; *H. P. Hood & Sons* v. *U.S.*, 307 U.S. 588.

measure at least to two other principles of organization in the American system of government. There is first the principle that there are some things which no government may touch, a principle enshrined in the Vth and XIVth Amendments to the Constitution in the words that no person be deprived 'of life, liberty and property without due process of law'. It is not possible to discuss the history of the meaning of this Due Process Clause here. It is enough to say that the Supreme Court's interpretation of it has resulted at times in the invalidation of measures, passed by state and general legislatures, to regulate economic life. On this ground it declared unconstitutional in 1905 the State of New York's maximum hours law which proposed a ten-hour day for bakers.[1] As Congress could not regulate their hours either—because they were not employed in inter-state commerce[2] —it looked as if no government could. In this way governmental control of economic affairs became restricted in the United States, but it was not because of federalism.

Similarly a second principle has restricted control. It is the principle, dealt with in a previous chapter, of the 'separation of powers'. Legislative power is vested in Congress, subject to the President's veto, and it is therefore unconstitutional for Congress to delegate legislative power to the President or indeed to any other body. Now all comprehensive economic control involves inevitably some delegation of rule-making power to officials and administrators. But, according to the Constitution as interpreted by the Supreme Court, this rule-making must not amount to actual legislation. The N.R.A. code-making powers were declared invalid in 1935 on this ground as well as on the ground that they purported to deal with intra-state commerce.[3] This principle of the 'separation of powers' is concerned not merely with the exercise of legislative powers by the executive, but also of judicial powers by the executive. The whole process of administrative rule-making and adjudication is governed by the Constitution and the effectiveness of much of the administration of economic control is accordingly reduced.[4]

It has seemed necessary to mention, even so inadequately, these two restrictions upon economic control in the United States in order that it should be clear that federalism alone is not responsible for the difficulties of the general government in dealing with these questions. It is not only and not mainly because the Americans wanted federal government that the general government's control over economic affairs is restricted; it is because they wanted weak government also;

---

[1] *Lochner* v. *New York*, 198 U.S. 45. Similarly the legislatures were denied the power to fix minimum rates of wages in certain circumstances by the decision in *Adkins* v. *Children's Hospital*, 261 U.S. 525, decided in 1923. This decision was overruled in 1937 by a majority of 5 to 4 in the case of *West Coast Hotel Company* v. *Parrish*, 300 U.S. 379.
[2] Even if they had been, Congress itself was restricted by the Fifth Amendment.
[3] 295 U.S. 495 at pp. 541–2 and at p. 551. Compare also *Panama Refining Co.* v. *Ryan*, 293 U.S. 388.
[4] See Blachly and Oatman, *Administrative Legislation and Adjudication*, and *Opp Cotton Mills* v. *Administrator*, 312 U.S. 126, cases cited at p. 146.

they wanted as little government as possible.[1] And although outside observers may say that nowadays they need more government and stronger government, it is doubtful even yet if the Americans themselves think so.

6

The contrast between the United States and Australia is interesting. Both began with the power to regulate inter-state and foreign commerce. Both find in that power great potential capacity for controlling economic affairs. The High Court of Australia has given the phrase its full significance. It declared in one case that the term has never been confined to the mere act of transportation of merchandise over the frontier. That the words include that act is, of course, a truism. But that they go far beyond it is a fact quite as undoubted. All the commercial arrangements of which transportation is the direct and necessary result form part of 'trade and commerce'. The mutual communings, the negotiations verbal and by correspondence, the bargain, the transport and the delivery are all, but not exclusively, parts of that class of relations between mankind which the world calls 'trade and commerce'.[2] The High Court has followed the Supreme Court in giving a wide meaning to the term. In the result the power has been used by the Commonwealth to legislate upon monopolies and agreements in restraint of trade, carriage of goods by sea, compensation to seamen for injuries suffered in the course of their employment, the licensing of water-side workers; it extends to transportation by land, sea and air, as well as to the purchase or sale of commodities, to the regulation of contractual rights and obligations, and the relations of employer and employees in inter-state commerce.[3]

But here the resemblance ends. The first difference arises from the fact that though the powers under inter-state commerce are wide in both countries, they operate upon economic systems which are different in one important respect at least. This difference is simply that in the United States there is much more inter-state commerce than there is in Australia. . . . 'The States of the Commonwealth are, on the average, larger than those of the United States and have their own coastlines, and as much of the trade and commerce of Australia in manufactured goods is in the capital cities of the States, which are large centres of population, and between the capital city and the rest of the State, the powers of the Commonwealth parliament are in fact more restricted in this respect than those of Congress. In the United States it has proved in some instances so difficult to draw a distinction between inter-state and intra-state commerce that Federal legislation has superseded that of the states. This condition is not so likely to prevail in Australia, and has become less likely as the concentration

---

[1] See Chapter V, p. 81, above.
[2] *McArthur's Case* (1920) 28 C.L.R. 530 at pp. 546–7.
[3] *Report of the Royal Commission on the Australian Constitution*, 1929, p. 144.

of the population in the great cities of New South Wales, Victoria and South Australia has increased.'[1]

The second difference works the other way. In the United States the wide powers given to Congress under inter-state trade and commerce are restricted by other provisions of the Constitution, particularly the Due Process Clause and the Separation of Powers. In Australia the powers under inter-state trade and commerce are unexpectedly supplemented by other parts of the Constitution and in particular by the power given to the Commonwealth parliament to legislate in respect of 'conciliation and arbitration for the prevention and settlement of industrial disputes extending beyond the limits of any one state'.[2] Under this power the Commonwealth parliament established a Court of Arbitration and Conciliation. Its powers have been gradually extended by judicial interpretation in the High Court of Australia, and as a result the Commonwealth, through the Arbitration Court, has been able to regulate hours of labour and rates of wages in a great number of industries which are completely and obviously operating intra-state. The category of disputes extending beyond the limits of any one state has come to be greatly enlarged.[3] Further it was decided in 1926 that an award of the Commonwealth Arbitration Court prevails over not only a state award for the same industry but also over a state statute regulating the industry, to the extent to which it is inconsistent with the federal award.[4]

But it would appear that the contrast with the United States may be exaggerated. Recent judicial decisions suggest that just as Congress is restricted by the Due Process clause, so also the Commonwealth parliament is restricted by the proviso in section 92 of the Constitution that trade, commerce, and intercourse among the states shall be absolutely free.[5]

The powers of the Commonwealth have been extended also by constitutional amendment. It is true that this has proved difficult. Three attempts—in 1911, 1913 and 1919—to remove the inter-state restrictions upon the trade and commerce power and to extend the Commonwealth's powers over monopolies were rejected by the people. An attempt in 1937 to extend the control of the Commonwealth to aviation (it is at present restricted to 'inter-state' so far as civil aviation is concerned) and to remove certain restrictions on its powers in respect of marketing was similarly defeated. Unsuccessful attempts at further amendment were made in 1944, in 1946 and in 1948, of which something is said later.[6] But one amendment was carried and that

[1] Ibid., pp. 141–2.
[2] Constitution s. 51 (xxxv).
[3] O. de R. Foenander, *Solving Labour Problems in Australia*, p. 131.
[4] *Clyde Engineering Co.* v. *Cowburn*, 37 C.L.R. 466. See also Ex parte *McLean*, 43 C.L.R. 472 and *Tasmanian Steamers Proprietory Ltd.* v. *Lang*, 60 C.L.R. 111.
[5] *James* v. *Cowan*, (1932) A.C. 542; *James* v. *Commonwealth* (1936) A.C. 578; *Commonwealth* v. *Bank of New South Wales* (1950) A.C. 235.
[6] See pp. 143–4 below.

has proved more important than many others might have been, viz. the Financial Agreement Amendment of 1928, which, as explained in the previous chapter,[1] has given the Commonwealth large powers over loan policy and consequently over the economic policies in general of the State governments.

7

It must be apparent that it is not easy to generalize about the efficiency of the control which federal governments exercise over economic affairs.[2] There are obviously certain inefficiencies, at first sight, which can be detected. There is, for example, the duplication of services which results from the division of the same industry between two sets of authorities. The division of navigation and shipping between the Commonwealth and the States in Australia is one example. The Commonwealth is confined to inter-state and foreign shipping; the States deal with intra-state shipping. This involved, it was claimed, 'unnecessary expenditure of public monies in that it necessitates the maintenance in each State of two sets, Federal and State, of administrative, clerical and highly qualified technical officers, when one set would suffice'.[3] It means diversity of laws in such important matters as wireless installations, survey of hull, engines and equipment, load lines or depth of loading, life-saving appliances and boat drills, manning and accommodation. And there are undoubtedly many other economic activities which are subject to the same duplication and diversity of control.

There is, secondly, much uncertainty about the respective powers of general and state governments, because of the conflicting and ambiguous language adopted, especially in the United States and Canadian Constitutions. The conflict between the terms 'trade and commerce' and 'property and civil rights in the province' in the case of Canada is the classic example.

The rigidity of constitutional amendment is another characteristic. In the United States only one amendment—that relative to income tax—can be said to have extended federal economic powers, and President Roosevelt's reluctance to propose amendments, in spite of the great majorities with which he was elected for his first two terms of office, illustrates the difficulties which exist in this direction. Similar difficulties exist in Canada and Australia, and the exception in the latter case—the Financial Agreement of 1928—only emphasizes the earlier and later failures, of which that in 1937 to give even aviation to the Commonwealth parliament is conspicuous.

And yet these defects are not conclusive. If federal government is

[1] See pp. 92–100 above.
[2] For an interesting discussion of the problem in relation to underdeveloped countries, see U. K. Hicks *et. al.*, *Federalism and Economic Growth* (1961).
[3] Evidence of the Secretary of the Maritime Branch, Department of Trade and Customs of the Commonwealth, quoted in *Report of the Royal Commission on the Australian Constitution*, p. 153.

appropriate to the conditions of a country, it involves necessarily division and duplication of control. It is true that the division should be as clear and simple as possible and that it should be capable of adaptation. But so far as economic affairs are concerned, if the federal principle is to operate at all, some control of economic affairs must remain with the regional governments. How to define what the share of each authority shall be is obviously very difficult, but on the whole it seems reasonable to conclude that the granting of inter-state trade and commerce to the general government is a good way of doing it. This formula has worked well, on the whole, in Australia. What lack of powers there has been in the United States, can be traced more to the Due Process Clause and to the Separation of Powers than to the Commerce Clause itself. Much of the criticism of the Commerce Clause has overlooked this point. But the fundamental point which is often ignored is that the United States is still, politically, a federation. It is not ready for unitary economic control. The Constitution already confers powers upon Congress to control economic affairs which Congress is not willing to use.

Criticism of the amending process is sometimes exaggerated. The example of Switzerland shows that this need not be an insuperable obstacle. For that matter the example of the United States in the case of the XVIIIth amendment which authorized the prohibition legislation shows that if a substantial majority of the people and the states want a change they can get it quickly, while the XXIst amendment which removed the XVIIIth rapidly in 1933 proved the same point. Those who remind us that a small minority of the population can hold up important changes draw attention only to the fact that in a federal government this is an inescapable safeguard. The integrity and stability of a federal country depends upon agreement to travel if need be at the pace of the slowest and smallest.

The obstacles which President Roosevelt's New Deal legislation encountered in America have led many people to declare that federal government is unsuited to the control of economic affairs. They point to the unity of economic life and to the multiplicity of the political authorities in a federation. There is much truth in what they say. Their criticisms are justified to this extent—that the actual division of powers in some federal states is unsatisfactory; secondly, that the interpretation of those powers at times by the Courts has been too narrow and has nullified effective control; and thirdly, that in some cases the amending process is too cumbersome. All this shows a need for reform in many federal states, a need which is usually recognized. But it does not prove that the federal principle should be abolished. Nor is this generally desired in any of the federal states themselves. The Labour Party in Australia may advocate unification but Western Australia, South Australia and Tasmania would never agree to it. President Roosevelt may speak of a constitution devised for 'horse and buggy' days, but for all his popularity and power, he was defeated as soon as he attempted to lay hands upon the great symbol and safeguard of federalism, the Supreme Court.[1] The Prairie Provinces may complain in Canada of their sufferings under federation, but it is a better federation rather than no federation which they desire. It is clear that reforms are needed and demanded in all the federations, not excluding Switzerland, but these reforms will be within federalism.

The boldest attempt at reform in recent years was that undertaken by the Labour Government of Australia in a campaign from 1942–44. It was put forward as part of the post-war reconstruction plans of the government, which maintained that if the urgent economic and social problems which would face the Commonwealth after the war could not be dealt with by the general government, whose control during the war over economic affairs had inevitably extended, then a period of chaos might set in. One proposal of the Commonwealth government was that the states should refer powers over certain economic and social matters to the Commonwealth for a period of five years from the cessation of hostilities. When this proposal could not be put into effect, the Commonwealth government initiated a constitutional amendment. It proposed that the general parliament should be given legislative power—again limited to a period of five years—to deal with a list of fourteen specified subjects, including the following economic matters:[2] employment and unemployment; the organized marketing of commodities; companies; trusts, combines and monopolies; profiteering; the production and distribution of goods, though in the case of primary products with the consent of the state concerned; overseas exchange and investment; air transport; uniformity of railway gauges; and national works. This was a comprehensive and extensive list. It is clear that some of the topics, such as overseas exchange and investment, combines, trusts and monopolies, and air transport, might very profitably be given to the general parliament. But the full list meant really the transfer of the fullest economic powers to the Commonwealth. It was not surprising, therefore, that the amendment was rejected. It asked for too much.

In 1946 a further attempt at amendment was made on a more modest scale. Proposals were submitted for the transfer to the Commonwealth parliament of power to legislate upon the organized marketing of primary products and upon the terms and conditions of

---

[1] In March 1937 President Roosevelt proposed a reform of the federal judiciary which included a provision for the appointment of one new justice to the Supreme Court for every justice who did not retire when he reached the age of seventy and had served 10 years, up to the limit of a total of fifteen justices on the whole bench. (The existing total was 9.) The bill was rejected by the Senate Committee on Judiciary and failed to pass. This was a remarkable defeat for a President who in the previous November had been re-elected for a second term by 523 votes to 8 in the Electoral Colleges—a greater majority than any predecessor. It is important to add, however, that although the Bill was defeated, one justice resigned and his place was filled by a more acceptable judge.

[2] The social matters in the proposal are dealt with in the next Chapter. The whole campaign is described in *The Round Table* for December 1944.

employment in industry. But both these proposals were defeated, for although they obtained a majority of all the electors voting, they failed to obtain the support of more than three of the six states. In 1948 a proposal to give to the Commonwealth power to legislate with respect to rents and prices failed to obtain either a majority of the electors in its support, or a majority in a single state. None the less, it cannot be denied that the need for reform remains.

Chapter VIII

FEDERAL GOVERNMENT AND THE SOCIAL SERVICES

1

THE term 'social services' is not exact or definite. I use it here to describe services which deal primarily with the protection and welfare of citizens, and I include such topics as police, education, health, insurance or assistance for old age, invalidity, unemployment or accident, workmen's compensation, prisons, and the control of alcoholism. It is true that legislation upon economic affairs lies within the field of social relations just as much as does legislation on these topics just enumerated. 'Social' is, however, used frequently in this narrower sense, and it may be adopted here without necessarily implying that it does not also include a wider range of subjects. The questions so collected together are a miscellaneous lot. Indeed just as the Home Office in the United Kingdom is the residuary legatee of all other government departments and deals with a range of subjects even more heterogeneous than those mentioned above, so also this chapter may tend to collect those topics which other chapters do not cover.

It is the practice even in unitary states to devolve social administration to local authorities, whether those authorities be controlled locally or not. The same principle is followed in federal systems. But when it comes to legislation upon social questions, the problem in a federation is different from that in a unitary state. In the latter there is no doubt that the power to legislate must be with the general legislature, no matter how much it may decentralize that power to provincial councils or legislatures. It will always be able to exercise an ultimate controlling power in the last resort. In a federal system, on the other hand, it has to be decided whether this ultimate controlling power is to be with the regional legislatures or with the general legislature. For since the division of powers, once made, is strict, it is important to share or divide the control in the proper way. It is proposed to see how this has been done in the federal systems of to-day.[1]

The most striking thing about them is that the older they are the less were the powers over social legislation which were confided to the general legislature in the original constitution. Thus in the Constitution of the United States it is difficult to find any specific

---

[1] See A. H. Birch, *Federalism, Finance and Social Legislation* (1955) for an interesting discussion of the subject in relation to Canada, Australia and the United States.

grant of power to the Congress to deal with social affairs. The nearest one gets to it is the authority to raise and spend money for 'the general welfare of the United States'.[1] That was the attitude of 1787. When the Swiss drew up their Constitution of 1848 they specified one topic in the social sphere which the general legislature could deal with. It was authorized to conduct a federal university and a federal polytechnic school.[2] But the rest of the educational sphere was left to the cantons. There was in addition a power to contribute to the cost of works of public utility and it was conceivable that this might be thought to cover such works as building hospitals or asylums.[3] The Canadians in their Constitution of 1867 emphasized their desire to keep social questions in regional control by enumerating as matters exclusively within the powers of the legislatures of the Provinces: the establishment, maintenance, and management of public and reformatory prisons in and for the province; of hospitals, asylums, charities, and eleemosynary institutions, other than marine hospitals; education, subject to certain safeguards; solemnization of marriage (but not 'marriage and divorce', which is given to the Dominion); the administration of justice in the province, though this did not include the criminal law, but did include the organization of the courts, civil and criminal; and finally the important head of property and civil rights. The most important social services were thus allotted to the exclusive control of the provincial legislatures. Any that remained were in the control of the Dominion, and in particular a few were enumerated: quarantine and the establishment and maintenance of marine hospitals; marriage and divorce, as already mentioned; the criminal law; and the establishment, maintenance and management of penitentiaries, that is of prisons for long-sentence criminals.[4] The Australian Constitution of 1900 envisaged roughly a similar division, though the method of enumeration, as stated earlier, was different. The Commonwealth was given power to deal with quarantine, with marriage and divorce;[5] and with the influx of criminals. But it is not given the criminal law, as in Canada. One topic is conceded, however, which was not found in the original constitution of preceding federations—invalid and old-age pensions—rather a startling innovation, which perhaps symbolizes the difference in outlook of 1900 from 1867.[6]

At a first glance, then, it would seem that the intention of all these federal constitutions was to leave the regulation of social affairs almost entirely to the regional authorities. The federal government was expected, as Alexander Hamilton put it, 'to be exercised princi-

---

[1] Art. I (8).
[2] Art. 27.
[3] Art. 23.
[4] See Sections 91 and 92.
[5] This power was used in 1959 to provide, for the first time, a uniform law of divorce for the whole of Australia.
[6] See Section 51.

pally on external objects as war, peace, negotiation and foreign commerce; with which last the power of taxation will, for the most part, be connected. The powers reserved to the several states will extend to all the objects which, in the ordinary course of affairs, concern the lives, liberties and properties of the people, and the internal order, improvement and prosperity of the state.'[1]

2

How has this original division stood the test of time? The answer is that in the sphere of social affairs much the same process appears to have occurred as in the sphere of economic affairs. The powers of the general government have, on the whole, increased; they have increased in much the same degree in the different federations; they have increased by much the same methods; and they have been restricted by much the same obstacles. This of course is not surprising. There is an obvious connection between economic and social changes. There are, moreover, certain fundamental principles of constitutional organization in each of the federal systems, which we saw to be operative either to extend or to restrict federal power in the control of economic affairs, and it is to be expected that they might operate similarly in respect of social matters.

Thus in Switzerland the powers of the general government have increased by the amendment of the Constitution through the referendum. For example, in 1885 the general government was given power to establish a monopoly in the manufacture and sale of spirituous liquors and this power has been extended from time to time down to 1930.[2] In 1890, powers were granted to deal with accident and sickness insurance;[3] in 1897 to regulate the sale of foods and thereby to protect public health in this respect;[4] in 1913 to deal with contagious and infectious diseases and epidemics;[5] in 1925 to introduce old age and survivors' (i.e. widows') insurance and invalid insurance;[6] in 1928 to regulate gambling.[7] There has thus been a steady increase in federal powers over social affairs if the letter of the Constitution alone is considered and this has taken place by the same method as in the case of economic affairs.

In the United States and Australia judicial interpretation has discovered within the words of the Constitution powers to deal with social affairs as with economic affairs. Thus under its power to deal with inter-state commerce, Congress has been held to be competent to legislate for safety in inter-state railways, for the regulation of

---

[1] *The Federalist*, No. XLV, p. 237 (Everyman ed.). But Hamilton did not anticipate that these state powers would prove so expensive.
[2] Art. 32 bis.
[3] Art. 34 bis.
[4] Art. 69 bis.
[5] Art. 69.
[6] Art. 34 quater.
[7] Art. 35.

hours of labour in certain cases,[1] to regulate lotteries,[2] to prevent the white-slave traffic[3] and to ensure purity of food and drugs.[4] Under its power to tax and to appropriate money for the general welfare of the United States, Congress was held in 1937, by a 5 to 4 majority of the Supreme Court, to be entitled to establish a system of social security which included a system of old age and survivors' insurance, administered entirely by the general government; and provisions for old age assistance, aid to dependent children, aid to the blind, and unemployment insurance, in which the general government was to co-operate with the state governments.[5] This decision was the more remarkable because a similar attempt by the use of taxing power to prevent child labour had been held unconstitutional in 1922.[6] Under its power to regulate post offices, Congress may determine what classes of things may be transmitted by post and in this way attempt to protect the morals of the people.[7]

And similarly Congress has been restricted in its powers to regulate social affairs by the Due Process Clause; and social administration has been hampered by the impossibility of delegating truly legislative and judicial functions to the President and his officers, since this would contradict the Separation of Powers as established in the Constitution. These obstacles have not always proved as difficult as might be expected, but they could never be safely neglected. Just as in the economic sphere it was found necessary and possible after much obstruction and contradiction to extend the powers of Congress by an amendment of the Constitution which made possible the imposition of income tax 'without apportionment among the several states and without regard to any census or enumeration',[8] so also in the social sphere after much trouble and piecemeal legislation, the XVIIIth Amendment came to be adopted in 1919[9] prohibiting the manufacture, sale or transportation of intoxicating liquor throughout the United States and giving Congress and the States concurrent power to enforce this provision.

In Australia the quarantine power has been interpreted to include legislation in respect of plants and animals as well as human beings, and in respect of isolation, segregation and disinfection not only on the outside borders of Australia but also between states and within states and indeed in any part of Australia.[10] The commerce power has been used to justify legislation providing compensation to seamen for

[1] *Baltimore and Ohio R.R. Co.* v. *Inter-state Commerce Commission* (1911) 221 U.S. 612.
[2] *The Lottery Case* (1903) 188 U.S. 321.
[3] *Hoke* v. *U.S.* (1913) 227 U.S. 308.
[4] *McDermott* v. *Wisconsin* (1913) 228 U.S. 115.
[5] *Steward Machine Co.* v. *Davis*, 301 U.S. 548. See also *Helvering* v. *Davis* (1937) 301 U.S. 619.
[6] *Bailay* v. *Drexel Furniture Co.*, 259 U.S. 20.
[7] *Public Clearing House* v. *Coyne* (1904) 194 U.S. 497.
[8] Amendment XVI, in effect 1913.
[9] It was declared adopted actually on January 29, 1920.
[10] *Report of Royal Commission on the Australian Constitution*, p. 168.

injuries suffered in the course of their employment, and to regulate
the importation of goods so as to protect the health of the population; and the power to legislate for industrial arbitration and conciliation has resulted, through the medium of the awards of the Arbitration
Court, in the control of conditions of labour in a great number of
industries. The power to legislate on external affairs, too, would
seem to make possible the carrying into effect of international convention relating to hygiene, and thus lead the way to regulation
by the Commonwealth of many matters of health, morals and
welfare. One amendment of the Constitution has been carried
granting increased powers to the Commonwealth over the social
services. In 1946 the Commonwealth parliament was granted power
to legislate for the provision of maternity allowances, widows'
pensions, child endowment, unemployment, pharmaceutical, sickness and hospital benefits, medical and dental services (but not so
as to authorize any form of civil conscription), benefits to students
and family allowances.

Canada, in its turn, followed in social affairs a course similar to that
followed in economic affairs. The Dominion Parliament has exercised
considerable powers, but the outstanding feature has been the
restriction imposed upon its powers by the wide construction placed
upon provincial powers and in particular upon property and civil
rights. This was symbolized by the invalidation in 1937 by the Privy
Council of the Employment and Social Insurance Act which had
provided for a nation-wide scheme of unemployment insurance supported in part by compulsory contributions from employers and
employed and partly by contributions from the Dominion Government. It was held that it encroached unconstitutionally upon the
sphere of property and civil rights in the provinces exclusively
reserved to the provincial legislatures.[1] It required a constitutional
amendment in 1940 to give the Dominion powers in this sphere, and
this amendment was in any case confined to unemployment insurance.[2] A further amendment gave powers to legislate on old-age pensions to the Dominion in 1951.[3]

But it would be misleading to consider the changes that have
occurred only in the law of the constitutions, both by amendment
and judicial interpretation. The powers of the general governments in
respect of social affairs have increased by one other important
method and that is the method of financial inducement and control.
The fact is that with the demand for the social services, which since
the middle of the nineteenth century appears to have occurred in all
these countries, the resources of the states have proved inadequate to

---

[1] *Attorney-General of Canada* v. *Attorney-General of Ontario* [1937] A.C. 355.

[2] *British North America Act*, 1940.

[3] *British North America Act*, 1951. It is significant that the grant to the Dominion parliament
was not exclusive but concurrent, with provincial laws prevailing in case of conflict.

the performance of the tasks allotted to them by the constitutions. This subject has already been discussed from the financial point of view in Chapter VI.[1] It is enough to say here just which social services receive support from the general government, so that some idea may be gained of the extent to which, by the indirect means of financial penetration, the general government enters the sphere of the social services.

Thus in Switzerland the general government has made grants to the cantons for education, police, sickness and unemployment insurance, unemployment assistance, public health, physical education and the combating of tuberculosis.[2] In the United States the general government has made grants to the states almost from its inception. Its first important assistance to the states in the social sphere was the Morrill Act of 1862 which made grants for agricultural and technical education. These grants were unconditional. But later extensions or amendments of the Morrill Act brought rather more control. In the twentieth century not only has the scale of the assistance greatly increased but also the degree of control which it entails. Grants were made for the prevention of venereal diseases in 1912, for maternity and infant hygiene in 1921, and the original grants for education were increased. Under President Franklin D. Roosevelt there was a tremendous increase. Grants were offered for old age assistance, public health and the care of the blind, unemployment insurance, slum clearance and rehousing, crippled and dependent children, while the grants already offered were greatly increased.[3]

In Canada the Dominion government, without acquiring any additional jurisdiction over social affairs, took on in 1930 the provision of 75 per cent of the funds needed for a scheme of old-page pensions, the provinces administering the service. In the depression years of the 1930s the burden of relief expenditures upon provincial and municipal authorities became excessive and Dominion assistance in the form of grants, loans and direct expenditure proved essential. In 1937 the Dominion was paying 44 per cent of the cost of the total expenditure in Canada on welfare services. Yet it had very little control over the actual outlay of the funds, which was left largely in the hands of the provinces and municipalities.[4] In Australia during the same period of depression a similar process occurred. Thus in the financial year 1936–7 the Commonwealth was contributing by grants about one-third of the states' expenditure on social services, in addition to which it was providing, on its own authority, for old-age and invalid pensions.[5]

[1] See pp. 109–16 above.
[2] See *Statistisches Jahrbuch der Schweiz*, 1940, pp. 339 ff.
[3] See article by Austin F. MacDonald already cited above, p. 114 n.
[4] *Rowell-Sirois Report*, Book I, p. 216.
[5] See Chapter VI above, espec. p. 111.

3

The relation between general and regional governments in the federations has been affected thus by three principal factors: the extension of the general government's powers by judicial decision and by constitutional amendment, and the extension of its power by financial participation. But there are one or two other aspects of the relations between general and regional governments in the sphere of social services which are worth mentioning.

There is first of all legislative co-operation. The general government and the regional government have sometimes agreed to work together, each using its respective powers to cover some aspect of a social service. One example is the treatment of housing in the United States. On the one hand Congress established a United States Housing Authority in 1937 and offered aid in the construction of low rent houses and slum clearance. But this would have been ineffective alone. States passed acts enabling them to take advantage of the loans and grants made available by Congress. By the end of 1945 about forty of the states had enacted such laws.[1] Another example is the co-operation between the Commonwealth and the states in Australia to prescribe uniform standards of food and drugs for the whole country, the Commonwealth dealing with food and drugs imported from outside the Commonwealth and in inter-state trade, the states dealing with those in intra-state trade, and uniformity being achieved by agreement at conferences followed by legislation in the respective parliaments.[2] These conferences between the general and regional governments are obviously a method by which co-operation and uniformity can be secured between governments in regard to social questions over which authority is divided. They have been increasing in the United States and Australia.[3]

A second aspect of the relations between general and regional governments in regard to social services has shown itself in an application to some degree of the principle enunciated by J. S. Mill to regulate the division of functions between central and local authorities in a unitary state. 'The principal business of the central authority,' he said, 'should be to give instruction, of the local authority to apply it. Power may be localized, but knowledge to be most useful must be centralized.'[4] It has become common for the general governments to devote themselves to research and to make available to the regional governments the results of their research; to go so far even as to prepare draft bills for state governments upon matters in which the general government is interested and which, usually, it is ready to support financially. Thus in the United States the general government has an Office of Education which collects information,

[1] See *Book of the States, 1948–49*, p. 275.
[2] *Report of the Royal Commission on the Australian Constitution*, p. 174.
[3] See Chapter XI below for a further discussion of this point.
[4] *Representative Government* (Everyman ed.), p. 357.

makes special investigations, and issues publications, gives advice to state and municipal authorities—although, apart from the case of Indians and the territories, the general government is not empowered to deal with education. Similarly, the Department of Labour and the Department of Commerce through their various bureaux carry out investigations, compile statistics, suggest laws and regulations in matters of social and commercial legislation which, without doubt, fall within state control. In Canada and Australia, also, the general governments have established Councils for Scientific and Industrial Research whose results are made available to state governments. These bodies deal constantly with matters within exclusive state jurisdiction. Much of their work is similar to that undertaken by the Bureau of Agriculture in the United States.

A most important function that the general governments can perform in this respect is clearly the collection, upon some uniform plan, of statistics, and, in the sphere of social service, of vital statistics. In all the federations there has been a good deal of overlapping and variety in the method of collecting these statistics and useful information cannot easily be obtained from them. The general governments have attempted, mainly by persuasion, to promote uniformity and they have, as in the Census Bureau and the Public Health Service of the United States, themselves endeavoured to produce a coherent and useful statistical service to assist and supplement the work of the states.

There may be mentioned finally the administrative co-operation that is possible between both sets of governments in social affairs. The notion that federal officers should administer federal laws and state officers state laws may operate well in certain cases, especially when the laws deal with subjects exclusively within the jurisdiction of one authority, or in matters where the loyalty of the officers concerned to their own government is likely to be tested. But where such topics as health, quarantine and safety of life at sea are divided between two sets of authorities it would often seem best that the administration of all the laws upon one subject should be confided to the administration of one set of officers. This has not always been done. But there are examples in the United States, Canada and Australia of co-operative administration especially in the health services, in spite of the existence of separate departments for each of the governments.[1] On the whole, however, this aspect of co-operation has been developed too little. Thus duplication of personnel has followed the division of authority.

So far an attempt has been made to explain the respective functions of the general and regional governments in the control of social legislation, the limits of their powers, the trends visible in the development of their relations, and the relative importance of one authority

[1] See below, pp. 161–2.

as against another. It may help to make the position more intelligible if now we leave the discussion of the subject according to the authority entitled to perform the service, and consider instead some of the important services in turn and discover not only where the responsibility for their performance rests but how far and how well it is carried out.

4

We may begin with education. This is in all federations a matter substantially in the hands of the regional governments and it seems best that it should be. More particularly is this so in federations where, as in Canada and Switzerland, there are religious differences which are territorially distributed, and where minorities may therefore be protected to some extent by their own provincial government. It is, of course, true that a national minority which is a provincial majority may not respect in its turn the rights of the minority within its own province; that Protestants in Quebec may fare worse in regard to education under a provincial government dominated by Catholics than they would under the Dominion government which is supported by a Protestant majority. Perhaps it is because of this that in the Constitutions of Switzerland and Canada there are guarantees for religious minorities, and that the responsibility for seeing that these guarantees are effective is laid upon the general government. Thus by Article 27 of the Swiss Constitution the privilege of attending the public schools is secured to the adherents of every denomination and the general government is required to take the necessary measures against cantons which do not fulfil these obligations. In Canada, by section 93 of the Constitution, the rights and privileges which any class of persons had in respect of denominational schools by law at the time the federation was established were safeguarded, and it was declared that where in any province a system of separate or dissentient schools existed by law at the union or was established thereafter by the legislature of the province, an appeal should lie to the Dominion executive government from any act or decision of any provincial authority affecting any right or privilege of the Protestant or Roman Catholic minority in relation to education. Further, to make the supervision of the Dominion government effective in this matter, it was provided that the parliament of Canada may make remedial laws for the due execution of its power under section 93.

The questions that arise over education in communities where language and religion differ are many. If there is only one set of schools, whether provided by the government or by religious bodies, there may be a demand that there should be no religious instruction; or, that if there is, it should be given by clergy of the different denominations, or be undenominational, or be optional. Or there may be a claim to establish separate schools, and if this is granted, a further claim that those who contribute to establish denominational schools should not be taxed by the government to provide state schools which are, in effect, the schools of the majority denomination in the province or canton.

It seems clear from the Swiss Constitution that it would be possible for the cantons to prohibit denominational schools, to require the attendance of children at cantonal schools only and to prohibit religious instruction at such schools. The Constitution does not guarantee the right to establish denominational schools or to require religious instruction. But the practice of the Swiss cantons has been wise. The characteristic of their policy since 1848 has been greater and greater tolerance. The problem is solved by different methods in different cantons. There are denominational schools in most cantons and side by side with them state schools. In some cantons there are mixed schools, attended by Catholics and Protestants alike. These appear to have worked well. At those in Berne, elementary religious instruction is given to all children. In the state-provided schools of Geneva and Neuchâtel there is no religious instruction during school hours. The greatest variety of organization exists but there appears general agreement that there is toleration and accommodation, which is all the more remarkable when one recalls the fierce religious struggle which existed in Switzerland right up to 1848.

In Canada the position is not so clear. The Constitution appears to guarantee the right to have separate schools if it existed by law in any province at federation. This applied therefore only to the original provinces of the federation, viz. Ontario, Quebec, Nova Scotia and New Brunswick. The Dominion parliament attempted when later provinces came to be formed to guarantee a similar right. In the Manitoba Act of 1870 it was provided that nothing in any law of the province of Manitoba respecting education should affect prejudicially any right or privilege with respect to denominational schools which any class of persons had by law *or practice* in the province at the Union. The addition of the words 'or practice' was necessary because there was no law in force in Manitoba at that time in respect of education although in fact denominational schools did exist. Up to 1890 there prevailed a system of separate denominational schools, each receiving state aid. In 1890 the provincial legislature passed acts abolishing this system and setting up undenominational schools. This deprived the Roman Catholics of the province of their system whereby they had their own state-aided schools, while requiring them to contribute to undenominational schools which they did not use. There was a great controversy. The Judicial Committee of the Privy Council decided against the Roman Catholics, holding that the only right they had in 1870 was that of paying for the education of their children, and this they still could do.[1] In the end the Dominion government was

[1] *City of Winnipeg* v. *Barrett* [1892] A.C. 445.

appealed to under section 93 of the Constitution. It attempted courageously, if too aggressively, to do its duty, but the bill it introduced failed to pass and the government itself was defeated. The new government under Sir Wilfrid Laurier was able to arrange a compromise, under which religious teaching could be given at the state schools by clergymen or Roman Catholic teachers.

There were similar bitter contests when Saskatchewan and Alberta came to be admitted as provinces in 1906, and the Dominion government was not able to obtain all the protection it desired for minorities. But the right to have separate schools and to be exempt from the obligation to contribute to the upkeep of the schools of other denominations, was guaranteed, together with a provision for optional religious instruction at a stated time for those who desired their children to have it.[1] There was also in Canada a bitter controversy on the use and teaching of English in certain districts of the Province of Ontario, and, in the years from 1912–16, the Dominion government was pressed to use its powers of disallowance to nullify the legislation of Ontario which, on the whole, was too severe upon the French-speaking minority.

The religious and linguistic aspects of education have caused acute controversies in Canada. It is clear that they have not been abolished yet. But it is also clear that the system of confiding education to the provinces with guarantees for denominational minorities is better than giving the whole topic to the general government; while at the same time experience has justified the plan of giving to the general government a responsibility to see that the rights of minorities are safeguarded. It seems certain that so long as a substantial minority of members in the Dominion House of Commons represent Roman Catholic constituencies in Quebec, Ontario and, to a less degree, in other provinces, no Dominion government can neglect their interests.

The share of general governments in education has not been confined to the exceptional function of intervention. In all federations the general government makes some direct contribution itself, either by directly carrying out educational work or by financing its conduct by others. Examples of direct educational work are the Swiss Polytechnic at Zurich, and the Australian National University established at Canberra by the Commonwealth Government. Indirect assistance through grants has been given in the United States for agricultural education and for vocational education; in Australia by grants to universities in the states and by the provision of scholarships for university students on a large scale; in Switzerland by grants, since

[1] The result in Canada is that separate school systems, each financed by taxation of its own denominational adherents, are found in all the provinces except British Columbia, Manitoba, Nova Scotia, New Brunswick and Prince Edward Island. The last three provinces have a minority of French-speaking people and the lack of a separate system is something of a hardship. It is to be noted that as Catholics are both English-speaking and French-speaking, there are consequently separate schools for each linguistic sub-division, a factor which has tended to make the Irish 'the most compact and homogeneous racial unit next to the French in the Dominion'. B. K. Sandwell, *Canada*, p. 66.

1903, towards primary schools in virtue of powers granted by constitutional amendment in 1902.[1] These grants were greatly increased in 1930. In Canada grants have been made by the Dominion government to the provinces for agricultural, technical and vocational education.[2] In the wider aspects of education, through radio, libraries, museums and art collections the general governments in the United States, Canada and Australia have all had some share. The general governments have power to control radio in all the federations. The Library of Congress, the National Library at Canberra, the departments for scientific research, all play their part in education.

On the whole the conclusion may be stated thus: Education is generally for the most part under regional control and this is wise.[3] Some supervision and assistance by the general government is advisable and has been justified. Whether education is well or ill done in these federations may be disputed. But if it is ill done, that is not because of any error in the federal principle so far as the division of functions is concerned. The division of financial resources may be incorrect, but the division of functions appears to have been well done and to point the way in general terms to the proper principle of division.

5

The problems of social insurance and social assistance may next be considered. Social insurance covers workmen's compensation for industrial accidents and occupational diseases, sickness insurance, invalidity, old age, widows' and orphans' insurance, unemployment insurance and schemes of voluntary insurance. Social assistance covers much the same field, but the help given does not depend upon contributions from the persons benefited or from employers. It includes, therefore, non-contributory pension schemes, for invalidity, old age, widows and orphans; unemployment relief; assistance to the blind, aged and infirm and to poor persons who have no other means of support. These are problems which are complex enough in unitary states. The peculiar federal problem is how they should be allocated as between general and regional governments.

It is clear that uniformity in all these services is desirable. A blind or aged or infirm person in any part of the United States, for example, should have an equal claim with all other such persons upon the assistance of the government and the nature and extent of the assistance should be calculated upon the same principles. That is not to say that all such persons must get the same amount. Differences in

---

[1] Art. 27 bis.

[2] Agricultural Instruction Act, 1913; Technical Education Act, 1919; and Vocational Education Act, 1931.

[3] It is noteworthy that even in the sweeping proposals for reform in the distribution of powers in the Australian Constitution which the Labour Government proposed (see above, p. 143) in 1942–44, it was not proposed that education should be transferred from the states to the Commonwealth.

needs, in means, in cost of living, in obligations, must be taken into account. But these differences should be assessed upon uniform principles. Abstract justice takes us so far. It demands either the regulation of all these services by the general government or the co-operation of all the regional governments in their uniform regulation. And since it is so difficult to obtain action by all the regional governments together, or to persuade any one government to impose obligations upon its own citizens which the citizens of other states do not bear, it seems likely that regulation by the general government is essential if any provision is to be made for all these classes of deserving citizens.

But if abstract justice is seldom followed in unitary states, it is even less frequently heeded in a federation. The fact is that uniformity is not a popular conception in federal systems. Indeed one of the main objects of a federation is to avoid it. Unless it can be shown that a lack of uniformity will produce results which are of great disadvantage to the states, they are likely to claim the power to control these functions. Does lack of uniformity in the social services produce any such disadvantageous results? On the whole it seems that in the case of unemployment services this is likely to be so. In a time of great unemployment, states which offer the most liberal scheme of benefits are liable to attract the unemployed to them in large numbers and thus to incur a burden to which their tax-payers will object. It is doubtful whether the same can be said with truth of other social services. The aged, infirm, blind and sick are not likely to gravitate in such large numbers across the great spaces of a federation to states where the highest pensions are to be obtained. It is sometimes argued that this would happen as a result of lack of uniformity, but there is little in the argument and in any case it would be of little avail in itself to persuade states to hand over the control of such services to the general government. The unemployment insurance and assistance services alone appear to be affected by this argument, and thus far there is a case for their control by the general government.

The next question is: Which of the authorities is better able to meet the cost of these social services? A preliminary answer to this question is found by considering a further question: Which authority is most likely to be in a position to finance these services when they are most needed? There unemployment marks itself off from the others. The regions where unemployment payments will be most necessary will usually be least able to provide them. There is a clear connection between the amount of unemployment in a region and the amount of revenue which the regional government can raise by taxation and loans in its territory.[1] There does not appear to be the same connection between the amount of sickness (apart from grave epidemics), old age, widowhood and the like, and the financial capacities of a state.

[1] See Chapter VI, p. 112, above.

The provision of assistance and insurance for the unemployed therefore seems to mark itself off as a service which the general government may most appropriately deal with. And this presumption is further supported by this fact, that it is the general government which is armed with the economic powers necessary to deal with economic depression in the control of imports and exports, banking and currency, public works and so on. The general government alone has available the greatest power for attempting to reduce the volume of unemployment and it seems fitting therefore that the care of the unemployed should be in its hands.

The experience of federal systems seems to support this view. In the United States under the Social Security Act, the control of unemployment insurance was shared between the general and the state governments. The general government provided grants in aid, prescribed conditions which state schemes were to fulfil if they were to obtain the maximum financial assistance under federal taxation, and the administration was carried out by the states. All the states took advantage of the scheme and as a result of it 48 different schemes came into operation, each separately administered. It is the view of the authorities who have studied its working, that the division of responsibility is not successful and that all the disadvantages suggested above are operating in the United States. 'It may be predicted,' says one student, 'that complete reconstruction on a national basis will come, either by the evolutionary process or by drastic revision in time of stress.'[1] Canada, on the recommendation of the Royal Commission on Dominion-Provincial Relations, decided to make unemployment insurance a Dominion matter. The British North America Act, 1940, placed the subject under the Dominion's exclusive control and thereafter the Dominion parliament passed the Unemployment Insurance Act, 1940. Indeed the Royal Commission went further. It recommended that the whole responsibility for unemployed employables should be a Dominion function.[2] But no action, beyond that in respect of unemployment insurance, had been taken up to 1950.

In Australia during the economic depression of the 1930s the states attempted to deal with unemployment relief. There was no unemployment insurance scheme except in Queensland, where it had been in operation since 1922. The burden on the states was very heavy; a grant from the Commonwealth was necessary; and it is clear that in this service as in others the states had to sacrifice in independence what they received in financial assistance.[3]

If the care of the unemployed is most appropriately a function

---

[1] Bryce Stewart, *Planning and Administration of Unemployment Compensation in the United States* (New York, 1938), p. 550. Quoted in *Rowell-Sirois Report*, Book II, p. 38.

[2] *Rowell-Sirois Report*, Book II, pp. 24 ff.

[3] In the reform proposals of 1942–44 the topics of employment and unemployment were to be transferred to the Commonwealth government. See above, p. 143.

of the general government, what should be said of the other services mentioned? In practice the question has to be settled largely on financial grounds. Which authority can afford it? And as the general government has proved in all federations, for reasons already discussed in Chapter VI, the stronger financial unit, the argument has seemed to lead towards its assumption of these functions. In Australia, by the Constitution of 1900, old age and invalid pensions were given to the Commonwealth government; and in the United States under the Social Security Act the financing and control of the old age and survivors' insurance schemes has been taken over entirely by the general government. There are, as has been seen, good arguments for this, apart from finance. But it is probable that it is the financial argument which has been decisive. This result has not been accepted without dispute by the states. They have argued that although the general government has taken over these services because it alone can afford them, this is not a good thing. Some of the services should be performed by the states and the states should be made financially capable of performing them. A redistribution of financial resources is necessary, not a redistribution of functions. This argument cannot be neglected. It has much practical force in any federation because there is an inherent tendency in all federations for the states to cling tenaciously to their allotted functions. The forces that make federalism necessary make this inevitable.

But even if we accept as an axiom that functions should remain with state governments unless sufficient cause be shown for their transfer to the federal government, the financial factor is not irrelevant. For the fact is that in most federal systems the general government will become the strongest authority financially. This fact cannot be ignored in any allocation of the social services. It means that, purely on the ground of expense, some of these services must be allotted to the general government, if not in form, at any rate in fact. It alone can finance them.

If this fact is admitted, as I believe it must be, it is then a question of deciding which services are most appropriately handed over. There is no fixed rule here. It may be best perhaps to hand over the social assistance, that is to say, the non-contributory, services and to retain the social insurance or contributory services (other than unemployment) with the regional governments. Even then some help may be needed from the general government in contributory insurance schemes, for the burden of payments in the early years before the fund has been well established may fall with undue severity on the regions. Or it may be thought best to retain in the hands of the regions those services such as sickness insurance and assistance, orphans' allowances and blind persons' pensions, which are more appropriately administered by the regions through hospitals and homes, working in conjunction with local voluntary organizations

of visitors, welfare workers and the like. These questions of allocation are similar to those involved in a unitary state in determining the
the proper functions of central and local authorities.

However the allocation is made, it seems clear that a substantial
financial burden must rest on the general government. Already in
Australia since 1946 the bulk of the social services are Commonwealth
matters,[1] in Canada and the United States old-age pensions are
similarly treated. Canada has begun to take over the field of unemployment. In July 1945 it began the payment of family allowances.
Switzerland as long ago as 1890 amended the Constitution to give
accident and sickness insurance to the general government and these
powers were extended further in 1925.

The line between general and regional services is difficult to draw.
So much depends on the circumstances of a particular place and time.
For this reason there is a case for treating the social services which
have been discussed above as matters upon which a concurrent
jurisdiction might appropriately be permitted in a federal system. The
objections to concurrent powers have been stressed already in Chapter V but there is more to be said for it in the social services than elsewhere.

6

It is appropriate to consider next certain general health services,
including the control of hospitals, infectious diseases, and epidemics,
medical practitioners, public medical services, pure food regulation,
poisons, drugs, patent medicines, and the like. Generally speaking
these are shared between the general and regional authorities upon
principles which are understandable, and, although there is bound to
be overlapping and a lack of uniformity, it need not be concluded that
this is necessarily avoidable or inefficient. Thus the general governments through their powers, express or implied, to regulate foreign
commerce, navigation and shipping, quarantine and defence, deal
with those aspects of health which involve medical inspection of
immigrants and travellers from abroad, hospitals for sailors, care of
the armed forces, the control of foods, drugs and poisons imported
into the country and so on. In all these countries there seems no
doubt that the powers conferred on the general governments by the
Constitutions are adequate to protect the health of the country
against invasions from outside. There are powers also to protect
health in similar ways within the country by the control of inter-state
or inter-provincial commerce and these are substantial. For the rest,
the powers over public health remain with the regions, and, in spite of
particular examples of inefficiency, this appears the sound general

[1] In the Australian proposals of 1942–43 'Social Security' was to be transferred to the
Commonwealth's control; in the proposed amendment of 1944 it had been changed to 'family
allowances'.

rule. What was said of Canada by the Royal Commission on Dominion-Provincial Relations in 1940 may be endorsed for most federal systems: 'Provincial responsibilities in health matters should be considered basic and residual. Dominion activities on the other hand should be considered exceptions to the general rule of provincial responsibility, and should be justified in each case on the merit of their performance by the Dominion rather than by the province. Mere importance of a service does not justify its assumption by the Dominion.'[1]

There are certain matters in which uniformity seems essential if they are to be regulated efficiently. Such are the registration of medical practitioners, the regulation of poisons, and the imposition of standards in respect of pure food and drugs. If the regions have different standards, and if the general government also imposes different standards, say on foods imported from abroad, it is impossible to regulate these matters effectively. In such cases it would seem that the general government must either itself impose the regulations or should give the lead in encouraging uniformity among the different authorities. Thus in the United States, Canada and Australia, each region has control over the qualifications required for registered doctors, dentists, pharmacists and nurses, although in Canada the Dominion's control over criminal law gives it some power on certain aspects. Although the difference in qualifications is not great, and although registration in one state is usually accepted as sufficient qualification for registration in another, it would be the better for some co-ordination by the general government and for the provision of a single register imposing some minimum of qualifications. The same is true of the pure foods and drugs acts. In Switzerland this is a matter for the general government, by constitutional amendment, but in the other three federations the subject is shared between general and regional governments roughly according to the principle of the distinction between inter-state and intra-state commerce. Differences in matters of this kind have been dealt with so far by conferences of the governments concerned and it has been usual for the officials who meet to reach agreement upon the principles which uniform legislation should embody. But it has not been so easy to get legislation passed.

This promotion of co-operation, with a view to uniformity has been the peculiar function of the Departments of Health set up by the general governments in the United States, Canada and Australia. Regular conferences with the regional departments are held, information is exchanged, and co-operative schemes for research have been carried out. It would seem that, on the whole, this method of dealing with the subject is preferable to that of placing health completely

---

[1] *Rowell-Sirois Report*, Book II, p. 34. In the Australian proposals of 1944 'national health in co-operation with the States' was to go to the Commonwealth.

under the control of the general government. It is true that there is overlapping and uncertainty of jurisdiction. Opinions differ about the efficiency of the system. Jealousy between state and federal departments does lead to obstruction and friction, just as it does between different departments within the government of a unitary state. But the sphere of health appears to be one in which co-ordination by co-operation is preferable to co-ordination by a single authority. The need for co-operation in the health service has been realized in the federations. Regular institutions have been established to ensure it, such as the Dominion Health Council in Canada and the National Health and Medical Research Council in Australia, upon which all the governments are represented.

A similar situation exists in respect of the regulation of conditions of labour, such as safety, cleanliness and sanitation of factories, ventilation, and the mass of detailed regulation covered by factory acts. Jurisdiction is divided between general and regional governments, and the general government's authority is derived either from a specific grant[1] or follows from its power to regulate inter-state and foreign commerce, navigation and shipping, the criminal law (in Canada) or to carry out public works. In the result there is inevitably a lack of uniformity in these regulations and there is often confusion as to which code of rules—general or regional—is applicable in a given industry. It is apparent that co-operation can do much in these matters, but its effectiveness depends of course upon a similarity of attitude among the regions towards governmental regulation of industry. In Australia all governments—regional and general—have had what may be called a 'collectivist' attitude towards the subject, and legislation has been passed in all the states and by the Commonwealth to improve conditions of labour. There is little obstruction to co-operation from this point of view. Where difficulty arises is in the lack of uniformity in details and in the conflicts and overlappings of jurisdiction.

In Canada, on the other hand, there is considerable difference of 'social philosophy' between the provinces, and this has made it difficult to get as much progress in the field of labour legislation as there has been in Australia. But it may be doubted whether any increase of the Dominion's powers in these matters is desirable. It would be difficult to frame the amendment providing for the increase in such a way as to safeguard the provincial field, and it may well be that where social philosophies vary so much, progress can only be hoped for by co-operation under the leadership of the general government. For this purpose conferences between the ministries and officials concerned are held in the federations, and in Canada itself the first conference of the Canadian Association of Administrators of

---

[1] For example, Art. 34 of the Swiss Constitution gives power over most of these topics to the general government.

Labour Legislation was held in Ottawa in May 1938. The existence of the Association itself, composed of officials of the provincial and Dominion labour departments, is important. It has as its objects: 'to serve as a medium for the exchange of information and to encourage co-operation among its members; to promote the highest possible standards of law enforcement and administration; and to attain uniformity of legislation and regulations thereunder.'[1] It is along these lines of co-operation rather than by any amendment of jurisdiction that this aspect of social legislation seems most likely to progress in the federal systems of the United States, Canada and Australia.

7

An aspect of social legislation which has produced some interesting federal problems is the control of the manufacture and consumption of alcoholic liquors. In Switzerland the subject has been placed almost entirely under the control of the general government by constitutional amendments,[2] the first of which in 1885 gave power to it to establish a monopoly in the manufacture and sale of alcoholic liquors. As this meant some loss of revenue in cantons where taxes were imposed on alcohol, some payments were made to indemnify them. Half the net receipts which the general government draws from the taxation of distilled beverages is distributed among the cantons proportionately to population, and each canton is obliged to contribute at least 10 per cent of its share to combat alcoholism in its causes and effects. The other half of the general government's receipts was earmarked for old age and survivors' insurance schemes. The cantons are empowered to regulate inns[3] and to this extent have control of the trade in alcoholic liquors, but the powers of the general government are elsewhere exclusive and substantial. None the less, what power the cantons have is important so far as controlling consumption of alcohol is concerned and, in the opinion of some experienced students, this division of control in Switzerland has made it difficult for the general government to exercise an effective control over the subject. Even so, Switzerland has not encountered the difficulties, not to say the evils, of divided jurisdiction and piecemeal legislation, such as occurred in the United States.

Unless the general government can act and is willing to act, it is difficult for any separate state to make its regulations effective. It may prohibit the manufacture and sale of alcoholic liquors within its borders, but it cannot prohibit their importation from another state as part of the process of inter-state commerce, for this latter topic, in federations such as the United States and Australia, is reserved to the general government. And it was held by the United States' Supreme

[1] *Rowell-Sirois Report,* Book II, pp. 45–49.
[2] Arts. 32 bis. ter. and quater.
[3] Art. 32 quater.

Court in 1888 that where alcohol was imported by post from another state, and was delivered in its original packages, this constituted inter-state commerce, and the transaction could not be regulated by the state into which the importation had occurred.[1] Congress came to the assistance of the states concerned by an act of 1890[2] which empowered such states to exercise police power over liquor imported from other states, even when sold in its original packages. In 1913 Congress went further and prohibited the transportation in inter-state commerce of any liquor intended to be received, sold or used in violation of the laws of the state to which it was sent. The Supreme Court upheld this act[3] although it seemed on the face of it to contain a delegation by Congress of its power over inter-state commerce.[4]

To difficulties of divided jurisdiction there are added difficulties of enforcing such a law when some states have it and others have not. These difficulties were notorious in the United States. In the end after Congress had, during the war and under the defence power, prohibited the manufacture and sale of intoxicants, the XVIIIth Amendment to the Constitution, which came into force in 1919, was passed and empowered Congress, concurrently with the states, to make laws to enforce the prohibition of the manufacture, sale or transportation of intoxicating liquors within, the importation thereof into, or the exportation thereof from, the United States or its territories, 'for beverage purposes'. When this amendment was repealed in 1933, the control of this subject was returned to the states, but their powers were supported by a provision that 'the transportation or importation into any State, territory or possession of the United States, for delivery or use therein of intoxicating liquors in violation of the laws thereof, is hereby prohibited.' This gives a constitutional power which the act of 1890, referred to above, had assumed, with doubtful authority, to exist already.[5]

In spite of the difficulties of divided jurisdiction, which the experience of the United States has illustrated, it cannot be concluded that authority to regulate this topic should necessarily be confided exclusively to the general government of a federation. It seems clear that the regulation of alcoholic liquor is a matter which depends almost more than any other form of social legislation for its effective administration upon almost the unanimous support of those subject to it. It is therefore not lightly to be undertaken, and the method of advance by piecemeal legislation, and divided jurisdiction, with all its difficulties, may be a necessary preliminary to the establishment of any effective system of regulation by the general government. Then, as the movement develops and more powers become necessary, the co-

---

[1] *Bowman* v. *Chicago & Northern R.R.* (1888) 125 U.S. 465; *Leisy* v. *Hardin*, (1890) 135 U.S. 100.
[2] Called the Wilson Act. Upheld by the Supreme Court, 1891, *In re Rahrer*, 140 U.S. 545.
[3] Known as the Webb-Kenyon Act.
[4] *Clark Distilling Co.* v. *Western Md. Ry.* (1917) 242 U.S. 311.
[5] A similar power rests with the States of Australia in Constitutions, sec. 113.

operation of other states and the assistance of the general government may be sought.

8

Some words may be said in conclusion about the allied topic of law enforcement in federal systems, and in particular about police and prison services, and the criminal law. The practice in the different federations differs on these questions. In Switzerland both police and prisons are under cantonal control. So far as prisons are concerned this results in great differences in treatment, varying in accordance with the religious and moral outlook of the cantons concerned, and also, in general, in a tendency not to spend sufficient money on the service. Not all cantons have established prisons, so that their prisoners have to be accommodated in the gaols of other cantons. On one point the constitution prescribes a rule which is of general application: corporal punishment is abolished throughout Switzerland. In Australia a similar system of control by the regions prevails. There are no Commonwealth prisons. The Constitution actually provides[1] that every state shall make provision for the detention in its prisons of persons accused or convicted of offences against the laws of the Commonwealth, and for the punishment of persons convicted of such offences, and the parliament of the Commonwealth has power to make laws to give effect to this provision. Police are similarly under state control. It would appear that this system works effectively. No doubt there is always extra expense involved in running six systems instead of one, but as the criminal law is, in Australia, a matter within state control there are arguments for saying that this extra expense results in extra efficiency. There is satisfactory co-operation between the police departments of the different states. Very few criminals would be found to regard federalism as their ally.

Canada and the United States are alike in having a dual system of prisons. Indeed the Canadian Constitution expressly gives penitentiaries to the Dominion government and reserves public and reformatory prisons to the provinces. This means that long sentence prisoners are under the charge of the Dominion government. The distinction does not correspond exactly to that between offenders against the Dominion laws and offenders against provincial laws, although, since in Canada the criminal law is a Dominion matter, and not provincial as in Australia, there is a tendency for most long term prisoners to be Dominion offenders. Some short term prisoners are Dominion offenders also, and the provinces have protested occasionally against the expense of maintaining them in their prisons. The Maritime Provinces particularly have protested against the expense involved in enforcing such Dominion statutes as the Customs Act, offences against which naturally occur in provinces with a coastline.[2]

[1] s. 120.   [2] *Rowell-Sirois Report*, Book II, p. 182.

In eight of the ten Canadian provinces the police services are performed entirely[1] by the Royal Canadian Mounted Police, a Dominion force, their services being rendered in return for provincial payments under agreements made between the Dominion and the Provinces. The provinces of Ontario and Quebec maintain their own separate forces for the administration of provincial laws, while the Dominion police operate in their territories also for Dominion purposes. It has been demonstrated in Canada that provinces which employ Dominion forces to do their police work have been able to cut their police costs in half. It has been estimated that there would be some saving—difficult to calculate precisely—if the two provinces of Ontario and Quebec were to join in the system in which the others have joined.[2] No general proposition can be asserted on this matter. The division of responsibility makes for some inefficiency sometimes, but it does not seem sufficient to warrant any transfer of power to the Dominion government.

The United States stands at the opposite end of the scale from Switzerland and Australia so far as police are concerned. There are federal police for the enforcement of federal laws and state police for the enforcement of state laws. The federal organization has grown steadily, particularly during the prohibition period, and it was about 20,000 all told in 1938. But it has not been working in complete isolation from the state police. By a series of six Crime Control Acts of 1934 close co-ordination of federal and state authorities in connection with the enforcement of criminal law was provided for.

The passing of these acts draws attention to the problems which arise when criminal law in a federation is placed almost entirely under the control of the regions, as it is in the United States and Australia. The problem has become most acute in the United States because the developments of modern transportation have been used there in the cause of crime much more than in other federations. State boundaries mean nothing—except a hope of escape—to the criminal who is equipped with the automobile or the motor-cycle or the aeroplane. Law enforcement becomes increasingly difficult if it is to be split up into independent, sometimes non-co-operative units. One example of the difficulty in the United States may be seen in the working of the constitutional provisions for the rendition of criminals.

The Constitution of the United States provides that 'a person charged in any state with treason, felony or other crime, who shall flee from justice, and be found in another state, shall, on demand of the executive authority of the state from which he fled, be delivered

---

[1] With the exception of urban centres of reasonable size which have their own municipal forces, paid for out of local taxation.

[2] It is fair to add that, the total Canadian tax bill would not be relieved to the same extent, for the Dominion government performs the service for the provinces at considerably less than cost. Ibid., Book II, pp. 178-9.

up, to be removed to the state having jurisdiction of the crime'.[1] By congressional legislation the duty of arresting and delivering up a fugitive from justice is placed upon the Governor of the state to which he has fled. It has been decided by the Supreme Court that this duty is a 'moral duty'; a governor cannot be directed by a writ of the Supreme Court to arrest and deliver a fugitive.[2] None the less, although extradition has been refused in some cases, the Governors have usually discharged their duty conscientiously. But it is obvious that the power is clumsy. Once across a state boundary a criminal has a breathing space while the legal machinery of extradition is set in motion, and, after a little, he may move on into another state. The spectacle of the police pulling up at a state boundary while the criminal drives off seems a denial of common sense.

With the alarming growth of crime in the United States, an attempt was made to obtain co-operation. Many states have enacted uniform laws to modify the process of rendition. About half the states permit the officers of one state in pursuit of a criminal to cross their borders and arrest the fugitive on their own soil. More than a third of the states have legislated to waive the formal requirements for rendition proceedings in the state of arrest and they permit the easy transfer of the fugitive back to the state in which the crime was committed. Uniform state action has therefore removed some of the obstacles. But it seems clear that co-ordination through the general government by such means as the Federal Crime Control Acts is likely to be more effective. And here, fortunately, the fact that crime has become inter-state, makes it possible for the general government to take a hand in its control. The powers available to the general government in the constitution are sufficient to authorize its action.

The problem has not been so troublesome in Australia, chiefly because the population is concentrated for the most part in large cities separated from each other by hundreds of miles, and crime has tended to be intra-state and not inter-state. But the same difficulties could arise and the same measure of co-operation and of co-ordination by the Commonwealth government would be permitted by the Constitution.

On the whole there seems no insuperable difficulty in permitting the regional governments to control a great part of the criminal law. The weaknesses of divided jurisdiction have been illustrated in an extreme form in the United States, but they can be overcome to a large extent by co-operative action. Where differences of outlook upon social questions are important—and they are in the United States—it may be wise to permit some freedom to the states to frame criminal justice as they think right, provided always there resides in the general government a power to protect the interests of other states and of the

---

[1] Art. IV, sec. 2, par. 2.
[2] *Kentucky* v. *Dennison* (1860) 24 Howard 66.

union as a whole. Not all students of federal government concur in this opinion but in my view the balance of the argument is that regional control of the criminal law, with the safeguards mentioned, is workable, and in a federation like the United States, with so great a population, desirable also.

Chapter IX

FEDERAL GOVERNMENT AND THE CONTROL OF FOREIGN RELATIONS

1

It is usually assumed that the foreign relations of a federation will be controlled predominantly, if not exclusively, by the general government of the whole territory. Indeed one of the arguments for establishing a federation is usually that it will provide for a unified foreign policy. So important is this thought to be that in most federations there is an explicit provision in the Constitution absolutely forbidding the component states from entering into obligations with foreign states, or permitting it only with the consent of the general government, in which case potentially exclusive control rests with the general government. Thus, in the United States, the Constitution declares that 'no state shall enter into any treaty, alliance, or confederation', and, a little later, that 'no state shall, without the consent of Congress, enter into any agreement or compact with another state or with a foreign power'.[1] The first and absolute prohibition appears to be directed against political agreements either between the states or with foreign states, and the second and qualified prohibition applies to non-political agreements. The confederation of the Southern States in the American Civil War was illegal because it conflicted with the first provision; boundary agreements between states could be illegal if they were not consented to by Congress. Similar arrangements are found in other federations. Although there are differences in detail, more particularly in the degree to which the states are permitted to make arrangements among themselves or even with foreign states,[2] there is found everywhere a recognition of the principle that the exclusive control, actually or potentially, of relations with foreign states rests with the government of the whole country.

This will not seem surprising. Indeed it may be well to admit at once that it is generally essential. But although it is easy for those who make a constitution to decide where the exclusive control of foreign relations should rest, it is not so easy for those who work the constitutions to decide just what this means. Problems arise at once.

[1] Art. I, s. 10.
[2] See Swiss Constitution, Arts. 7–10.

2

The control of foreign relations includes most obviously the control of treaties. But what is meant by the control of treaties? It involves at least two processes. There is first the contracting of obligations between the government of the federation and the government of the foreign state, the making of the treaty, the formation of obligations. That is a matter between governments and it operates in the sphere of international law. There is secondly the carrying into effect of these treaty obligations by the governments which have formed them, the performance as opposed to the formation of the obligations.[1] This is a matter between the government of a federation and the people of the federation and it operates in the sphere of national law.[2] For example, a treaty of commerce is first negotiated and signed by the representatives of the governments concerned, but it is not necessarily binding upon the citizens of their countries there and then. Usually it requires legislation making the necessary alterations in the customs and commercial laws of the country concerned before it can be carried into effect. There are clearly these two distinct processes in the control of treaties. It will depend on the provisions of the constitution of a country whether both processes are carried out by the same organ and at the same time, or whether they are controlled by different organs or shared between different organs.

What is the importance of this distinction to federal government? It is just this. If the general government of a federation is given the exclusive power to control both these processes, to make treaties on any matters which it thinks fit, and to pass the legislation necessary to carry these treaties into effect, then it means that the legislative power of the general government extends to any subject upon which it can make a treaty. In these days the subjects upon which treaties come to be made are manifold. They embrace many important questions in the social and economic field, such as hours and conditions of labour, rates of wages, health, education and religion, as well as marketing, migration, shipping, air navigation and the like. It would follow, therefore, that the general government by the use of its power to make treaties on these subjects would obtain power, if it had not already got it, to make laws on such subjects to the extent necessary for carrying these treaties into effect. But supposing these treaties are made on subjects which, by the constitution of the federation, are given to the exclusive control of the states or provinces, does not this mean that the general government is, through its use of the treaty power, entering the sphere of the regional legislatures? And does not this reduce the regional field considerably? And unexpectedly?

This is a problem which has arisen in at least three modern federations—the United States, Canada and Australia. Its practical impor-

[1] I adopt the words used by Lord Atkin in *Attorney-General for Canada* v. *Attorney-General for Ontario* [1937] A.C. 326 at p. 347.
[2] Or, to use the technical term, 'municipal' law.

tance can be illustrated most clearly perhaps by the Canadian experience.[1] In Canada, as I have mentioned already, one of the matters which, in the Constitution, was given to the exclusive control of the provinces was 'property and civil rights in the province'. Any legislation of the Dominion Parliament which invades the sphere of property and civil rights in the provinces is accordingly invalid. On March 1, 1935, the Dominion Executive of Canada ratified two conventions which had been adopted by the International Labour Organization, one limiting the hours of work in industrial undertakings and one concerning the application of the weekly rest in industrial undertakings. On April 12, 1935, it ratified a convention concerning the creation of minimum wage-fixing machinery. It is clear that these treaties dealt with subjects which affected property and civil rights within the provinces of Canada. So far, however, the treaties were only made or the obligations formed. They had next to be carried into effect or performed. If this was to be done, legislation, admittedly affecting property and civil rights within the provinces, must be passed. If it were a fact that the Dominion parliament of Canada had legislative power to carry into effect treaties made on any subject by the Dominion executive, then that parliament could, to this extent and for this purpose, enter the sphere of property and civil rights within the province, a sphere expressly stated by the Constitution to be reserved exclusively to the provincial legislatures. If on the other hand it were a fact that legislation on property and civil rights could be dealt with by the provincial legislatures only, then the position was that the Dominion executive could form treaty obligations on behalf of the whole of Canada, but the Dominion parliament could not carry them into effect, if, to do so, it was necessary to make laws on subjects exclusively assigned in the Constitution to the legislatures of the provinces. The answer to this question was important. For if the first alternative were true, the powers of the provinces of Canada were much smaller than they had thought, and they must submit to a regulation of their economic and social life by the Dominion parliament, a regulation of which many of them disapproved. If the latter alternative were true, then the Dominion parliament was handicapped not only in carrying out any uniform economic planning through the whole Dominion but also in forming treaty obligations on such matters with foreign states, because it would be unable to guarantee the performance of obligations so formed. Whatever view might be taken of the desirability of either alternative, it is clear that the question was important. It is not a mere argument about words. It is an argument about policies. Much depends, therefore, on what a federal constitution has to say on this aspect of the control of foreign relations.

[1] Some reference to this matter has already been made in Chapter VII dealing with the control of economic affairs, see p. 133 above.

3

The question has been considered by the supreme tribunals of the United States, Canada and Australia, and it is worth while stating what the position is in each. In the United States the position is governed by Article VI of the Constitution which runs: 'This Constitution and the laws of the United States which shall be made in pursuance thereof, and all treaties made, or which shall be made, under the authority of the United States, shall be the supreme law of the land; and the judges in every State shall be bound thereby, anything in the Constitution or laws of any State to the contrary notwithstanding.' This article confers upon the President and two-thirds of the Senate the power both to 'form' and to 'perform' treaty obligations with foreign countries. In many cases, however, an act of Congress is used to ensure the performance. Moreover, it looks like a fairly sweeping power, and appears to justify the words used by the Supreme Court as early as 1796 when it said: 'A treaty cannot be *the supreme law of the land,* that is, of all the United States, if any act of a State legislature can stand in its way. If the constitution of a State, which is the fundamental law of the State and paramount to its legislature, must give way to a treaty and fall before. it, can it be questioned whether the less power, an act of the State legislature must not be prostrate? It is the declared will of the people of the United States that every treaty made by the authority of the United States shall be superior to the Constitution and laws of any individual State, and their will alone is to decide.' 'If this were not so,' said the Court, 'the will of a small part of the United States may control or defeat the will of the whole.'[1]

This is the view which has always been held by the Supreme Court. Indeed it expressed in 1890 an opinion which did admit some limitations. Mr. Justice Field said: 'The treaty power, as expressed in the Constitution, is in terms unlimited except by those restraints which are found in that instrument against the action of the government or of its departments, and those arising from the nature of the government itself and of that of the States. It would not be contended that it extends so far as to authorize what the Constitution forbids, or a change in the character of the government or in that of one of the States, or a cession of any portion of the territory of the latter without its consent. (*Fort Leavenworth R. Co.* v. *Lowe,* 114 U.S. 525 at p. 541.) But with these exceptions, it is not perceived that there is any limit to the questions which can be adjusted touching any matter which is properly the subject of negotiation with a foreign country.'[2] This surely means that the treaty-making power is subordinate to, among other principles, such rules as that of the 'Due Process Clause', and the separation of powers. The Court's reference to restraints imposed

---

[1] *Ware* v. *Hylton,* 3 Dall., 199. See also *Fairfax* v. *Hunter* (1813) 7 Cranch, 603.
[2] *Geofrey* v. *Riggs,* 133 U.S. 258, at p. 267.

by 'the nature of the government itself' suggests that the separation of powers was in its mind. On this interpretation the power of the United States extends much further than to make and perform treaties which deal with subjects allotted to the legislative power of Congress by the Constitution.

There are other cases which support this view. The most recent case, in 1920, expressed in the words of Mr. Justice Holmes, though in cautious language, a tendency which has shown itself at times in certain decisions: 'Acts of Congress,' he said, quoting Article VI already transcribed above, 'are the supreme law of the land only when made in pursuance of the Constitution, while treaties are declared to be so when made under the authority of the United States. It is open to question whether the authority of the United States means more than the formal acts prescribed to make the convention. We do not mean to imply that there are no qualifications to the treaty-making power; but they must be ascertained in a different way. It is obvious that there may be matters of the sharpest exigency for the national well-being that an act of Congress could not deal with, but that a treaty followed by such an act could, and it is not lightly to be assumed that, in matters requiring national action, "a power which must belong to and somewhere reside in every civilized government" is not to be found.'[1]

No certain pronouncement can be made, however, of the position in the United States. If the limitations which Field, J. maintained in 1890 are to be given full effect, the power of the general government will not be absolute, it is true, but there is little limit to the encroachment which the general government could make. President Roosevelt's New Deal could have been imposed to a large extent by the implementing of conventions of the International Labour Organization as Mr. Bennett, the Prime Minister of Canada, tried to do.[2] So far the question has not been put to the direct test as it was in Canada. It can be surmised of course, that the tendency shown by the Court in the case of 1920 will be continued.[3] But such surmises cannot take us very far. The fact is that the issue has not arisen directly in an important question of economic or social legislation so far. In my view, the true interpretation seems to be that enunciated by the Court, through Field J., in 1890.

The position is well summarized in a modern text book in the following passage: 'It is an undetermined issue what, if any, are the

---

[1] *Missouri* v. *Holland*, 252 U.S. 416. In this case the Court held valid an act of congress regulating the killing of migratory birds and passed in fulfilment of a treaty between the United States and Great Britain on this subject.

[2] President Roosevelt did not attempt to use the treaty power in this way. It would be interesting to know whether the matter was ever considered.

[3] I may add that, in my view, the remarks of Holmes, J. quoted above, should be treated as *obiter dicta*; the *ratio decidendi* of the case was that the treaty and the act which implemented it dealt with 'a subject matter which is only transitorily within the state and has no permanent habitat therein'. It was not a matter within the competence of the states. See ibid., 252 U.S. 416 at p. 435.

limits on the treaty-making power of the United States. It is clearly not limited to subject matter concerning which Congress could legislate under the powers conferred upon it. The cases sustaining treaty provisions that conflicted with state laws governing matters the regulation of which was reserved to the states shows this. . . . There is no decision holding invalid any provision of any treaty made "under the authority of the United States". It will probably be long before the question is settled whether the constitutional guarantees may be infringed by exercises of the treaty-making power.'[1]

The position in the United States, then, is not yet clear. In Australia, in spite of constitutional differences, the position is much the same. Treaties are not, as they are in the United States, given by the Constitution the force of supreme law, but the Commonwealth parliament has power to make laws respecting external affairs. This power involves, by a decision of the High Court of Australia in 1936,[2] the power to carry treaties into effect and extends far enough to bring within the scope of the powers of the Commonwealth parliament subjects which, without a treaty, would be beyond those powers. If the Commonwealth executive makes a treaty, the Commonwealth parliament has power to make laws to carry that treaty into effect. The precise limits of the power have not been decided. There is vagueness here as in the United States. Expressions were used by some of the judges which re-echoed the view of the United States Supreme Court that treaties and laws made in pursuance thereof which dealt with matters expressly prohibited by the Constitution would be invalid. But there was no general decision on this point and the case must not be quoted as authority for more than the point which it decides. The most that it established is that it is possible in Australia for the general government, by making a treaty, to obtain power thereby to pass laws on matters which, without a treaty, would be beyond the powers of the Commonwealth.[3] It may be mentioned that this appears to be the only case where this point has arisen in Australia, and that, as in the United States, the question has not yet assumed important dimensions. Australia, like the United States, has carried out its regulation of economic life to a great degree, as was explained in a previous chapter, but it has done so by the use of other powers in the Constitution than that relating to the implementing of treaties.

4

In Canada the words of the Constitution had led to a more complicated result. The Dominion parliament and government, in section 132 of the Constitution, were given all powers necessary to perform 'the obligations of Canada or of any province thereof, as part of the

[1] H. Rottschaeffer, *American Constitutional Law*, pp. 384–5.
[2] *Rex* v. *Burgess*, ex parte *Henry* (1936) 55 C.L.R. 608.
[3] See note by K. H. Bailey in (1937) *British Year Book of International Law*, XVIII, 175.

British Empire towards foreign countries arising under treaties between the Empire and foreign countries'. But apart from this section there is no explicit grant of power to deal with external affairs as there is, for example, in Australia and the United States. Now this section intended, it seems clear, that the Dominion parliament, in legislating to carry into effect, in Canada, treaties made by the British Empire, might make laws on matters exclusively assigned to the provinces, matters which, except in pursuance of a treaty, it would not be entitled to touch. And in 1867 this power covered the whole of Canada's foreign relations. But since 1918 Canada has advanced to the status of a distinct treaty-making power and has incurred obligations under treaties not made by the British Empire. By the judgement of the Judicial Committee of the Privy Council in 1937[1] a distinction must be drawn between the 'legislative powers given to the Dominion to perform obligations imposed upon Canada as part of the Empire by an Imperial executive responsible to and controlled by the Imperial Parliament, and the legislative power of the Dominion to perform obligations created by the Dominion executive responsible to and controlled by the Dominion Parliament'.[2] These latter obligations which Canada alone creates 'are not obligations of Canada as part of the British Empire, but of Canada by virtue of her new status as an international person, and do not arise under a treaty between the British Empire and foreign countries'.[3] Consequently they are not covered by section 132 quoted above. In the performance of these obligations a different rule applies. Since there is no specific power of carrying treaties into effect, apart from that in section 132, the powers of Dominion or provincial legislatures to pass laws for that purpose must be sought in their capacity to make laws on certain classes of subjects. 'As a treaty deals with a particular class of subjects, so will the legislative power of performing it be ascertained.'[4] Any treaty other than a 'British Empire' treaty, therefore, can be carried into effect only by that legislature which has power to make laws upon the subject with which the treaty deals.[5]

'It must not be thought,' said the Judicial Committee in conclusion, 'that the result of this decision is that Canada is incompetent to legislate in performance of treaty obligations. In totality of legislative powers, Dominion and Provincial together, she is fully equipped. But the legislative powers remain distributed, and, if in the exercise of her new functions, derived from her new international status Canada incurs obligations, they must, so far as legislation be concerned, when they deal with Provincial classes of subjects, be dealt with by the

[1] *Attorney-General for Canada* v. *Attorney-General for Ontario* [1937] A.C. 326.
[2] [1937] A.C. 326 at pp. 349–50.
[3] At p. 349.
[4] At p. 351.
[5] It should not be thought that this decision of the Privy Council in the case of Canada is inconsistent with that of the High Court of Australia referred to above. The different result arises from a difference of wording in the constitutions. See Evatt, J. in *Ffrost* v. *Stevenson* (1937) 58 C.L.R. 528, at pp. 596–601.

totality of powers, in other words by co-operation between the Dominion and the Provinces. While the ship of state now sails on larger ventures and into foreign waters she still retains the water-tight compartments which are an essential part of her original structure.'[1]

The consequences of this view upon the Canadian 'New Deal' legislation discussed above[2] may now be seen. The conventions limiting hours of work and providing for a weekly rest and for minimum wage machinery in industry were not British Empire treaties. They had been negotiated by Canada acting separately. They could be carried into effect in Canada therefore only by the legislature competent to deal with their subject matter. That subject matter affected property and civil rights in the provinces of Canada and this topic is reserved by the Constitution to the exclusive control of the provinces. The Dominion parliament acting alone could not therefore carry these conventions into effect and its acts purporting to do so were therefore invalid.

This view of what the Constitution of Canada meant aroused great criticism.[3] Our concern is not so much with its soundness in law,[4] but with the question whether, assuming it to be a correct statement of the law of the Canadian Constitution, it is in accordance with good federal government. Its obvious advantage is that it guarantees completely the power of the regional governments in a federation to the exclusive control of the matters which are set out as theirs. There is no possibility of encroachment upon these matters by the general government through its use of the treaty power. Having divided the subjects in the federal constitution, the provinces can feel that they know what is theirs, and that their control of a particular matter is not qualified by the power of the general government to make a treaty on that matter with some foreign country. This is an undoubted advantage and there can be little doubt that if a federation is formed of units which desire to retain the exclusive control over certain matters entirely, a desire to regulate these matters according to their own lights, then provision must be made in the Constitution whereby the general government cannot invade these fields by legislation to implement a treaty.

It seems clear, therefore, that a choice has to be made in framing a federal government about the way in which the power to carry treaty obligations into effect is to be distributed or deposited in the federation. If the rights of regional governments are to be fully and jealously safeguarded then the principle stated by the Judicial Committee for Canada in 1937 must be preferred: if the general government is to be entrusted with the possibility of increasing its powers, however

[1] At pp. 353-4.
[2] See p. 171 above.
[3] See, for example, a special issue of *The Canadian Bar Review*, 1937.
[4] I may be permitted to say, with respect, that in my view the decision contains the correct interpretation of the Canadian Constitution.

gradually and discreetly, then the provisions embodied in the constitutions of the United States and Australia will be preferred.

It is interesting to see how this matter has been dealt with in the
more recent federal and quasi-federal constitutions. In the Constitution of India of 1950[1] and in that of Rhodesia and Nyasaland of
1953[2] the general parliament was given full power to implement
treaties, irrespective of whether or not the subject matter of the treaty
fell within the general or the regional legislatures' lists. A similar
power was given to the general parliament of the West Indies, though
at the same time a territorial legislature had power to implement
agreements whose subject matter was not within the exclusive legislative list of the general parliament. In Malaya and Nigeria some
restrictions were placed on the power of the general legislature in
implementing treaties. The parliament of Malaya could make laws
with respect to matters on the state list for the purpose of implementing a treaty but no such law could deal with Muslim law or the custom
of the Malays, and any such law could not be introduced until the
government of the state concerned had been consulted.[3] Nigeria went
further and, while giving the general parliament power to make laws
on any matter in implementation of a treaty, provided that any such
law should not come into operation in a region unless the Governor
of the region consented to its having effect[4]—a provision which,
incidentally, had been found in the quasi-federal Indian constitution
established by the Government of India Act, 1935.[5]

5

Those who are critical of the result obtained for Canada by the
decision of 1937 support their view by a variety of arguments.
One is that it is obviously absurd to give the general government of a
federation power to enter into treaty obligations which it is powerless
of its own motion completely to perform. Does not the Canadian
system produce the ridiculous and dangerous result that the parties
with power, the Provinces, have no international status, while the
party with status, the Dominion, has no power, or not enough
power?[6] How can the general government regulate foreign relations
if it cannot be sure, and foreign nations cannot be sure, that it can
perform what it promises? There is no doubt that this is inconvenient
and that it should be avoided if possible. But it may be unavoidable.
It is one of those inconveniences which are the price of federal
government. Indeed those circumstances which make federalism
essential and unavoidable are likely to make this division of power in
the control of foreign relations also essential and unavoidable. For

---

[1] Art. 253.
[2] Constitution, Second Schedule, Part I. 1.
[3] Art. 76.   [4] Art. 69.   [5] S. 106 (1).
[6] See e.g. Norman Mackenzie in (1937) *British Year Book of International Law*, XVIII
pp. 174–5.

certain of the factors which make federation essential—differences of language, race and religion, resulting in differences of nationality; differences of economic interest; strong regionalism; separation by sea or large land areas—are factors which produce differences of outlook also on foreign relations as well as on internal social and economic organization. The regions may not be willing, therefore, to hand over entirely the control of foreign relations, and with it some consequential power of controlling internal relations, particularly in the economic sphere, to the general government. The more appropriate federalism is to their circumstances, the more nearly will a division in the power to control foreign relations become inevitable.

To this the critics have an answer. They realize quite well that there are strong differences of opinion about foreign relations in a federation and that the regional units will not be prepared to trust their conduct to a general government completely unchecked. But they maintain that the best kind of check upon the actions of the general government is supplied not by a crippling division of the legal power to control foreign relations but by other forms of safeguard, particularly political safeguards. Critics of the Canadian system, for example, say this: 'No Dominion executive or legislature is likely to introduce by the treaty route, or any other route, any questionable measures or legislation unless it has pretty general support throughout the country—that is, the Provinces. To do so would mean political annihilation and no democratic government or party is prepared to face that.'[1] This argument admits the greatness of the power conferred upon the general government but asserts that it can be trusted to use its power carefully from the very nature of the political forces in a federation upon which it depends. There is truth in this.

In Canada and Australia the executive is chosen from the elected legislature, and it holds office because and for so long as it keeps the confidence of the legislature. These legislatures are representative of the whole country and the differing interests in the federation are likely therefore to be able to express their views by votes in parliament either through their organization into separate parties, like the Labour Party or the Country Party in Australia, or within the confines of parties which, like the Liberal and Conservative parties in Canada are themselves so far as foreign relations are concerned, by no means homogeneous in opinion So long, therefore, as the political factors exist which make federalism necessary, for so long will the parties upon which the government depends in these two federations find it necessary to pay heed to regional differences of opinion. The dependence of the Liberal Party in Canada upon the support of the liberals of Quebec is the most striking example perhaps of the restraining influence which a provincial interest can have on the foreign and consequential domestic policy of a national party. It is

[1] Norman Mackenzie, loc. cit.

worth recording perhaps that the Canadian Conservative Government which in 1935 enacted the legislation to carry into effect the I.L.O. conventions about hours of work, weekly rest and minimum wages, was itself utterly defeated soon afterwards at the general election. This seemed to show that the policies which the legislation embodied did not arouse the interest or support of the electorate. It seems likely, too, that the Liberal party, on its return to power with a large majority, would have repealed the legislation in question, had it not been declared invalid by the Judicial Committee.[1]

But one must be careful not to exaggerate the value of the check which cabinet government—with its foundations in a party system—can provide against the abuse of powers by the general government. In both Canada and Australia the cabinet depends predominantly upon its majority in the lower house of the legislature. This house is composed of representatives allocated, as I have explained, not upon a basis of equal representation for each unit in the federation but upon a population basis. It is composed, therefore, predominantly of representatives of the more populous regions. Thus in Canada, Ontario and Quebec, the two most populous provinces, have 160 members in a House of Commons of 265; the three maritime provinces of Nova Scotia, New Brunswick and Prince Edward Island have 26 between them; the three prairie provinces of Alberta, Manitoba and Saskatchewan have 48 all told, and British Columbia has 22.[2] In Australia, New South Wales and Victoria, the most populous states, have 79 members out of a House of Representatives of 124, Queensland has 18, South Australia 11, Tasmania 5 and Western Australia 9.[3] That there is wisdom and justice in this arrangement can easily be argued. But the results from a federal point of view can be appreciated. There is the danger that the general executive and legislature, depending primarily on numbers, may adopt policies in foreign and consequently in domestic affairs, which might be opposed but ineffectually opposed by the less populous states which are less strongly represented in the lower house.

It cannot be assumed, therefore, that because a federation is governed by a cabinet system based upon representative and party government, the general government can be trusted to use an unqualified power to control foreign relations in a way which will respect the views and interests of the great majority of the regions of which the federation is composed. It may happen, but it need not. Legal safeguards in the form of a division of responsibility in the power of controlling foreign relations may be essential if regional rights are to be respected and the spirit as well as the letter of the federation be

[1] See Chapter VII, p. 132 above.
[2] The total is made up of seven representing Newfoundland, one representing the Yukon territory, and one to North West Territories.
[3] With one each from the Northern Territory and the Australian Capital Territory, entitled to debate but not to vote.

maintained. Of course it may be thought preferable that divided authority in these matters should be avoided or gradually softened. That may be wise politics in certain circumstances. But, if that is not desired, if, on the contrary, it is desired to maintain regional interests in this sphere, then it must be realized that the political conventions of democratic cabinet government may not be enough, without the assistance of appropriate legal safeguards.

6

The arrangement of institutions in the United States has proved most effective in safeguarding the interests of the regions. One reason for this appears to be that although the United States, like Canada and Australia, has democratic representative government, it does not have cabinet government. Its chief executive is not, like the executive of Canada and Australia, chosen from the legislature, nor does he hold office because and for so long as he commands the confidence of the legislature. Consequently he does not depend for his tenure of office on either house of the Congress and in particular he is not under the predominant control of the lower house, in which, as in Canada and Australia, the more populous states have the predominant share of the representation. This rules out one factor which might lead to the neglect of the interests in foreign affairs of the less populous states.

Added to this is the fact that the upper house of the legislature, the Senate, in which each state, irrespective of its population, is represented by two members, is given special powers in the matter of the control of foreign relations, powers which are not possessed by the lower house. The American Constitution provided, as is generally known, that the President shall have power to make treaties, but that that power must be exercised by and with the advice and consent of the Senate, and that the consent of the Senate must be signified by two-thirds of the Senators present. This ensures that no treaty can be made under the authority of the United States, and become thereby part of the supreme law of the land, unless the consent has been obtained of that house in the general legislature which is so organized as to compensate the less populous states for their numerical inferiority.

And finally this Senate which has special powers in foreign affairs is, unlike the Senates of Canada and Australia, more powerful than the Lower House.[1] For a variety of reasons, including the length of a senator's term of office—six years—in comparison with the very short two years for a member of the House of Representatives, and the smallness of its size, 100 as against 437 for the House, the Senate is in any case the more powerful chamber.

At first sight this seems a good system. It ensures that there is one

See Chapter V, pp. 89–90 above.

general government which can speak for the United States in foreign affairs, but it ensures also that no obligations will be formed on behalf of the United States unless they are approved by the great bulk not only of the people of the country but also of the area of the country. No strongly organized regional minority can be overlooked. If the general government of the United States, through the President and two-thirds of the Senate, accept obligations in foreign affairs, two things are practically certain. Firstly, foreign nations with whom the obligations are contracted can feel sure that these obligations can be and are carried into effect in the municipal law of the United States, provided, of course, that they do not contradict prohibitions in the constitution. Secondly, the regional governments in the United States can be sure that everything that can reasonably be done in a federation to assert and defend their interests, may be done, and experience has shown that it can be done effectively. The system of the United States thus provides certainty for the foreign states and security for the federated states.

But does it provide certainty for foreign states? It does if, and only if, the condition set out in the preceding paragraph is fulfilled— that the president and two-thirds of the Senate agree to accept the obligations. And here the notorious difficulty of the American system comes to light. The constitution empowers the President to negotiate with foreign states, but he can give no guarantee that what he accepts in negotiation will be accepted by the Senate. Foreign states can have no certainty that when they have negotiated with the agent with whom alone the constitution allows them to negotiate, anything will have been achieved. It is for reasons like this that Professor Laski has written that 'the treaty-making power displays the whole American scheme of government at its worst. It multiplies all the difficulties that are inherent in the separation of powers'.[1] And it is on these grounds that one can legitimately criticize the working of the American system in the case of the Treaty of Versailles in 1919–20. The mere fact that the Senate rejected the treaty is not in itself a criticism of the system. If the treaty as negotiated and accepted by President Wilson committed the United States to obligations in foreign affairs which even a substantial minority of the people objected to, then it was well that these obligations should be rejected by the Senate. But the weakness of the system lay in the fact that the authorized negotiator was shown to be unable to implement what he had undertaken. There was a division of authority which destroyed responsibility and multiplied uncertainty and confusion.[2]

[1] *The American Presidency*, p. 193. See also R. J. Dangerfield, *In Defence of the Senate*; D. F. Fleming, *The Treaty Veto of the American Senate* and an article by the same author, 'The Role of the Senate in Treaty Making' in *American Political Science Review*, Vol. XXVIII, No. 4, August 1934; and W. S. Holt, *Treaties Defeated by the Senate*.

[2] The number of times that the Senate has rejected treaties is often exaggerated, under the influence perhaps of the example of the Treaty of Versailles; between 1789 and 1934, 682 were accepted, 173 amended and 15 rejected, while of those amended only 18 per cent were vitally altered. Laski, op. cit., p. 189.

These weaknesses in the American system are well recognized in the United States, and they lead to two developments in the conduct of foreign relations by the President. The first, largely explained by the example of the Treaty of Versailles, is that the President attempts to associate the Senate with him in his negotiations, by discussing them either with influential members of the Foreign Relations Committee of the Senate, or with a group of representative senators. The latter method was adopted in 1944 by Mr. Cordell Hull, President Franklin D. Roosevelt's Secretary of State, in the preparation of the plans for a post-war world organization—an obvious attempt to profit by the failure of President Wilson. The practice was continued after 1945 and was a leading feature of the bi-partisan foreign policy. It is clear that along this line some integration of the two essential institutions in American foreign relations should be attempted.

The restraints of the Senate have led presidents to seek a way round the barrier of the two-thirds majority and this has produced the second development—executive agreements. An executive agreement is an agreement between the President and a foreign government which, not being technically a treaty, does not need to be submitted for approval to the Senate.[1] It was by executive agreement, for example, that President Franklin D. Roosevelt transferred fifty destroyers to Great Britain in September 1940, in return for a ninety-nine year lease of Atlantic bases in British territories; it was by executive agreements with the Danish Minister to the United States that he obtained the right in 1941 to establish bases in Greenland and to occupy Iceland.[2] This device of the executive agreement is of great importance. It is the reaction of the Presidency to the particularistic and divergent forces which, organized through the Senate, paralyse action in foreign affairs. But it is well to recall the limitation upon the President's powers in this direction. He cannot regulate by executive agreement, unfettered by Congress, any matter the regulation of which to be effective needs legislative action. If legislation is needed, he must invoke the aid of Congress.

But although presidential action is limited, it is well to emphasize its importance. The President is, after all, the sole intermediary of the United States in its relations with foreign states. He has a 'very delicate, plenary and exclusive power',[3] said the Supreme Court. He has the power, for example, to recognize new governments or not to recognize them, and this power he has exercised very many times on his own entire responsibility. 'At times, indeed,' says Professor Corwin, 'this prerogative has proved a most potent instrument of foreign policy, a remark which applies as well to its non-use as to its use. President Wilson encompassed the downfall of Huerta's regime

---

[1] None the less they can have force of law. *U.S.* v. *Belmont* (1937) 301 U.S. 324.
[2] In these matters the President was using his powers as Commander-in-Chief also. See the discussion in the next chapter, below, p. 188.
[3] *U.S.* v. *Curtiss-Wright Corp.* (1936) 299 U.S. 304 at p. 320.

in Mexico in 1915 by refusing to recognize it as even a government *de facto*, and the pivotal feature of our relations with both Mexico and Russia for some years was the refusal of successive administrations at Washington to recognize as *de jure* the governments of these countries.'[1] The President exercises an influence, too, by his messages to foreign governments, his appeals, his warnings. President Wilson's Fourteen Points, the enormous influence of which has been too easily forgotten, as a result perhaps of the rejection of the Treaty of Versailles, were no more than a manifesto from the chief negotiator of America's foreign relations, but they had their effect in international affairs. Then again the President has the power, with the advice and consent of the Senate, to nominate ambassadors to represent the United States abroad, but, although the Senate has not frequently rejected his nominations, he has asserted his independence of it by appointing also his 'personal agents', a device comparable to that of executive agreements, for evading the restrictions which the constitution has imposed. This practice has been adopted by all Presidents from the time of Washington. In recent times there has been President Wilson's Colonel House; Mr. Norman H. Davis has been ambassador-at-large for more than one President; Mr. Myron C. Taylor has been the personal representative of President Franklin D. Roosevelt at the Vatican and elsewhere. Through these representatives the President can be informed and can himself influence foreign affairs, quite independently of senatorial control. It seems necessary to stress the existence of this sphere of independent action to show how much room there is potentially for presidential initiative. In the conduct of foreign affairs it is the President who symbolizes the unity of the United States, and it is the Senate which symbolizes its multiplicity. And it is natural that each should try to curb the power of the other.

7

There are thus at least two important problems confronting the framers of a federal constitution in respect of the conduct of the foreign relations of the federation. There is the problem of whether the power to control foreign relations should be given in its entirety to the general government or divided between general and regional governments, more particularly so far as the carrying of treaties into effect is concerned. And there is the problem of how the power of the general government in foreign affairs, whatever its extent may be, is to be so controlled that in its exercise the divergent interests of the component regions in the federation shall be duly safeguarded. The first problem has been met in Canada by dividing the power, so that while the executive of the Dominion has power to make treaties, the power to carry them into effect is divided between Dominion and provincial

---

[1] *The President: Office and Powers*, p. 322. The whole of Chapter VI is most interesting on this subject.

legislatures.[1] The general government has both powers in the plan of the United States and Australia. Which is the better plan and which shall be adopted in any given federation will depend on the factors in each case. The second problem has been solved most satisfactorily, in my view, in the United States, chiefly because of the fact that the Senate there has proved effective.

Whatever the machinery adopted, however, it appears essential that the powers of the general government of a federation in foreign affairs, more especially if they are extensive, should be surrounded by safeguards to the end that they may be exercised in accordance with the wishes of the greater part of organized political opinion throughout the country. Unless this is secured there is a risk that prompt and decisive action by the general government in foreign affairs, spectacular and efficient as it may appear, will merely impose strains on the loyalty of certain regions in the federation, strains which may prove intolerable. This principle has been recognized most in the United States Constitution. For in addition to the powers of the Senate, there are powers shared by the Senate and the House of Representatives which affect the President's action in foreign relations, directly or indirectly. The two houses have some power to modify treaties;[2] their consent to the appropriations necessary for action taken to implement treaties is required; acts and resolutions of Congress may limit the freedom of the President in conducting foreign negotiations, as in the neutrality resolutions of 1935, 1936 and 1937, and the Neutrality Act of 1939; Congress alone has the power to declare war, and it would seem that it has the power also to declare a state of war at an end. All these provisions ensure what may be called effective parliamentary control of foreign relations, a control which seems an essential consequence of federal government and an essential pre-requisite of good federal government in this sphere.

It is this intrusion of the numerous and representative assembly into the conduct of foreign relations which seems to mark off federal representative government from unitary representative government. In the United Kingdom the freedom of the executive in the conduct of foreign relations has always been asserted and it is rare that the House of Commons is required to do more than express its approval of a *fait accompli*. That is conceived to be its normal role, and the system is defended on the ground that, as the executive is chosen from parliament and holds office because it has the confidence of the House of Commons, it may be trusted to act in accordance with the views of the House. Or the system may be defended in another way. It may be said that foreign negotiations are matters which are essentially unsuitable for parliamentary control and that it is better therefore that they should be conducted by ministers, who can act in secret and

[1] Excluding 'British Empire Treaties'. See above, p. 175.
[2] That is, to deprive them of effect in the law of the United States; they would still be obligatory in international law.

with the assistance of skilled advisers. The advantages of this sort of system are well known. But it must not be assumed that it can be adopted to the same extent in a federation. The experience of the United States illustrates this. But there is evidence too from Canada. A constitutional convention appears to have become established there in the years since 1918 that no obligations in foreign affairs will be incurred by the Dominion executive without the consent of the Dominion parliament. This principle has been asserted by Canadian prime ministers on many occasions, and its most striking example occurred in 1939 when the decision whether Canada was to enter the war against Germany was postponed until the parliament met and voted upon the question. The strongest sanction for this procedure is not a legal sanction. It is the fact that Quebec, with its 75 members in the Canadian House of Commons, is strongly opposed to the contracting by Canada of political obligations in Europe, and so strong and determined a block of votes can never be neglected. In Australia, parliamentary participation in the conduct of foreign relations has not developed so fully as in Canada. But it is clear that there too the executive cannot act with that independence of parliament which is characteristic of the system of the United Kingdom. The reason for this is not specially concerned with foreign affairs at all. It is that, with a House of Representatives of only 124 members, no cabinet can have a large majority, and the vote of each individual member is more important. Half a dozen malcontents can place a cabinet in jeopardy.

But it is in Switzerland that the extreme is found. For in this federation there has been introduced not the halfway house of parliamentary participation, but the full principle of democratic participation in determining certain of the country's foreign obligations. The question of Switzerland's accession to the League of Nations was submitted to the people by a referendum in May 1920, and, by a narrow majority, the proposal was approved. By an amendment to the Swiss Constitution in 1921[1] it was provided that treaties concluded on behalf of Switzerland which purported to bind the state indefinitely or for more than fifteen years must be submitted for approval to the people in a referendum before they could come into effect, if 30,000 voters or 8 cantons demand it. Here is a strong safeguard of regional interests. And the power has not been a dead letter. A treaty was submitted to the electorate in 1923 and rejected. It is probable that nowhere but in Switzerland would such a power be given to the people to control foreign relations, nor would it be wise to do so. But the Swiss people are familiar with the use of the referendum,[2] and, more important in this case perhaps, Switzerland has no foreign policy.

---

[1] Art. 89.
[2] Many would say that their use of it in 1923 was unfortunate and perverse.

8

This leads one to remark in conclusion: Happy is the federation which has no diplomatic history. Switzerland is here most fortunate. It is of course an exaggeration to say that it has no foreign policy. It has a simple policy—to preserve its territorial integrity and political independence. But its chief instrument in realizing that policy is not its own diplomatic manoeuvres, but the guarantee of its territorial integrity and political independence which neighbouring great powers have given it, and which will last for so long as these powers are able or willing to maintain it. Its chief diplomatic move must always be, therefore, to keep out of foreign affairs. So situated, Switzerland can afford this luxury of democratic participation in decisions upon foreign affairs.[1]

For the United States it has never been so easy. There has been a conflict there from the beginning between those who want to keep out and those who want to take a hand in the affairs of other continents. And it is clear that the more the United States has been forced to participate in foreign affairs, the harder the problem of determining its policy has become. The United States became and continues a federation because of its divergent regional interests. Once a question of foreign policy arises these divergent interests come more sharply into conflict than ever. Isolation, neutrality or any similar policy must always have a strong appeal in this and other federations, for it keeps the peace among the United States, though it may encourage or ignore a breach of the peace among foreign states. Canadian isolationism has similar origins, similar manifestations, similar justifications. Federalism and a spirited foreign policy go ill together.

[1] For a short account of the development of Swiss foreign policy see Rappard, *The Government of Switzerland*, Chap. XIII. 'Switzerland and the League of Nations' is dealt with by Walter R. Zahlen in *American Political Science Review*, August 1936.

Chapter X
FEDERAL GOVERNMENT AND THE WAR POWER

1

THE working of federal government in war-time would seem likely to exhibit in extreme form the peculiar problems which a federal system produces. For, while it is the essence of federalism to be pluralistic, it is the essence of the war power to be unitary, to be centralized and regimented, to be, in the modern word, 'totalitarian'. There is an immediate contrast between the multiplicity of federalism with its divisions of authority, and the unity necessary if war is to be conducted efficiently. Of all the topics which have been discussed so far, therefore, this present subject would seem to provide the most critical test of the efficiency of federal government.

2

One would expect that the control of defence in a federation would be granted to the general government. For one thing, it was the need for common defence which impelled the regions to join together in the modern federations. And for another, if the control of foreign relations has been given to the general governments, it seems reasonable to give them also the control of those armed forces which give to policies their influence and their final effectiveness. In fact, and speaking quite generally, the control of the war power has been given to the general governments in the four federations which we are discussing, but there are interesting differences of detail from case to case and there are certain qualifications of the truth of the general statement which come out upon closer study.

It is worth while to begin with one aspect of the topic—the power to declare war. In the United States and Switzerland this power is placed exclusively in the hands of the general government. What is more, it is the general legislature, not the executive, which is given the power. One advantage which can follow from this arrangement in a federation is that no war will be entered upon unless a majority of representatives of the regions agree, for in each case the consent of the upper house is required, and the upper house is composed of two representatives from each of the states or cantons.

Yet experience in the United States makes it necessary to speak of one important modification to the general statement that Congress alone can declare war. This is true, but it is also true that the President, by virtue of his powers as Commander-in-Chief, can engage in

war without waiting for Congress to declare war.[1] That in fact is what
Abraham Lincoln did in 1861. And the Supreme Court, though by a
majority of one, upheld him. In a famous passage the Court said:
'Whether the President in fulfilling his duties as Commander-in-
Chief, in suppressing an insurrection, has met with such armed
resistance, and a civil war of such alarming proportions as will compel him to accord to them the character of belligerents, is a question
to be decided *by him*, and this Court must be governed by the decisions and acts of the political department of the government to which
this power was entrusted.' And again: 'If a war be made by invasion
of a foreign nation, the President is not only authorized but bound to
resist force by force. He does not initiate the war, but is bound to
accept the challenge without waiting for any special legislative
authority.'[2] Since Lincoln's time it has come to be accepted that the
President must take the initiative in dealing with threats to the
security of the United States, from within or without.

It has become clear too that a President, by his use of the armed
forces, may bring about a situation in which war becomes probable.
He may present Congress with a *fait accompli*.[3] President Polk
brought on the Mexican War in 1846 by sending United States forces
into disputed territory; President McKinley, though he did not seek
war, had some share in the responsibility for the Spanish-American
War of 1898 by the sending of the United States battleship *Maine* into
Havana Harbour; President Franklin D. Roosevelt had brought the
forces of the United States into a situation where they were participat-
ing in the war, by his action in occupying Iceland in July 1941, although some months were to pass before Pearl Harbour. Similarly,
President Roosevelt, in September 1940, had transferred fifty United
States destroyers to Britain in return for a ninety-nine year lease to
the United States of Atlantic base sites in British territories. This
action was taken partly under his powers as Commander-in-Chief. If
it was not a warlike act, it was not a neutral act.

It is in the light of such events and tendencies that Congress's
power to declare war must be considered. There has been much
jealousy by congressional leaders throughout the history of the
United States of the use which Presidents have made of their powers
as Commander-in-Chief. It is a field where the struggle between
legislature and executive shows itself to a degree that is surpassed
only by that of foreign relations. It seems clear that Presidents have
stretched their powers beyond what Alexander Hamilton, at any
rate, intended.[4] It is an illustration of what we shall encounter again,

[1] See E. S. Corwin, *The President, Office and Powers*, Chapter V, and C. A. Berdahl, *War
Powers of the Executive in the United States*.
[2] *The Prize Cases*, 2 Black 635 (1863). See the discussion in J. G. Randall, *Constitutional
Problems under Lincoln*.
[3] See an article by Charles C. Tansill, 'War powers of the President of the United States with
special reference to the beginning of hostilities' in *Political Science Quarterly*, Vol. XLV, March
1930.
[4] *The Federalist*, No. LXIX.

the process by which the emergencies of war give opportuny to the unifying and integrating institutions in a federal government to assert their power.

The principal point in the Canadian and Australian cases is that the regions have no power to declare war and that the power in these federations to declare war is vested in or controlled by the general executives. These executives are responsible to their legislatures, and in the case of Canada, the formal prior consent of the legislature has been sought by the Prime Minister before the declaration of war has been made. In this way the differences of opinion are given a chance to express themselves.

3

To declare war is one thing. To wage war is another. How are the powers to wage war distributed? Consider a first requirement: the raising of armed forces on sea, land and in the air.

In the two later federations exclusive control over raising armed forces has been given to the general government. In Canada the Dominion government has exclusive power over 'the Militia, military and naval forces and defence'.[1] In Australia the states are denied the power to raise or maintain any naval or military force, without the consent of the parliament of the Commonwealth, and this consent, once given, may be withdrawn. The parliament of the Commonwealth is positively empowered to deal with 'the naval and military defence of the Commonwealth and of the several states, and the control of the forces to execute and maintain the laws of the Commonwealth'. The power of the general government is therefore potentially exclusive. In both cases the power to deal with the raising of an air force was naturally not mentioned, but the power over 'defence' in Canada and over 'the forces to execute and maintain the laws of the Commonwealth' in Australia would appear to be sufficient to authorize the raising of air forces in both cases.

In the two earlier federations, the United States and Switzerland, there was not the same clear-cut intention to hand over the entire control of the armed forces to the general government. In Switzerland between 1848 and 1874 the cantons had considerable control, but in the reorganization of the constitution in 1874 their powers were limited. None the less the cantons still exercise some powers. They enforce the laws which the general government makes for the organization of the army; they are responsible for the supply and upkeep of uniform and equipment, although their expenditure is re-paid to them by the general government. Unless military conditions make it undesirable, units must be formed of troops from one and the same canton. The cantons are responsible for the compensation of these

---

[1] 'Militia' here appears to mean voluntary or part-time troops, as contrasted with per manent corps or a standing army.

units; for the maintenance of their effectives and for the nomination of their non-commissioned and commissioned officers, up to the rank of captain. All these powers they must exercise subject to the broad control of the general government. There is, then, one army, but it is organized on a cantonal basis and there is co-operation between general and cantonal governments in its control. The supremacy of the general government seems assured in the last resort, but the composite nature of the army cannot be quite obliterated. To this it may be added that the Swiss army is not a standing army. The general government is forbidden by the constitution to maintain permanent troops. The cantons, on the other hand, may maintain up to 300 permanent troops, presumably as an insurance of internal order. They may not maintain more without the consent of the general government.

The Constitution of the United States left with the component states a power to raise a militia[1] and gave them the exclusive power to appoint the officers of the militia, and the authority to train the militia according to the discipline prescribed by Congress. It may be noted that the militia was evidently intended to be distinct from professional military forces, for the constitution expressly forbade the states, as in Australia, to keep troops or ships of war in time of peace. The power of the states over the militia is, however, not exclusive in all matters. Congress may call forth the militia 'to execute the laws of the Union, suppress insurrection and repel invasions; it may provide for organizing, arming and disciplining the militia; and for governing such part of them as may be employed in the service of the United States'. Over and above these powers in respect of the militia, Congress is empowered 'to raise and support armies, but no appropriation of money to that use shall be for a longer term than two years; to provide and maintain a navy; to make rules for the government and regulation of the land and naval forces; and to raise and spend money for the common defence of the United States'. There were thus contemplated by the Constitution of the United States two kinds of military forces in the country, the state militia under the command of the governor, and the army of the United States. Alone among federal governments, as I have defined them, the United States tolerated this dual system.

4

It is well worth while to consider at once how this dual system has worked in the United States, and whether such an arrangement is desirable in a federal union. Does not the existence of state troops lead to an assertion of state independence and, if need be, to defiance of the general government? And, to take the particular instance of the

---

[1] The militia was, in theory, composed of all men of military age. In practice it was composed of a small force of volunteers which spent part of its time in drill and encampment and received a payment for these services.

United States, does not the American Civil War itself prove that it is unwise to allow states to possess armed forces? This is an important question and it is one which is certain to need consideration in any proposal to federate existing sovereign states, say, in Europe. Should they be allowed to retain armed forces of their own distinct from the forces of the general government?

The argument for state troops is put in this way. They are needed to maintain internal order and to defend the state against external aggression, whether from other states, from the general government or from foreign countries. In the United States the constitution provided for these needs. It said that the state government might use its militia to preserve internal order, and that if the militia were not sufficient, its legislature or executive might call in the United States to its assistance.[1] So far as aggression from another state or foreign country is concerned, a state is permitted by the constitution to use its militia if actually invaded or in such imminent danger as will not admit delay. Otherwise it must obtain the consent of Congress before it engages in war and it is guaranteed also the protection of the United States against invasion.[2]

In Switzerland the cantons are given rather less freedom. Cantons are forbidden by the constitution to resort to force in settlement of their conflicts. But if a canton is threatened by another canton, it must inform the general executive at once, so that the latter may take the necessary steps or summon the general legislature. Similarly if the canton is threatened from outside the federation, or if it is threatened by internal disorder within the canton, it must inform the general executive at once. It is authorized also, in all cases, to call upon other cantons to come to its assistance and the other cantons are obliged to render such assistance.[3] If the government of a canton is not in a position to call for help, the competent authority of the general government is entitled to intervene without being called upon, and indeed it is obliged to intervene when the disturbances endanger the security of Switzerland. Thus in Switzerland the general government must be immediately associated with the use of military force by any canton.

In the cases of Canada and Australia it seems clear that the provinces and states respectively must rely upon the forces of the general government to protect them from internal violence and from external aggression, and that the constitution permits no province or state to raise any forces against the general government.

The experience of the American Civil War is instructive. In December 1860, before any of the Southern States seceded, the regular army of the United States consisted of about 16,000 officers and men. The militia—though by the constitution subject to be 'called forth' by the general government—had remained a state organization. In

[1] Art. IV (4).
[2] Art. I (10).
[3] Arts 14–17.

most of the states it was a nebulous affair with no effective organization.[1] There is no evidence that the states, in the North or South, devoted special attention to the equipment and extension of their state militias in the period which preceded the secession of the Southern States. Their first thought does not appear to have been: We have our own state forces and we will use them against those who oppose us. For many years there was talk of secession and resistance, of armed resistance too. And yet when the time came the state militias were unprepared. Most of the Southern leaders appear to have thought that the North would agree to part from them in peace. Throughout the long controversy state militarism did not exist. The threat of secession, even of armed resistance, does not appear to have been translated into or supported by a policy of state re-armament. To this extent, therefore, in the United States the power in the separate states to raise troops of their own was not used to destroy the authority of the general government.

What may be said, however, is that the existence of state troops and of the idea that each state should have its troops, with its Governor as Commander-in-Chief, and its officers appointed by state authority, did symbolize and strengthen state independence. It gave an outlet and an encouragement to state patriotism. It made it possible to conceive of dying for one's state. Troops gave a state a consequence which policemen did not. Admittedly the states of the American Union had not made the most of these possibilities. But it seems undeniable that the state militia did have some effect in encouraging the seceding states to resist the Washington government in the years before 1861. It is hard to assess the importance of this factor. It appears to me to have been of minor importance. But it was there. If there had been no state militia the task of the federal government in imposing its will on the rebellious states would have been easier.

This is not to say that it would have encountered no resistance at all. State loyalty could exist without state troops, and it is clear that if the federal government had attempted to enforce its decisions on the seceding states and there had been no militia there would still have been armed resistance. And it would have been led, as it was largely led, by men who had theretofore been in the Regular Army of the United States. About 300 officers (roughly one-third of the total) left the army to go with the South, though the number of privates who did so was negligible.[2] The case of General Robert E. Lee of Virginia is the classic example. The experience of the Civil War illustrates the fact that in a federal system where state loyalty is strong, the federal government and the state governments must act with constant vigilance to avoid forcing any deep dividing issue to the point where armed resistance comes into view. And if that point is reached no

[1] J. G. Randall, *The Civil War and Reconstruction*, pp. 406–9.
[2] Randall, op. cit., p. 406, n. 4.

constitutional provisions about the control of the armed forces can prevent armed resistance and a conflict of loyalties for those in the forces of the general government. If there are no state militias the task of the federal government is easier. But as long as there is state loyalty there is a danger of a break in the ranks of a federal army.

The development of the militia in the United States has shown, in fact, that the early compromise by which the states were allowed to retain some symbol of armed force has been justified. The tendency throughout has been for the armed forces of the states to be integrated gradually into one composite national force available for the service of the United States. The process has been long and by no means uninterrupted. The relations between the general government and the state governments in the control of the militia were much debated in the nineteenth century. It was not until the United States entered the war against Germany in 1917 that the question came up for final settlement. Congress passed a law providing for compulsory military service. Its validity was attacked upon the ground, among others, that it conflicted with the provisions of the constitution which left the control of the militia to the states. The Supreme Court of the United States dealt with this and other objections to the 'Draft' Law in a series of cases in 1918.[1] Their view was that Congress had power to use the militia, if it so desires, 'to execute the laws of the union, suppress insurrections and repel invasions', but this does not curb in any way the power of Congress to raise an army by conscription. The Court said: 'There was left, therefore, under the sway of the States undelegated, the control of the militia to the extent that such control was not taken away by the exercise by Congress of its power to raise armies. This did not diminish the military power or curb the full potentiality of the right to exert it, but left an area of authority requiring to be provided for (the militia area) unless and until, by the exertion of the military power of Congress, that area had been circumscribed or totally disappeared.'

The potential predominance of Congress was asserted in this judgement, and indeed the history of the relations between the general government and the militia in the twentieth century shows how the independence of the states has gradually been subordinated to the needs of the general government. In 1916, for example, Congress passed a National Defence Act which changed the name of the militia to the National Guard; the members of a National Guard of a state were also to be members of the National Guard of the United States which is 'a reserve component of the Army of the United States'. Organizations and members of the National Guard of the United States may be called into service, whereupon their status as parts of the National Guard of a state becomes dormant. This was

---

[1] *Selective Draft Law Cases* (1918), 245 U.S. 366.

done in 1940, for example, when the threat of war was still in the distance.[1] In 1946 the National Guard reverted to the states. The increase in control by the general governments is indicated, too, by the financial aspect. Throughout the nineteenth century Congress made grants to the states to furnish arms and equipment for the state militia, in accordance with its constitutional duty. But little attempt was made to control this expenditure. Since 1913, however, Congress has imposed a more detailed control of the way in which money is spent; 'the appropriations for National Guard training are disbursed to each state by a United States Property and Disbursing Officer who is a federal employee appointed on the nomination of the governor. The money does not go to the states, but is disbursed directly by the federal officer to individual members of the National Guard of the state for drill attendance and other activities incident to training. The state retains authority to determine the location of Guard units and power to use the Guard (without federal financial assistance) in quelling disorders.'[2] In 1940 the general government contributed about $42 million to the expenditure of the National Guard and the states about $12 million.[3] But in spite of this integration there is some friction and difficulty in controlling an organization through officers of the general government and officers of the state government. We are told that in some instances state political pressure has been exercised improperly on the corps and area commanders, themselves responsible to the War Department of the United States.[4] Nevertheless control by the general government is increasing. There is a regular system of inspection by officers of the United States. Although officers of the National Guard are state officials, appointed by the governor, they must meet the detailed requirements of the National Guard Bureau.[5] 'Thus,' says Professor Beard, 'the ancient symbol of independence, armed force, passes from the states to the Nation.'[6]

5

But the power to wage war comprises much more than the power to raise troops, equip navies and build air forces. It demands a control of the whole economic and social life of a people. How have the federal governments met this need? Has the plurality of authority over economic and social life which has been the characteristic of federal governments in peace been able to adapt itself to the totalitarian requirements of war? Experience has shown that the general governments in the federations have found themselves equipped with

---

[1] States are allowed to raise a state guard, with what men remain, to replace those members of the National Guard who are called into the service of the United States. They receive assistance, likewise, in training their state guard.
[2] V. O. Key, Jr., *The Administration of Federal Grants to States*, pp. 23–24.
[3] A. F. MacDonald, *American Political Science Review*, XXXIV, p. 490.
[4] J. P. Clark, *The New Federalism*, p. 188.
[5] Ibid., pp. 199, 200.
[6] *American Government and Politics*, 8th ed., p. 462.

substantial powers with which to wage war. The power to control defence has proved in war-time to be sufficient to bring within the ambit of the general governments matters which, without invoking that power, would have been beyond the powers of the general governments. A few illustrations may be given.

In the United States during the First World War the Federal Control Act was passed in 1918 giving the federal government power to fix both inter-state and intra-state rates of railroads. The Supreme Court, in dealing with the act, assumed without argument that this was a legitimate exercise of war power,[1] yet in time of peace it is doubtful if any such claim to control railroads could be substantiated under the guise of war power. But in war-time the courts are more easily convinced. Similarly the Supreme Court of the United States approved legislation which authorized the taking over by the federal government of all the telephone lines in the country;[2] which regulated the price of fuel;[3] which enforced nation-wide prohibition of the manufacture and sale of alcoholic liquor, before the Eighteenth Amendment to the Constitution was passed;[4] which provided for the commandeering of ships,[5] and for the commandeering of the output of factories.[6] All this legislation was upheld as a valid exercise of the war power of the general government, and in all cases it seems reasonable to say that in peace-time some part of this legislation would have been declared invalid on the ground that it invaded the area of state powers. The general government of the United States was thus able 'to commandeer essential industries and mines, requisition supplies, control distribution, fix prices, and take over the entire system of transportation and communication.'[7] The most complete regulation of economic and social life proved possible and there was practically nothing lacking in power to the government of the United States which was available to the government of the United Kingdom. And when the United States entered the war in 1941 the general government found itself once more possessed of the fullest powers which it has used to organize economic and social life on a more comprehensive scale than ever before. Congress in effect has the fullest powers, if it chooses to use them. Acts were passed to control manufacture, output and sale of articles even remotely connected with the waging of war; wages, prices and salaries were stabilized under Congressional control. Many of these powers are exercised by the President under a delegation from Congress, but the significant fact for our present purpose is that the general government claims power to deal with them.[8]

[1] *North Pacific Railway Co.* v. *North Dakota* (1919) 250 U.S. 135.
[2] *Dakota Central Telephone Co.* v. *Sth Dakota* (1919) 250 U.S. 163.
[3] *U.S.* v. *Pennsylvania Central Coal Co.* (1918) 256. Fed. 703.
[4] *Hamilton* v. *Kentucky Distillery Co.* (1919) 251 U.S. 146.
[5] *The Lake Monroe* (1919) 250 U.S. 246.
[6] *Moore and Tierney* v. *Rexford Knitting Co.* (1918) 250. Fed. 276.
[7] Morison and Commager, *The Growth of the American Republic*, Vol. 2, p. 471.
[8] See E. S. Corwin, *Total War and the Constitution*.

In Australia,[1] similarly, legislation was upheld in 1916 under which the Commonwealth parliament could fix a maximum price of bread.[2] The Commonwealth government exercised in practice a greatly extended power of control over the lives of people throughout the country. Further, legislation was upheld in 1917 under which the Commonwealth made an offence of any action encouraging the destruction of or injury to property,[3] and in 1918 legislation was upheld organizing the sequestration of enemy property.[4] In September 1939 the Australian parliament passed a National Security Act, drafted in the widest terms and giving to the government complete power to deal with any matter which affected Australia's war effort. The defence power was used to cover every variety of matter—prices, fair rents, capital issues, monetary control, reinstatement in civil employment, public safety and order, wheat requisition. One striking example of its extent was the taking over by the Commonwealth of the states' machinery for assessing and collecting income tax, an exercise of the defence power which the High Court upheld, though two judges dissented.[5] In another case it was held that the defence power was sufficient to cover the prohibition of all advertising in war-time.[6] Indeed it has been said by an authority that the defence power in Australia was 'so simply and largely conferred that in time of war the Parliament could itself make any laws whatever, unless they could be plainly shown to have no possible bearing on the military preparedness of the nation'.[7]

Yet it would have been wrong to think of the defence power as unlimited, although a succession of decisions by the High Court favourable to the extension of the power had given rise to that expectation. In 1942 limits began to be set. The High Court held that some regulations issued under the National Security Act obliging every person to work on a holiday could not validly be applied to public servants of the state of Victoria employed in a government department which was not engaged on war work.[8] In this case the Chief Justice said: 'If, under the defence power, the Commonwealth can control the pay, hours and duties of all state public servants, it is obvious that the Commonwealth can take complete control of all governmental administration within Australia. The result would be the abolition, in all but name, of the federal system of government which it is the object of the Constitution to establish.'[9] This had been said before but only by the dissenting minority. Now it seemed to be

---

[1] The best discussion is B. Sugerman and W. J. Dignam in *Australian Law Journal*, Vol. 17 1943, 'The Defence Power and Total War'.
[2] *Farey* v. *Burvett*, 21 C.L.R., 433, espec. Isaacs, J. at pp. 453, 455, 456.
[3] *Pankhurt* v. *Kiernan*, 24 C.L.R. 120.
[4] *Burkard* v. *Oakley*, 24 C.L.R. 422.
[5] *South Australia* v. *The Commonwealth* (1942) 65 C.L.R. 373. See also *Andrews* v. *Howell* (1941) 65 C.L.R. 255.
[6] *Ferguson* v. *The Commonwealth* (1943) 66 C.L.R. 432 per Latham, C. J., at p. 435.
[7] Professor K. H. Bailey, in *Studies in the Australian Constitution* (ed. Portus), p. 32.
[8] *Victoria* v. *The Commonwealth* (1942) 66 C.L.R. 488.
[9] At p. 507.

obtaining the support of the majority. Yet it is hard to distinguish this case from some of its predecessors where the action of the Commonwealth was upheld.

In 1943 further illustrations were given that the defence power is subordinate to the Constitution. In at least three important cases, the decision went against the Commonwealth.[1] In one case regulations restricting the admission of students to universities were declared invalid; in another the guarantee in the constitution of religious freedom was held not to be infringed by regulations restricting the sect of Jehovah's Witnesses, but the defence power was held insufficient to justify these regulations. The tests which the court had come to apply are summarized by recent writers as (1) whether the legislation has a real connection with defence; (2) the true character, object and effect of the legislation, to be ascertained from an examination of the legislation in its entirety; (3) whether the subject of the legislation has a specific relation to the subject of defence or whether that relation is general only and not specific.[2]

But before the end of 1943 a majority of the High Court had decided that the control of all industrial disputes and industrial unrest in war-time lay within the defence power of the Commonwealth, and the scope of the decision of 1942 was seen to be narrow.[3] In 1944 certain regulations imposing industrial conscription and controlling civil employment were brought before the High Court for consideration. They were unanimously upheld.[4] Some other decisions in the same year, though less far-reaching, showed that the tide had begun to run once more in favour of the Commonwealth, though there was some division of judicial opinion.[5]

In Canada the War Measures Act of 1914 gave the Dominion government authority to employ a wide range of powers, many of which were beyond its peace-time constitutional capacity. 'The fact of an unprecedented emergency insured the constitutional validity of the measures of economic regulation which were adopted.'[6] Price fixing, the control of the production, conservation and distribution of foodstuffs, the control of the export of wheat, the control of wages, and finally the establishment of the War Trade Board in February 1918, with sweeping powers authorizing it to carry out 'such supervision as may be necessary of all industrial and commercial enterprises'—all these are examples of powers the exercise of which the war emergency at once demanded and justified. Such measures must

[1] *R.* v. *University of Sydney,* ex parte *Drummond* (1943) 67 C.L.R. 95; *Adelaide Company of Jehovah's Witnesses* v. *Commonwealth* (1943) 67 C.L.R. 116; *Victorian Chamber of Manufacturers* v. *Commonwealth. (Industrial Lighting Regulations)* (1943) 67 C.L.R. 413.
[2] Su:erman and Dignam, loc. cit., at p. 212.
[3] *Pidoto* v. *Victoria* (1943) 68 C.L.R. 87.
[4] *Reid* v. *Sinderberry and McGrath* (1944) 68 C.L.R.
[5] e.g. *R.* v. *Commonwealth Court of Conciliation and Arbitration* ex parte *Victoria* (1944) 68 C.L.R. 485; *Gonzwa* v. *Commonwealth* (1944) 68 C.L.R. 469; *De Mestre* v. *Chisholm* (1944) 69 C.L.R. 51.
[6] *Rowell Sirois Report,* Book I, pp. 101 ff.

trench, for example, on property and civil rights in a province, yet this matter was normally in the exclusive control of a provincial legislature. The validity of exceptional measures in war-time was recognized by the Judicial Committee of the Privy Council. In a case which arose out of the war legislation, it said: 'However the wording of sections 91 and 92 (of the British North America Act) may have laid down a framework under which, as a general principle, the Dominion Parliament is to be excluded from trenching on property and civil rights in the Provinces of Canada, yet in a sufficiently great emergency such as that arising out of war, there is implied the power to deal adequately with that emergency for the safety of the Dominion as a whole.'[1] In this case the Judicial Committee upheld the validity of the Canadian War Measures Act, 1914, and Orders-in-Council made thereunder during the war for controlling throughout Canada the supply of newsprint paper by manufacturers and its price.

The War Measures Act of 1914 was in fact not repealed. When Canada entered the war in 1939, therefore, it was possible for the Dominion government to impose comprehensive and drastic measures of control over all aspects of Canadian life. No restriction upon the Dominion's legal powers has arisen to prevent its undertaking the most thorough organization of defence.[2] In June 1940, for example, the National Resources Mobilization Act was passed authorizing the Dominion executive to require all Canadians to put their persons and property at the disposal of the state. The needs of defence override the exclusive power which the provinces have over property and civil rights. No better illustration could be given of the adequacy of the powers available to the Dominion government to wage war in all its forms.

Switzerland did not abandon her neutrality in the wars of 1914 and 1939, but the maintenance of the neutrality did mean that the country was on a war footing, with the army mobilized for a good part of the time. War economy was imposed though an actual declaration of war was not made. On each occasion the federal assembly made a very wide grant of powers to the executive under which the country was governed during the war. On August 30, 1939, for example, it was enacted as follows: 'The Federal Assembly grants to the Federal Council the power and the duty to take the measures necessary to maintain the security, independence and neutrality of Switzerland, to safeguard the credit and economic interests of the country and to secure its supply of food. The credits necessary for this purpose are granted to the Federal Council. In addition, the power is granted to the Federal Council to contract the necessary loans.' These powers were exercised to the full from 1939–1945 and to a

[1] *Fort Frances Pulp & Power Co.* v. *Manitoba Free Press* [1923] A.C. 695.
[2] The decision in the *Fort Frances Case, supra*, was admitted without argument as justifying the wide powers of regulation exercised in 1943, in a case before the Supreme Court of Canada, *Reference concerning the Regulation of Chemicals* (1943) S.C.R. 1.

considerable extent for some years after 1945. It may be doubted whether they conform with the Constitution. They were not submitted to a referendum, however, being expressly excluded from it by the Federal Assembly.

6

It has proved possible, therefore, for federal governments to meet the demands of war-time in spite of the fact that by the operation of the federal principle their essential characteristic is multiplicity rather than unity of authority. The general governments have found available to them the fullest powers to wage war, both in respect of raising troops and in the even more important respect of organizing man-power, woman-power, economic resources and the whole complicated and intimate structure of social and domestic life.

But it is one thing to be able to wage war when war is raging. It is another to be able to prepare for war. It is well known from experience that states place themselves on a war footing before they declare war. They begin to prepare to wage war. Germany from 1933 to 1939 is only one example of a phenomenon well known in history, the state which prepared for war until it was ready to declare war. What powers have federal governments in this respect? Are they able in peace-time to exercise those large and comprehensive powers which, it is found, they possess when war is actually being waged? Can the defence power be exercised with the same all-embracing force in peace?

Switzerland, in this, as in other respects, appears to be fortunate. She is unhampered by judicial review, and is therefore able to exercise powers to prepare for war which in other federations might well be held unconstitutional. Not all these measures are submitted to a referendum though it should not be assumed that the Swiss people are powerless in this sphere. In considerable measure through their control over their government by the referendum they can ensure that these powers are not abused in peace-time.

Experience so far seems to show that the federal systems of Canada, Australia and the United States are at something of a disadvantage in this respect. The power to raise troops remains untouched, of course, in peace as in war. There have been one or two indications, however, of the difficulties that might beset any attempt in peace-time to prepare for war in any sense other than the raising of armed forces or the manufacture of armaments.

Two Canadian cases illustrate well how courts view the difference between the needs of defence in war-time and in peace-time. In a case, decided in 1923,[1] to which reference has already been made, the Privy Council approved Canadian legislation imposing control over paper, including an act of 1919 which continued the war-time control after

[1] *Fort Frances Pulp & Power Co. v. Manitoba Free Press* [1923] A.C. 695.

peace had returned. It expressed itself as unable 'to say that the Dominion Government had no good reason for thus temporarily continuing the paper control after actual war had ceased, but while the effects of war conditions might still be operative.'

On the other hand the Privy Council had declared void[1] in 1922 legislation designed to prevent hoarding and combines, passed in 1919 to deal with the conditions of the immediate post-war period. In this case they based their decision on the ground that 'the law is not one enacted to meet special conditions in war-time. It was passed in 1919 after peace had been declared, and it is not confined to any temporary purpose, but is to continue without limit in time, and to apply throughout Canada. . . . It may well be that the subjects of undue combination and hoarding are matters in which the Dominion has a great practical interest. In special circumstances such as those of a great war, such an interest might conceivably become of such paramount and over-riding importance' as to justify encroachment into what is normally the sphere of the provinces. 'It can, therefore, be only under necessity in highly exceptional circumstances, such as cannot be assumed to exist in the present case, that the liberty of the inhabitants of the provinces may be restricted by the Parliament of Canada. . . .'

That is the doctrine for Canada. The judges must be convinced that a very grave emergency connected with the defence of the country exists before they will extend the war power beyond its technical and limited bounds. What evidence is needed will be a variable matter. The experience of recent years, when war has come to be waged before it is declared, may lead judges to take a more liberal view. They may feel inclined to accept a declaration of the legislature that a state of emergency exists. But it is impossible to anticipate. In 1926, for example, it was held by the High Court of Australia that the defence power did not authorize the Commonwealth to establish a business for trade purposes in time of peace merely because it might assist in the maintenance of a naval dockyard and a naval workshop.[2] More recently an act to control communism and communists, passed in 1951, was held invalid on the ground, among others, that it could not be supported under the defence power, as the government contended.[3] In 1935, on the other hand, the High Court held that, where a clothing factory had been established to supply clothing for the military forces of the Commonwealth during the war, legislation authorizing the supply of clothing to Commonwealth government departments other than the Department of Defence, to the government departments of a state, and to the local authorities of the states could be regarded as incidental to the defence power.[4]

[1] *In re Board of Commerce Act* [1922] 1 A.C. 191 at pp. 197–8.
[2] *Commonwealth* v. *Australian Shipping Board* (1926) 39 C.L.R. 1.
[3] *Australian Communist Party* v. *the Commonwealth* (1951) 83 C.L.R. 1.
[4] *Victoria* v. *Commonwealth* (1935) 52 C.L.R. 533.

There is occasionally a similar decision in the United States supporting an extension of the defence power in time of peace. It was relied on as one of the grounds for justifying the federal government in authorizing the construction of national highways.[1] The Congressional legislation of 1933 which established the Tennessee Valley Authority was upheld by the Supreme Court partly under the war power, although it had been passed when the United States was at peace and although it dealt with other matters than defence in its narrower sense.[2] But it is true on the whole to say that the Courts have been careful to construe the defence power narrowly in time of peace; that they are slow to accept the view that, short of actual hostilities, a state of emergency exists; but that, once a state of emergency exists, they are slow to question the deliberate decision of the government as to the measures needed to deal with it.

These limitations upon the war power in peace-time are admittedly a restriction upon the three federations of Canada, Australia and the United States, in their capacity to prepare for what is called 'total war'. That is undoubted. And it is inevitable if the federal system is to exist at all. For if the war power is interpreted as widely in peace as in war, then the power of the general government extends to all important spheres of a country's life and destroys the division of powers upon which a federation is based. And if the Courts are to be denied the power to determine whether circumstances are sufficiently grave to justify a wide use of the war power, then the general government of a federation by a mere declaration that an emergency exists, may empower itself to invade at will the sphere of action of the regions. It is a case where courts should be slow to reject the views of a legislature unless there be clear evidence to the contrary. But if they are to perform their functions they must take care that the federal structure is not unnecessarily subordinated to one item of power of the general government.

It may be well to add that, although it must be admitted that in federations there are obstacles arising from federalism itself to the placing of a country on a war footing while a technical state of peace exists, these obstacles alone should not be taken as the sole explanation of the slowness with which Canada, Australia and the United States acted in response to the re-armament of Germany under Hitler's regime. There were other reasons for that, reasons, it may be suggested, which applied also in the case of the United Kingdom.

7

Some brief outline has been given of the working of federal government in relation to the war power in respect of declaring war, waging

---

[1] *California* v. *Pacific Railroad Co.* (1888) 127 U.S. 1 at p. 39.
[2] *Ashwander* v. *Tennessee Valley Authority* (1936) 297 U.S. 288.

war and preparing for war. What general conclusion may be stated about the effect of federalism upon the exercise of the war power, and, further, about the effect of the exercise of the war power on federalism?

It may be said in general, I think, that federal government is efficient in its exercise of the war power. It has been shown that there are ample powers available to the general governments for the waging of war once war has been declared. It is true, at the same time, that there are difficulties arising from federalism itself in regard to preparing for war, but it is doubtful if these are greater than those which are found in the unitary states. They should be recorded, however, on the debit side.

But then there are certain positive advantages arising from the existence of general and regional governments in a federal structure. Some indication of the value which a federal structure has in the conduct of war can be obtained from a study of the practice of the United States in the two world wars. In both cases the general government chose to delegate to the states almost the whole administration of certain services. In particular the 'call-up' of men for service was carried out by the states, subject to a general supervision by the government at Washington. In practice in the First World War the President did not give his orders direct to state officials but issued them through the state governors.[1] In the second war not only was the call-up delegated in the same way to the states but greater discretion was left to the state authorities in administering the system. Further, the complicated arrangements for civil defence[2] were similarly delegated. It is to be noticed that almost all appointments in these administrative agencies are made by the governors of the states, and that where appointments were made by the President, it is required by law or custom that the governor should make a nomination.

State co-operation in war after 1941 was carried out through such institutions as the Conference of State Governors and the Council of State Governments,[3] which co-ordinated policies between states and enabled them to work more easily with the general government. The states took charge of arrangements for safeguarding rubber resources, for example; they co-operated in the imposition of uniform speed limits; in concerting measures for law and order; in undertaking housing policies for war workers in co-operation with the administration of the National Housing Agency; in passing necessary war legislation and in co-ordinating their financial policies. In some cases states organized a state guard to replace the National Guard,

---

[1] Clark, *The New Federalism*, pp. 90–92.

[2] This service covered a wider field than in Britain. It included the equivalent of the Observer Corps and much of the security work in connection with public utilities which fell to the Home Guard in Britain.

[3] More is said of these co-operative institutions in the next chapter. See below, pp. 229–31.

then called up for service by the United States. These are a few examples of the use to which the state organizations have been put. It confirms the view of an Attorney-General of the United States 'that as a matter of practical administration, the strength of 130,000,000 people cannot be fully mobilized for the war programme, except through the mobilization at full capacity of state and local machinery'.[1] Similar use of regional governments was made by the general governments of Canada and Australia. It is not an exaggeration to say that, for the conduct of war by such large and complex organizations, if the regional governments had not existed, it would have been necessary for the general government to create them. I do not mean that if federalism had not existed, it would have been necessary to create it. What I emphasize is that the existence of these regional governments proved to be most valuable in the conduct of war administration. And the most striking illustration of it is the way in which the general governments actually delegate the administration to the regional authorities.

That is one aspect of the question. But there is one political factor which has to be remembered. There are usually deep, dividing issues in the political foundations of a federal state, and it may happen that these issues can affect the waging of war. After all, the conduct of foreign relations in a federation, as I explained in the preceding chapter, is for these reasons a delicate function, and the exercise of the war power is closely linked with this.

The illustration that comes to mind is that of Quebec in the Canadian federation. In the war of 1914 and again in the war of 1939 the issue of conscription came to the front in Canada and it was strongly opposed in the province of Quebec.[2] In the war of 1914 Quebec was not alone in its opposition to conscription. Organized labour and agriculture were also critical of it. But by 1917 the opposition had become most violent in Quebec and in the general election held at the time, Quebec, almost alone in the whole Dominion, returned candidates pledged to oppose conscription. The measure was passed in spite of their opposition and it was enforced. But the bitterness was intense. The experience of that time was in the minds of the Canadian ministers in the war of 1939 and they gave a pledge, as their predecessors had done, that conscription for overseas service would not be introduced. But after two years of war they were obliged to reconsider this pledge and in 1942 a referendum was held on the subject. Once again Quebec was in a hostile minority. The other eight provinces gave a 4 to 1 vote in favour of releasing the government from its pledge; Quebec gave a 2.5 to 1 negative. A conscription act was passed but its powers were used at first for home service only. In 1944 the issue became critical once more. The Liberal government was

[1] Francis Biddle, in *State Government*, April 1943.
[2] An instructive short analysis is in B. K. Sandwell, *Canada*, pp. 96–100.

obliged to conscript for overseas service and it incurred the deep hostility of Quebec.

There is no doubt that this difference of opinion lessened the war strength of Canada. But does that mean that Canada was handicapped because it was federal? Surely not. Canada's handicap in the matter of conscription came not from any lack of legal power to conscript men for military service. It came from a fundamental division of opinion among the Canadian people, a division which would have existed whatever the form of government, a division of the same kind as exists in South Africa between 'Dutch' and 'British' South Africans, where there is a unitary not a federal form of union. The point is well put in the words of the Canadian Royal Commission on Dominion-Provincial Relations. 'The French-speaking Canadians had been established in Canada for centuries. They were the oldest Canadians of European stock and they were much more firmly rooted in North America than their English-speaking fellow citizens. Their political connection with France had been severed 150 years before and they had never claimed a close sentimental attachment for republican France with its anti-clerical associations. Their undoubted loyalty to Great Britain was a reasoned rather than an instinctive loyalty. It lacked the emotional pull which was essential to command deep sacrifice in a remote European war. While the rest of Canada was deeply affected by living in remembered links with the British Isles and by United Empire Loyalist and Imperial tradition, their experience and memories were essentially North American. It was not unlikely, therefore, that the attitude of the French-speaking Canadians towards a prolonged war in Europe would differ from that which prevailed in the rest of Canada.'[1]

It was a division which handicapped Canada so far as conscription was concerned and it would have handicapped her whether her government was federal or unitary. At the same time it must be asserted that this division was also a reason why Canada was a federation and not a unitary state. Canada's handicap in war may be said to rest then not on the fact that she had adopted a federal system; rather it is true to say that both her handicaps in war and her federal system rest upon the fundamental division between French and English-speaking Canadians. To this one qualification may be suggested. It is probable that the adoption of federalism in response to the division between French and English-speaking Canadians, has done something to preserve and intensify this division, and to that extent the fact that Canada is a federation may indirectly have increased the difficulties of the conscription issue.

If other federal systems are studied a similar conclusion seems ustified. There are weaknesses in their conduct of war, but these

---

[1] *Rowell-Sirois Report*, Book I, pp. 94–95.

appear not to come directly from the fact that they have federal systems with their inevitable divisions of powers between general and state governments. Indeed, on the contrary, as we have seen, the legal powers of the general governments appear everywhere to be widespread. What is lacking is that political homogeneity which makes it possible for wide powers to be exercised. These divisions which, as we saw, paralyse the conduct of foreign affairs in some federations, continue for the same reason to weaken their exercise of the subsequent war power.

To quote some words again from the Canadian Royal Commission: 'The united effort required of a nation by modern war places a great strain on the political unity of any people. . . . If the common endeavour is one with respect to which deep impulse in the community arouses different conceptions, it is likely to break down and the consequent disharmony will embarrass all the common enterprises which have been entrusted to the common government. A population of common origin and tradition deeply habituated to think alike on fundamental issues, may be readily able to maintain the agreement necessary for collective action affecting the whole range of community life. Canada lacks that homogeneity and this, in turn, limits the extent of collective endeavour which can be effectively organized under Dominion control.'[1]

What is true of Canada may often be true of any other country which has deliberately chosen federal government and to which federal government is, in truth, appropriate.

8

The effect of the exercise of the war power upon federal government has been tremendous. Some indication of this has already been given in the chapter on public finance. It has been the experience of all four federations that war, and particularly the wars of 1914 and 1939, has made a greater difference in the financial relations of general and regional governments than any other single factor. It is not necessary to repeat the details of that chapter here. It is enough to say that in all four federations war has placed the general governments in a position of financial predominance, a position from which, in peace-time, they have been slow or unwilling or unable to retreat.

One equally striking result is the increase in the power of the executive—be it a cabinet or a single man—in war-time, and, as it is the executive which, of all institutions in a federal government, is by nature unitary and centralizing in its tendencies, the effect upon the working of federal government is important. Not merely does the general government increase in power, as I have shown, but within the general government itself the executive power is magnified as against the legislative. Some of this increase is, if not welcomed, at

---

[1] *Rowell-Sirois Report*, Book I, p. 97.

any rate acquiesced in by the legislature, for it delegates, of necessity, wide powers of regulation to the chief executive.

Even in the United States where, in normal times, such delegation might be considered unconstitutional, the necessities of war are held to validate it.[1] Professor Corwin writes that in the war of 1914–18, the entire life of the people of the United States was 'brought under the control of the government and their property put at its disposal on a previously unparalleled scale. And, in the main, this regimentation of the nation was accomplished by Congress through the simple device of transferring to the President its legislative powers'.[2] He goes on to give examples of this kind of delegation. The most striking, in his view, was the Lever Food and Fuel Control Act of August 17, 1917, which gave the President power to regulate by license the importation, manufacture, storage, mining and distribution of necessaries; the power to requisition foods, feeds, fuels and other necessaries; the power to purchase, store and sell certain foods; the power to take over factories, refineries, pipe lines, mines or other plants, and operate the same; the power to fix a minimum price for wheat; the power to limit, regulate or prohibit the use of food materials in the production of alcoholic beverages; the power to fix the price of coal and coke and to regulate the production, sale and distribution thereof. It is astonishing enough to see what a revolution war makes in the division of powers between general and regional governments, but it is even more astonishing to see the revolution made in the separation of powers in the United States. What has been written does not by any means cover the main part of the delegation of power to the President in the first war. And what was done in the first war was done still further in the second.

Thus, in the first war, an act authorized the President to take over and operate any factories or industries necessary for the production of military supplies if the owners refused to produce war supplies for the government.[3] In September 1940, before the United States was at war, an almost identical act was passed again. Within a fortnight of the United States being at war, the First War Powers Act delegated to the President complete discretion to regulate or prohibit any transactions whatsoever involving any property in which any foreign nation or citizen of a foreign nation has any interest. There was granted to him also power to order factories to produce certain specified articles and nothing else; he could control their supply of raw materials and their whole selling activity. An act of October 2, 1942, authorized and directed the President to issue a general order stabilizing prices, wages and salaries affecting the cost of living, subject to certain limitations and principles laid down by Congress in delegating the power. And most interesting of all perhaps was the Lease-Lend Act, passed in

[1] See C. A. Berdahl, *War Powers of the Executive in the United States*.
[2] *The President: Office and Powers*, p. 190.
[3] See further Corwin, *Total War and the Constitution*.

March 1941, before the United States was at war. By this act the President was empowered 'when he deems it in the interests of national defence' to authorize the manufacture or procurement of any defence article 'for the government of any country whose defense the President deems vital to the defense of the United States'. The terms upon which this aid is to be given are to be 'those which the President deems satisfactory', and in return the United States is to receive payments or repayments in kind or 'any other direct or indirect benefit which the President deems satisfactory'.

It is not possible to enlarge on this topic here. The examples of the increase in executive power by delegation from the legislature would fill many pages. What has been said illustrates, however, the enormous change in the operation of federal government which war and even the threat of war brings about. What has been done in the United States has been done as much in Canada[1] and Australia, but it attracts less attention, perhaps, because the notion of delegating wide powers to the executive in war-time is one commonly accepted under the system of cabinet government as it operates in the United Kingdom and in other members of the British Commonwealth. None the less it needs emphasis where the federal members of the Commonwealth are concerned, for it adds one more strong unifying factor to those which already operate in war.

There is one final aspect of this question which is most important. War leads to the transformation of a federal government into a unified state, with its plurality and multiplicity of jurisdictions coordinated for the unitary and totalitarian process of war. What is to happen in this complex system of unified governmental control when peace returns? The powers of the general government in law immediately contract. The structure must collapse unless by co-operation between regional and general governments some part or the greater part of it can be preserved. The post-war years for a federal government possess perils and problems more complicated therefore than those which confront a unitary government.

It was with these problems in mind that the Labour government of Australia in 1942 endeavoured to obtain for the Commonwealth powers to deal with a variety of matters which in war-time lie, in whole or in part, within the powers of the Commonwealth but which thereafter would fall from its grasp. The topics envisaged included the reinstatement and advancement of ex-service men and women, employment, unemployment, profiteering, prices, production and distribution of goods, marketing, trusts, combines, monopolies and family allowances.[2] Conferences were held between representatives of the Commonwealth and state governments, at which representatives

---

[1] The power of delegation to the Governor-General in Canada and his power further to delegate was judicially considered and upheld by the Supreme Court of Canada in *References as to Regulations in relation to Chemicals* (1943) S.C.R. 1.

[2] See above, Chapter VII, p. 143.

of the opposition also were present. An agreement was made that the states should delegate power over these subjects to the Commonwealth for a period of five years after the cessation of hostilities. The state legislatures failed to fulfil the agreement. In 1944, 1946 and 1948 the Commonwealth submitted proposals for constitutional amendment to the people by which power over most of these matters should be transferred from the states to the Commonwealth. The amendments save in the sphere of social services were not carried and the Australian parliament had to face the work of reconstruction with little more power than it had possessed heretofore. Yet if it be true that the problems which follow wars are as difficult and as serious as the problems of war itself, then there is need in all federal systems for providing some machinery to deal with them.

It need not be assumed, however, that a wholesale transfer of powers from the regional to the general governments is necessary if reconstruction is to be efficiently carried through.[1] War produces methods of co-operation which can survive, in some degree, into the peace. General governments, moreover, possess in some of the federations and notably in Switzerland and Australia, considerable powers of control over economic and social life, as I have already explained. Nor are the powers of Congress in the United States so limited as is sometimes suggested. There is often a good deal of exaggeration about the lack of powers of the general government to deal with these matters of economic and social reconstruction. In no case, except perhaps Canada, is this lack of power so great as to prevent a general government which is determined to exercise its full powers from going a long way towards economic and social reconstruction. It is true that a good deal must be left to the regions. Even so, the people of these regions will make demands upon their governments to regulate many activities which, before a war, they would not have wished to see regulated. It has been asserted that 'the war (of 1914) hastened considerably the acceptance of the philosophy of the social service state in Canada'.[2] People learn in war-time how governments can organize their lives, and if they wish it to continue in some form after a war, they are at liberty, in a federation, to demand it of their regional as of their general governments.

---

[1] The High Court of Australia recognized that 'the defence power includes not only a power to prepare for war and to prosecute war, but also a power to wind up after a war and restore conditions of peace. . . .' *Dawson* v. *Commonwealth* (1946–47) 73 C.L.R. 157, per Latham C. J. at p. 176. See also Dixon J. at pp. 83–84. But there were limits to it, and the Court unanimously invalidated certain controls, including petrol rationing, in 1949 in *R.* v. *Foster*; *Wagner* v. *Gall* and *Collins* v. *Hunter*. See article by G. Sawer in 23 *Australian Law Journal* 255. For some interesting divisions of opinion on this aspect of the war power in the United States Supreme Court see *Woods* v. *Miller* (1947) 333 U.S. 138 and *Ludecke* v. *Watkins* (1948), 335 U.S. 160.
[2] *Rowell-Sirois Report*, Book I, p. 111.

PART V

REVIEW

Chapter XI

FEDERAL GOVERNMENT:
RIGID OR FLEXIBLE?

1

THE point has come at which a brief review of the working of federal government may be attempted. Perhaps the best way in which to begin this review is to consider how far federal governments have shown themselves capable of being adapted to the needs of the communities for which they were established. It is a common criticism of federal government that it is too rigid, too conservative, too difficult to alter; that it is consequently behind the times. It is important to ask whether our study of the working of federal government supports this general criticism, and further, whether such excessive rigidity and conservatism, if it exists, is an inevitable consequence of a federal system.

There are in fact several methods by which changes may be brought about in federal governments. Some references to their operation have been made from time to time in previous chapters. I will deal with them one by one here in order to expose the processes by which change occurs. We may begin with the most obvious method—the amendment of the constitution. It has been the nature of the amending process itself in federations which has led political scientists to classify federal constitutions as rigid. A rigid constitution, they say, is one which enjoys an authority superior to that of the other laws of the state, and can be changed only by a method different from that whereby those other laws are enacted or repealed. Flexible constitutions, on the other hand, are those which stand upon an equal footing with other laws and which can be changed by the same process as other laws.[1] On this definition, the Constitutions of the United States, Switzerland, Canada and Australia would be classed as rigid, for they are intended to be supreme over the legislatures—general and regional —which they create or recognize, and they cannot be altered by these legislatures acting through the ordinary process of legislation.

Granted, then, that the process of amending the constitutions of the federations is a different process from that of amending their ordinary laws, has it proved in practice to be not only more difficult, but unduly difficult? To this question no generalized answer can be given.

[1] Bryce, *Studies in History and Jurisprudence*, Vol. I, p. 167.

Federal governments have had different experiences. In Switzerland, where amendment of the Constitution requires always the consent of a majority of the electors voting in a referendum, and of a majority of the electors voting in a majority of the cantons; and, on some occasions, the consent of the general legislature also,[1] the process has been used frequently and successfully. The powers of the general government have been increased from time to time to deal with new needs in the realms of economics, social services, defence and public finance, as the preceding chapters have abundantly illustrated. Some figures illustrate what has happened.[2] Since 1874, when the Constitution of 1848 was submitted to a general revision, there had occurred, up to 1962, 125 plebiscites in Switzerland upon constitutional questions. Of these sixty-four were referenda upon constitutional amendments submitted to the people by the general legislature. Forty-nine of these proposals were accepted. This is a high proportion indeed. Of the remaining plebiscites, forty-nine were proposals for amendment of the Constitution presented on the initiative of 50,000 voters. Seven only of these were accepted by the people. Then there were thirteen cases where the general legislature offered proposals as substitutes for those offered on the initiative of 50,000 voters, and in nine out of these thirteen cases, the proposals were accepted. It seems clear that in Switzerland proposals for amendment which commended themselves to the general legislature have in most cases been accepted by the people. If the Swiss Constitution is rigid, the Swiss people are flexible. They have been ready to use an amending process which, from its careful safeguards, might have proved a conservative and obstructive force, to adapt their Constitution to what they conceived to be the needs of their time.

By instructive contrast the people of Australia, with an amending process which is substantially the same as the Swiss and was borrowed from Switzerland, have refused on most occasions to alter their Constitution. From the foundation of the Commonwealth in 1901 until 1963 proposed constitutional amendments were submitted to the people by referendum on twelve separate occasions[3]—1906, 1910, 1911, 1913, 1919, 1926, 1928, 1937, 1944, 1946, 1948 and 1951.[4] Only four were carried by the requisite majority of all electors voting and of a majority of electors in a majority of states. Of these four, the first, in 1906, merely altered the date of Senate elections and was agreed to by majorities in all the states; the second, in 1910, enabled the Commonwealth to take over state debts irrespective of the date at which they were contracted, in place of the provision that the Commonwealth might take over the state debts in existence at the time of

---

[1] Swiss Constitution, Arts. 118–23.

[2] I base these figures on information in *Statistiches Jahrbuch der Schweiz*.

[3] In all, twenty-four separate proposals were put forward.

[4] Details of proposed amendments up to 1928 are given in the *Report of the Royal Commission on the Australian Constitution*, 1929, pp. 231–4.

federation, and this amendment was approved in all states except New South Wales; the third—the amendment validating the Financial Agreement of 1927—was most important.[1] The fourth, in 1946, confirmed the Commonwealth's power to legislate upon certain social services and was agreed to by majorities in all the states. This amendment, with that of 1928, constitute the two important affirmative results of the referendum.

But the negatives were impressive. From 1911 onwards successive proposals were made to increase the powers of the Commonwealth in the economic field and they were successively rejected. In 1911 it was proposed that the Commonwealth should be empowered to deal with trade and commerce generally without the restriction to 'inter-state' which the Constitution imposed; with corporations; with labour and employment, including wages and conditions of labour in any trade, industry or calling, and the prevention and settlement of industrial disputes in relation to employment on state railways; and with combinations and monopolies. These proposals were all rejected by a majority of all the electors voting and by a majority of the electors voting in all the states except Western Australia. In 1913 a similar set of proposals was submitted to the electors. They were again rejected by a majority of all the electors voting, but there were majorities in favour of the proposals in three states—Queensland, South Australia and Western Australia—and majorities against in the remaining three. In 1919 it was proposed to extend the powers of the Commonwealth over industrial disputes and monopolies. Again a majority of all the electors rejected the proposals, but in the three states of Victoria, Queensland and Western Australia majorities were cast in favour. In 1926 attempts to extend the Commonwealth's powers in regard to the settlement of industrial disputes; to empower it to deal with corporations and monopolies; and in addition to give it certain powers to maintain essential services should there be any attempt to interrupt them, were rejected by majorities of all the electors, though in two states, New South Wales and Queensland, majorities voted in favour. In 1937 proposals to give the Commonwealth increased power in regard to marketing and aviation were defeated. In the case of marketing, there was a majority against it of all electors and in all states. In the case of aviation, there was actually a majority in favour of it out of the total of electors voting, but there were majorities in favour in two states only, Victoria and Queensland, and the proposal therefore was rejected. In 1944 came the sweeping proposals already discussed by which powers over all important economic affairs and most social affairs were to be transferred to the Commonwealth. They failed to obtain a majority of all the electors voting, and they were approved in two states only—Western Australia and South Australia. In 1946, though the proposal for social services was

[1] See above, Chapter VI, p. 99

accepted, the other two—marketing of primary products and conditions of employment—were accepted in three states only, although, like aviation in 1937, each had a majority of the electors in its favour. In 1948 the proposal for rents and prices was defeated in all the states. In 1951 a proposal to give the Commonwealth power to make laws with respect to communists or communism was rejected by a majority of electors and by majorities in each of three states.

It can be seen that, with the exception of the proposals of 1910, 1928 and 1946 (social services), each proposal to extend the powers of the Commonwealth has been rejected, and in all cases, except three, this rejection was registered by a majority of all the electors voting. This will seem a surprising fact to those who have read in previous chapters of the extent to which the Commonwealth controls economic affairs in Australia and of the dominance in the sphere of public finance which it has attained. The explanation is that the Commonwealth has increased its powers and position by other methods than that of the amending process. The majority of the Australian electorate, in so far as it has expressed its views upon the matter in referendum, has been, in general, opposed to the encroachment of the Commonwealth upon the sphere reserved by the constitution to the states. In this respect while the Swiss electorate has been liberal in its use of a rigid amending process, the Australian electorate has been conservative.

Whereas in Australia attempts were made to obtain alterations in the Constitution to extend the powers of the Commonwealth parliament over these matters, in the United States no comparable attempt has been made to alter the distribution between the general and state governments. Even President Franklin D. Roosevelt at the height of his powers never proposed such an alteration. Only one change of note in the sphere of public finance can be recorded. That is the XVIth Amendment which removed from Congress certain restrictions upon its power to levy income tax.[1] But it would be a mistake to conclude that the powers of the general government had not been extended by other constitutional amendments. To do so would be to overlook or ignore an important sentence which appears in the XIIIth, XIVth, XVth and XVIIIth Amendments, among others: 'Congress shall have power to enforce this article by appropriate legislation.' In each of these cases some increase of power was given to the general government. Amendment XIII (1865) abolished slavery and gave Congress power to enforce this abolition; Amendment XIV (1868) applied the 'Due Process Clause' to the states in the words: 'No State shall make or enforce any law which shall abridge the privileges or immunities of citizens of the United States; nor shall any State deprive any person of life, liberty or property, without due process of law; nor deny to any person within its jurisdiction the

[1] See Chapter VI, p. 101.

equal protection of the laws.' If the amendment had said no more than this, the powers of Congress would not have been increased, though the jurisdiction of the Supreme Court would have been extended into spheres of state activity which it had not been authorized to review formerly. But the amendment actually gives Congress power to enforce its provisions; and a study of the provisions shows that Congress is authorized, if a state fails to observe the prohibitions placed upon it, to make laws on many matters which normally lie in the very heart of state administration. Congress is entitled to enforce due process upon the states; only the Supreme Court can enforce due process upon the general government. Amendment XVIII, the Prohibition Amendment (1919), gave a concurrent power to Congress and the states to enforce its provisions, but the increase in the power of Congress was not less great on that account. It became authorized to exercise a police power and to enforce a criminal law which formerly had belonged largely to the states.[1] These amendments all deserve emphasis, the more so because their potential effects have not yet been fully exploited. But at the same time it is necessary to admit that the predominant influence in increasing the powers of the general government in the United States has not so far been the process of constitutional amendment.

Yet it may be doubted whether the amending process in the United States is more rigid in its requirements than that of Switzerland, and consequently of Australia. Amendments may be initiated, as I have explained earlier,[2] at the instance of two-thirds of both Houses of Congress or by a convention called by Congress at the request of the legislatures of two-thirds of the states. Amendments initiated by Congress or by a convention may be ratified either by the legislatures of three-fourths of the states or by conventions in three-fourths of the states, as the one or the other mode of ratification may be proposed by Congress. In practice all amendments so far have been initiated by Congress. In all cases except the Twenty-first—that repealing prohibition—they have been submitted for the approval of the legislatures of the states. The Twenty-first amendment was submitted to conventions in the states. There are perhaps some signs of a greater rigidity in this process than in that of Switzerland and Australia. The legislatures of the states may be more tenacious of their powers than the people of the states; the three-fourths majority is more difficult to obtain than the simple majority required in Switzerland and Australia. But on the whole it would seem that it is the conservatism of the people, not the rigidity of the amending process, which explains the relatively few changes made in the American Constitution so far as the division of powers between general and state governments is concerned. When Congress chooses to propose an amendment it is

[1] Nor was this police power entirely withdrawn when the XVIIIth Amendment was repealed in 1933.
[2] See above, Chapter IV, p. 55.

usually successful. Out of the twenty-eight amendments proposed by Congress twenty-two have been accepted. When it does propose an amendment, action upon it has not been unduly slow in recent years. Six amendments came into effect in the twenty years from 1913 to 1933, although only three had been adopted in the hundred years before 1913. Of the six recent amendments, the first, concerning the income tax, was proposed by Congress in 1909 and proclaimed in 1913; the second, concerning direct election of Senators, was proposed in 1912 and proclaimed in 1913, the third, imposing prohibition, was proposed in 1917 and proclaimed in 1919; the fourth, granting votes to women, was proposed in 1919 and proclaimed in 1920; the fifth, adjusting the terms of office of the President and Vice-President and of Congress, was proposed in 1932 and proclaimed in 1933; and the sixth, repealing the prohibition amendment, was proposed in February 1933 and proclaimed in November 1933. After an interval of nearly twenty years, another amendment, the Twenty-second, relating to presidential terms of office, was proclaimed in 1951. But it had been proposed by Congress on March 24, 1947 and took nearly four years to come into effect.

Canada provided until 1949 the extreme example of a federation with, in law, no amending process under its own control. And even now the parliament of the United Kingdom alone has power to alter the British North America Act in respect of the division of powers between Dominion and provinces. Of all the amendments made in the Canadian Constitution up to 1963, two only related to the division of powers. The first, in 1940, transferred unemployment insurance to the general parliament, and the second, in 1951, gave it power in relation to old-age pensions. There were two amendments— those of 1907 and 1930—adjusting the amount of the grants payable by the Dominion to the provinces. For the rest the Dominion has not succeeded in persuading the provinces to transfer any other powers. An unsolved question in Canada is how much consent is requisite before the Dominion parliament may ask the United Kingdom parliament to legislate and before that parliament may itself feel free to accede to the request. At present it would seem that any amendment to which Quebec objected, would not be pursued. The same is probably true of Ontario. This veto by a single province imposes a greater rigidity in practice upon the amending process in Canada than is imposed by law in the other three federations. Yet it seems unlikely that a change will be made in the process unless very strong safeguards for Quebec at any rate are made part of a new amending process.

The case of Canada raises in the extreme form the argument used against the amending processes in these federal systems—that they make it possible for the will of a majority to be obstructed by a minority. It is explained how, in the United States, for example, thirteen states with a combined population less than that of the single state of New York, can prevent the remaining thirty-five states from realizing their will; that one-tenth of the population can obstruct nine-tenths.[1] Similar calculations can be made for Australia and Switzerland. But this is only part of the question. For one thing, federal government is based upon the principle that government by a bare majority of the people is not the only way in which to govern well and in some cases is equivalent to bad government. Majorities of regions have a significance which majorities of people have not; two-thirds and three-quarters majorities have a significance which bare majorities have not. There is, of course, no special magic in these figures, though people sometimes speak as if there were. But a combination of these types of majorities may produce a result in a federal government which is wiser than that provided by a simple majority of people. Such a system can be abused. But on the experience of the three systems of Switzerland, the United States and Australia no evidence to that effect seems to be found. The Swiss have used their powers of change freely. In Australia in three cases only has a majority of all the electors found itself obstructed by a minority.[2] In the United States the significant fact is that Congress has been slow to demand changes in the division of powers and that there has in fact been no case where a tiny minority has obstructed the will of the majority. The reverence of Americans for their Constitution has imposed a check upon the initiative of Congress far greater than that provided by a minority of thirteen states. In Canada admittedly the veto of Quebec and Ontario is great in practice, though in their case it is the veto not of sparsely populated provinces, but of the two most populous of all. None the less the need for some method of amending the Canadian Constitution in Canada and by Canadian majorities of some appropriate kind, is urgent. And the reason for this urgency becomes clear when we turn to consider another method by which constitutions are adapted and developed.

2

It was remarked earlier that although the general governments of the United States and Australia had been able to extend their powers over new fields in the course of years, this process had not been predominantly the result of explicit amendments to the Constitution. What, then, had made it possible? It was the result, in large measure, of the interpretation of the constitution by the courts. In the view of the judges of the Supreme Court of the United States and of the High Court of Australia, the original constitutions of these federations had conferred power upon their general governments to undertake legislation and administration in many new spheres of economic

[1] See C. A. Beard, *American Government and Politics*, 8th ed., pp. 35–36.
[2] The aviation proposal of 1937 and the marketing and conditions of employment proposals of 1946 referred to above, p. 212.

and social life. That is, of course, a general statement. It is necessary to emphasize that the process was not always continuous. There were ebbs and flows in the tide of judicial opinion. But if the position to-day is compared with that of a hundred years ago in the United States, for example, it can be seen that the general government has been able to regulate activities over a much wider range and that this exercise of its powers has been possible not only because the legislature wished it, but because the judiciary also upheld it. In Canada, on the other hand, the net result of judicial interpretation has been to restrict the sphere of action of the general government. Here again it is important to emphasize that there are exceptions to the general statement. But the trend of judicial review has been towards limiting the powers of the general government. Canada, therefore, has been doubly restricted. Like Australia and the United States, she has obtained comparatively little alteration from the amending process itself, but, unlike them, she has obtained no room for expansion from the exercise of the function of judicial review by the courts.

The Judicial Committee of the Privy Council until 1950 had the last word in deciding what was meant by the division of powers drawn up in 1867 and embodied substantially in Sections 91 and 92 of the British North America Act. In the seventy years from 1867 to 1937 the Judicial Committee decided about 120 cases involving disputes about the meaning of the British North America Act. Many of these are not relevant to our discussion of the division of powers. Of those that are relevant it is not possible to attempt a careful analysis here. The most that can be done is to recall some of the main lines of development, to which indeed incidental reference has been made from time to time in previous chapters.

The major task before the Judicial Committee has been to reconcile the words of sections 91 and 92 of the Constitution. Section 91, it may be recalled, gave to the Dominion power 'to make laws for the peace, order and good government of Canada, in relation to all matters not coming within the classes of subjects by this act assigned exclusively to the legislatures of the provinces'. This means that the residue of powers not expressly given to the provinces was reserved to the Dominion. Then there follows in section 91 an enumeration of 29 classes of subjects to illustrate but not to restrict the scope of the general words empowering the Dominion to make laws for peace, order and good government. In section 92 certain classes of subjects were enumerated and the provinces were given exclusive power to make laws in relation to matters coming within these classes of subjects. When these two sections are placed side by side difficulties arise. To begin with, if the Dominion makes a law for the peace, order and good government of Canada it is almost certain that it will affect, in some way, matters assigned exclusively to the provinces in section 92. Conversely laws made by the provinces on their exclusive field would frequently affect the peace, order and good government of Canada, or might overlap some topic actually enumerated in section 91 as falling within the Dominion's sphere. When the conflicts occur, which power is to prevail? This has been the dilemma before the Privy Council since 1867. One or two examples are worth quoting to illustrate the way in which the dilemma has been faced.

In 1882 the Privy Council had to decide the validity of an act of the Dominion parliament which forbade the sale of intoxicating liquor in municipalities which chose by 'local option' to apply the provisions of the act.[1] Now, from one point of view, this act interfered with property and civil rights in the provinces. On the other hand the Dominion parliament asserted that the object of the Act was to promote public order throughout the Dominion. The Privy Council upheld the act. It said that legislation genuinely 'deemed to be necessary or expedient for national safety or for political reasons' or 'designed for the promotion of public order, safety or morals', fell within the power to make laws for peace, order and good government. They admitted that such legislation inevitably would affect property and civil rights in an incidental way. Thus 'the true nature and character' of the legislation in the particular instance under discussion must always be determined in order to ascertain the class of subject to which it really belongs. Here was a decision which favoured the primacy of the power of the Dominion to make laws for peace, order and good government. It appeared to favour the view that if the Dominion parliament genuinely asserted its view that its legislation was for the peace, order and good government of Canada, the courts should accept the legislation.

Had this line of interpretation prevailed, the powers of the Dominion parliament of Canada would have been held to cover a sphere much wider indeed than that made available to the general legislatures of the United States or Australia by the judicial interpretation of their supreme tribunals. But in fact the trend in Canada was soon reversed. In 1896[2] the Privy Council had to decide the validity of an act passed by the legislature of Ontario which regulated the liquor trade in similar terms to that passed by the Dominion and held valid in 1882. The Privy Council upheld the Ontario act and in the course of its judgement asserted a different view of the force of the general words 'peace, order and good government' in section 91. It decided that the Dominion when legislating under the 'peace, order and good government' clause 'has no authority to legislate upon any class of subjects which is exclusively assigned to the provincial legislatures by section 92'. If the Dominion were legislating under the *enumerated heads* of section 91, then it could validly enact legislation which affected subjects assigned exclusively to the provinces in section 92.

---

[1] *Russell v. The Queen* (1882) 7 A.C. 829.

[2] *Attorney-General of Ontario* v. *Attorney-General of Canada* (1896) A.C. 348.

But apart from these circumstances the primacy of the general power was denied. It was not completely expelled. It could be invoked for 'such matters as are of unquestionably Canadian interest and importance'.

The justification of this interpretation was and is that it maintains a division of power between Dominion and provinces and forbids the steady encroachment of the Dominion legislature upon the provincial field by the use of the wide and vague term 'peace, order and good government'. 'If it were once conceded,' said the Privy Council, 'that the parliament of Canada has authority to make laws applicable to the whole Dominion, in relation to matters which in each province are substantially of local or private interest, upon the assumption that these matters also concern the peace, order and good government of the Dominion, there is hardly a subject enumerated in section 92 upon which it might not legislate, to the exclusion of the provincial legislatures.'[1]

As a result of this decision, then, the powers of the Dominion came to be restricted to the topics enumerated in section 91 with an exceptional power available in emergency under the general clause. This result need not of itself, however, have restricted the Dominion very closely. If the enumerated heads of section 91 could have been interpreted widely and the enumerated heads of section 92 narrowly, and if the requirements needed to constitute an emergency had been moderately and broadly conceived, Dominion powers might have been elastic, while provincial powers could have been safeguarded from gradual extinction. This has not happened. Instead the head of 'property and civil rights in the province' in section 92, has been widely construed, the head 'the regulation of trade and commerce', given to the Dominion in section 91, has been narrowly construed,[2] and the general power to make laws for peace, order and good government has been confined to occasions of emergency legislation in the stress of great national crises.[3] How extreme these emergencies must be is illustrated by the decisions of 1937 in the cases involving the Bennett New Deal legislation, where it was held that the economic dislocations with which the legislation purported to deal did not amount to an emergency of such extremity that the general power could be validly invoked to justify the legislation. The general power is operative only in temporary and overwhelming emergencies such as war, pestilence or famine.[4] 'Temporary evils of great magnitude may be grappled with by Dominion legislation under the general clause of section 91 but an enduring and deep-rooted social malaise, which requires the mobilizing of efforts on a nation-wide scale to

---

[1] At pp. 360–1.
[2] See discussion in Chapter VII, at pp. 129–33 above.
[3] See, e.g., *Toronto Electric Commissioners* v. *Snider* [1925] A.C. 396 at p. 412.
[4] *Attorney-General of Canada* v. *Attorney-General of Ontario* [1937] A.C. 326 and ibid. [1937] A.C. 355.

deal with it, is beyond the power of the Dominion unless it is comprised in the enumerated heads of section 91.'[1]

Such has been the general trend of judicial interpretation in Canada. But it is important to mention that there have been cases now and then when a wider view of the Dominion's powers prevailed. In the years from 1930 to 1935 some decisions suggested that the Privy Council was beginning to modify its views. In 1932 it upheld the Dominion's power to deal with radio[2] and aviation[3] in judgements which adopted a generous interpretation of Dominion powers, while in the case *In re Silver Bros.*,[4] to which reference was made in the chapter on public finance, it gave priority to Dominion taxation over provincial taxation when the claims of both came into conflict. The keynote of the trend in these cases[5] was exemplified in a passage from the judgement in the *Aeronautics Case* where the Privy Council said: 'But while the Courts should be jealous in upholding the charter of the Provinces as enacted in section 92 it must no less be borne in mind that the real object of the Act was to give the central government those high functions and almost sovereign powers by which uniformity of legislation might be secured on all questions which were of common concern to all the Provinces as members of a constituent whole.'[6] These words suggested that the need for uniformity, or the fact that matters were of common concern to Canada, might be sufficient to justify legislation under the general clause of section 91. But the decisions of 1937 ruled out any such hope.

I have dealt with the trend of Canadian interpretation because it appears to illustrate well the whole problem of judicial review. It shows that the choice before the judges is difficult. There is little help to be found in referring to the intentions of the founders of the Constitution, for in the case of Canada strong historical arguments can be adduced on both sides. But Canada illustrates also the fact that the judges have a discretion. They decide how widely property and civil rights should be construed; they decide what constitutes an emergency of sufficient gravity to justify the exercise of the general clause in section 91. In matters like this everything depends upon opinion and a great deal upon the personal views of judges concerning what is politically wise or what is necessary. On this aspect of the matter there has been much criticism of the Privy Council's decisions. It has been said that where they have had a discretion they have exercised it to narrow the powers of the Dominion, whereas it would have been wiser for them to use it to widen these powers. And it is here that critics point to the decisions of the Supreme Court of the

[1] *Rowell-Sirois Report*, Book I, p. 249.
[2] *In re Regulation of Radio Communication* [1932] A.C. 304.
[3] *In re Regulation of Aeronautics* [1932] A.C. 304.
[4] [1932] A.C. 514.
[5] Other cases are *Edwards* v. *Attorney-General of Canada* [1930] A.C. 124 and *British Coal Corporation* v. *The King* [1935] A.C. 495.
[6] [1932] A.C. 54, at pp. 70–71.

United States and the High Court of Australia which they believe show more wisdom in exercising the discretion admittedly and perhaps inevitably conferred upon judges who have to interpret constitutions.

It is not possible to enter upon a detailed examination of the decisions of the American and Australian courts. One or two examples may be given to illustrate points. To begin with, some decisions in the United States may be mentioned in order to show how discretion has been exercised there in relation to a problem of interpretation similar in some respects to that just discussed in Canada.

In the Constitution of the United States, Congress was empowered 'to lay and collect taxes, imposts and excises, to pay the debts and provide for the common defence and general welfare of the United States'. Now what was the effect of this reference to providing for 'the general welfare of the United States'? 'Madison asserted it amounted to no more than reference to the other powers enumerated in the subsequent clauses of the same section, that, as the United States is a government of limited and enumerated powers, the grant of power to tax and spend for the general national welfare must be confined to the enumerated legislative fields committed to the Congress. In this view the phrase is mere tautology, for taxation and appropriation are or may be necessary incidents of the exercise of any of the enumerated legislative powers. Hamilton, on the other hand, maintained the clause confers a power separate and distinct from those later enumerated, is not restricted in meaning by the grant of them, and Congress consequently has a substantive power to tax and to appropriate, limited only by the requirement that it shall be exercised to provide for the general welfare of the United States.'[1] It can be seen that both contentions are reasonable. Each has had strong support. But until 1936 the Supreme Court had not been required to decide which was the true construction. In that year it had to decide upon the validity of the Agricultural Adjustment Act which included in its provisions appropriations for agriculture. The court decided in favour of the view which Hamilton had supported. 'The power of congress to authorize expenditure of public moneys for public purposes,' the Court said, 'is not limited by the direct grants of legislative power found in the Constitution.'[2]

But the exercise of discretion does not end there. May not Congress, under pretext of taxing and appropriating, actually attempt to legislate for some matter which it is not authorized to regulate? For it is a power to raise and spend money for the general welfare and not to legislate apart from such raising and spending, which the general welfare clause conferred. The court must therefore decide in a particular case whether an act is in truth a taxing and appropriating

[1] This passage is extracted from the judgement of the Supreme Court in *U.S.* v. *Butler* to which reference is made below.
[2] *U.S.* v. *Butler* (1936) 297 U.S. 1, at p. 66.

act, or whether it is a regulating act. And, further still, if it is in truth a
taxing and appropriating act only, the Court must decide whether its
objects are for the general welfare or not—obviously a matter of
opinion. Thus, in 1936, in the case just mentioned, the Court decided,
as I have said, that Congress might appropriate and tax for matters
beyond those upon which it was given powers to legislate, but it went
on to say by a majority of six to three that the Agricultural Adjustment Act was not a mere appropriating and taxing act. 'It is a statutory plan to regulate and control agricultural production, a matter
beyond the powers delegated to the Federal Government.'[1] The
majority therefore declared it invalid. The minority—Justices Stone,
Cardozo and Brandeis—took the opposite view. They held that the
act was an appropriating act and that any regulation involved in its
operation was purely incidental to its main purpose of aiding agriculture. 'The power of Congress to spend is inseparable from persuasion
to action over which Congress has no legislative control. . . . It is a
contradiction in terms to say that there is power to spend for the
national welfare, while rejecting any power to impose conditions
reasonably adapted to the attainment of the end which alone would
justify the expenditure '[2]

Such was the difference of opinion over the A.A.A. in 1936. It
was found again in 1937 when the Court had to deal with the Social
Security Act, but on this occasion the minority had become the
majority. The Court decided that appropriations and taxation for
unemployment insurance and old-age pensions fell within the power
of Congress to provide for the general welfare.[3] It emphasized that it
was not always easy to know whether an appropriation was for the
general welfare or not. But it asserted that Congress should be given
the benefit in doubtful cases. 'Nor is the concept of the general welfare
static. Needs that were narrow or parochial a century ago may be
interwoven in our day with the well-being of the nation. What is
critical or urgent changes with the times.'[4]

One final example from the United States. In 1923 the Supreme
Court declared invalid a Minimum Wage Act passed by Congress
for the District of Columbia on the ground that it interfered unduly
with freedom of contract contrary to the Fifth Amendment of the
Constitution which had provided that Congress had no power to
deprive a person of life, liberty or property contrary to due process of
law.[5] Freedom to buy and sell labour unrestricted by law was held to
be part of the notion of liberty. In 1937 the Supreme Court overruled
this decision by a majority of five to four, and upheld minimum wage
legislation. It asserted a different view of liberty, a view which, in

[1] At p. 68.
[2] Stone, J., at pp. 83 and 85.
[3] *Steward Machine Co.* v. *Davis* (1937) 301 U.S. 548, and *Helvering* v. *Davis* (1937) 301 U.S.
619.
[4] *Helvering* v. *Davis* (1937) 301 U.S. 619, at p. 641.
[5] *Adkins* v. *Children's Hospital*, 261 U.S. 525.

other cases, it had also asserted from time to time. The liberty which the Constitution safeguards, it said, is 'liberty in a social organization which requires the protection of law against the evils which menace the health, safety, morals and welfare of the people'.[1]

Or take two examples from Australia which illustrate the discretion which judges have and the room there is for justifiable differences of opinion. From the establishment of the High Court of Australia in 1903 until 1920, a majority of the court maintained the principle that the federal nature of the constitution required that the Commonwealth should in no way interfere with the states in the execution of their powers and vice versa. Commonwealth arbitration awards were not to apply to state railway servants, for example.[2] Commonwealth officers were not liable to state income tax.[3] This was the principle of the immunity of state instrumentalities, and it was adopted from the decisions of the Supreme Court of the United States. But its application in particular cases raised difficulties; the further the immunity was extended the more crippling the restriction became. In 1920 the High Court reversed its decision.[4] It adopted a principle of interpretation which gave fuller scope to the Commonweath's powers. They were not to be restricted in future by implied prohibitions or governing principles not explicitly enunciated in the Constitution. The Supreme Court of the United States still maintains the doctrine of the immunity of instrumentalities, but its application of the doctrine is becoming narrower and less reverent.[5]

Then there were the cases involving the defence power in Australia in 1942 and 1943. In one case[6] two justices held that the proposal of the Commonwealth to take over the state income tax machinery was not authorized under the defence power; three justices held that it was. In another case two justices held that the defence power authorized the Commonwealth to make certain regulations affecting enrolment at universities; three justices held that it did not.[7]

Many examples of this kind can be quoted. Those already given are sufficient to illustrate how far the flexibility of a federation depends upon the manner in which judges exercise their function. They have it in their power in many cases to adapt the Constitution to the changing needs of the time. They can do this without violating their oath to the Constitution. The words they have to interpret are flexible; there is a wealth of judicial precedents upon which they can fall back; and they are none of them bound irrevocably by their previous decisions. They can overrule themselves.

Yet it is wise to recall what the function of a court is and how far

[1] *West Coast Hotel* v. *Parrish* (1937) 300 U.S. 379, at p. 391.
[2] *State Railway Servants Case* (1906) 4 C.L.R. 488.
[3] *D'Emden* v. *Pedder* (1904) 1 C.L.R. 91.
[4] *Amalgamated Society of Engineers* v. *Adelaide Steamship Co.* 28 C.L.R. 129.
[5] See the flippant remark of Frankfurter, J. in *Graves* v. *New York* (1939) 306 U.S. 646, at p. 489.
[6] *South Australia* v. *The Commonwealth* (1942) 65 C.L.R. 373.
[7] *R.* v. *University of Sydney*, ex parte *Drummond* (1943) 67 C.L.R. 95.

the judges, the politicians and the people should feel entitled to expect of a court that it should undertake the function of adapting a constitution to the needs of the time. Courts may adapt, but they may not amend. They may follow common sense, but they may not follow mere expediency. They may have opinions but they may not be partisan. They may choose to treat a constitution as a living instrument, but they must treat it first of all as a constitution. And, although it may be wise for a court to give the legislature the benefit of the doubt, where there is a doubt, it is no part of a court's duty to do for a legislature or for a majority of the electors what a Constitution has not done for them. Many of these restrictions upon a court's powers and duties are forgotten in discussions which emphasize the great powers which courts in a federal system do possess. It is true that their powers are great. But there are definite limits to their powers. They have a discretion, but it is a discretion within the law and not above the law. 'Courts may modify, they cannot replace. They can revise earlier interpretations as new arguments, new points of view are presented; they can shift the dividing line in marginal cases; but there are barriers they cannot pass, definite assignments of power they cannot reallocate. They can give a broadening construction of existing powers, but they cannot assign to one authority powers explicitly granted to another. . . .'[1]

3

The two factors determining the rigidity or flexibility of federal governments which have so far been discussed—the process of constitutional amendment and the exercise of judicial review—have this in common that they operate upon the actual law of the constitution. It is interesting to consider now factors which operate not upon the strict law of the constitution but upon its practice; factors which accept the existing division of legal powers, but operate upon the governments which exercise the powers so divided. These factors are conveniently grouped under the heading of usage, custom or convention. By usage I shall mean some usual way of behaving which governments follow but which they do not recognize as completely binding. By custom or convention I shall mean some method of behaving which is regarded as binding, though it lacks the actual force of law. How far can it be said that the operation of usage and convention have affected the rigidity or flexibility of federal governments?

At the outset it has to be affirmed that usage and convention cannot alter the rules of law which govern the distribution of powers between general and regional governments. They may nullify certain legal powers by making it constitutionally improper to exercise them, and in this way actually restrict in practice the extent of the

[1] Dr. O. D. Skelton, Under Secretary of State for Canada, in his evidence before the *Special Committee on the British North America Act: Minutes of Proceedings and Evidence*, 1935, p. 24.

powers of general or regional governments. They may establish certain rules which require that some powers should not be exercised except with certain consents or after consultation. Here again in practice the extent of a power may be affected, but in law the power is still there and it may be used. Above all, usage and convention cannot make it possible for a general or regional government to make laws on a topic which is, by the terms of the constitution, beyond its powers.

With these qualifications in mind, it is possible to detect certain effects upon the working of the federal governments which usage and convention produce. And first of all their effect is most noticeable in restricting the exercise of the powers of the general governments. Here Canada provides a notable example. The Canadian Constitution is in law at most quasi-federal, for the Dominion Government has a measure of control over the provinces, through the powers of reservation and disallowance, which is not consistent with the federal principle.[1] Yet in practice it operates as a federal government. These powers of control have been exercised so sparingly that it is not reasonable to deny the name of federal government to Canada. This check upon the exercise of the powers is the result of usage rather than of convention. No binding rule has been adopted so far which would enable one to say with certainty what limits the Dominion recognizes to its power. There have been differing usages. Between 1867 and 1896 the Dominion exercised the power of disallowance freely, and on a variety of grounds. Provincial acts were disallowed not only because they were regarded as *ultra vires* or in conflict with Imperial or Dominion interests or policies, but also because they were regarded as unjust or unsuitable. This gave a wide scope to Dominion control. Between 1867 and 1900, seventy-two provincial acts were disallowed. Then from 1896 to 1911 the Dominion government declared that it did not propose to disallow provincial acts on the ground that such acts were unjust or unsuitable. It proposed to confine itself merely to questions of *ultra vires* or of conflict with imperial or Dominion policies. From 1911 to 1924 the test of injustice came to be asserted again, though it was actually relied on in two cases only, one in 1918 and the other in 1922. From 1924 to 1937 the power was not exercised at all. Then in 1937, 1938 and 1939 legislation passed by the province of Alberta was disallowed and among the reasons given in respect of two of the acts concerned was their injustice. On the whole, however, the trend is towards less use of the power of disallowance. From 1900 to 1939, only thirty-five acts were disallowed. It may be said that there is a constitutional convention to this extent at least, that the power should be used sparingly and in exceptional cases; that it should not be used by the Dominion to unify the Canadian system of government. Yet in law no such restriction is imposed upon the

[1] See Chapter II, pp. 18–20 above.

power.[1] Every provincial budget might be vetoed in order to secure compliance with the Dominion's wishes. Convention forbids that. But the occasions when its exercise is appropriate may be described by usages and are not regulated by conventions.

From Canada again comes another example of the working of usage and convention. The amendment of the Canadian Constitution is in law in the hands of the parliament of the United Kingdom. By convention that parliament will not act except on the initiative of Canada. But what is meant by 'Canada'? Is it the Dominion or the Provinces, or both? Convention assures us, perhaps, that no action would be taken merely on the initiative of the provinces; the Dominion's consent would be required also. Convention would forbid also, perhaps, action on the initiative of the Dominion alone if all, or almost all, the provinces objected. But beyond this it is difficult to assert anything for certain. There have been several usages. Amendments have been made without provincial consent being asked; they have been made contrary to provincial consent. In recent years it has come to look as if the Dominion government feels obliged to propose no amendments at any rate affecting provincial powers, without obtaining unanimous consent.[2] Here usage and convention support on the whole the federal principle in the practice of Canadian government.

In the federations of the United States, Canada and Australia, constitutional usage and convention limit the general governments in the exercise of their legal powers by certain requirements that the interests of the regions or some group of regions should be represented or catered for. Thus an American President must remember in making appointments to his cabinet and to the administration that the interests of the Southern States, of the Middle-Western States and of the Farming States should be represented. In the making of a Canadian Cabinet 'no matter what may be the available material, it is politically essential that a Government position should be provided for every province except the diminutive Prince Edward Island, and that there should be French, English Catholics, and English Protestants in certain proportions'.[3] A similar necessity for regional representation in the making of an Australian cabinet is recognized. These conventions restrict the freedom of action and the strength of the general government.[4] They go further perhaps in the United States, where, by the practice of what is called 'senatorial courtesy', the President in making appointments 'will choose persons satisfactory to the Senator or Senators of the President's political party from the State in which the offices are located or from which the appointees

---

[1] *In re Disallowance and Reservation* [1938] S.C.R. 71, when the Supreme Court of Canada decided the question. For references, see note 2 on p. 19 above.

[2] See Chapter IV, pp. 56–57 above.

[3] B. K. Sandwell, *Canada*, p. 79.

[4] They are made matters of law in the Swiss Constitution, see Art. 96.

come'.[1] And, again, the control exercised over foreign relations by the Senate Committee on Foreign Relations, itself a creation not of the law of the constitution but of convention, weakens the executive of the general government and enables the differing opinions of the United States to be expressed. In Canada it has been practically established as a constitutional convention that no treaty obligations will be imposed upon Canada and that Canada will not be permitted to participate in any war without the consent of the Canadian parliament.[2] These are examples of usages or conventions which restrict the general governments in the exercise of their powers. They express the tendency in a federal government for the regions to desire that the general government should be weak.

On the whole the tendency of usage and convention has been predominantly that way. But there are examples in the opposite direction. By law in the United States the President is to be chosen by an 'Electoral College',[3] itself chosen by the people. But by convention the President is directly elected, the members of the 'Electoral College' doing no more than register the decisions of a majority of the voters in each state. This has made the Presidency into a strong national institution; it has made the Presidency into a more important office than the Governorship of any state. In Australia and Canada, similarly, the conventions of cabinet government operate to unify the general executive and to enable it to control the general legislature to a degree which would not be possible otherwise. In particular the working of cabinet government has led to the overshadowing of the upper house—which was supposed, in Australia at any rate, to safeguard the rights of the states—by the lower house, to which the cabinet is responsible and from which the Prime Minister and the leading ministers are drawn.

But usage and convention are not confined in their working to matters of this kind. They enter into the sphere which, for want of a more exact term, may be called inter-governmental co-operation. Here we are concerned not with the way in which the general and regional governments exercise their powers upon each other, or restrict each other in the exercise of their powers, but how each, operating within its own allotted sphere, is able to offer help to the other, or to receive help from the other. Some examples of this co-operation may be considered, for it is likely that along this line flexibility in the working of federal government may most easily be found.

4

There are two main areas in which there is room for inter-governmental co-operation in a federation. There is the area of relations between

[1] Lindsay Rogers, *The American Senate*, p. 25.
[2] See Chapter IX, p. 185 above.
[3] Strictly speaking by electoral colleges, one in each state.

the general and regional governments, where, through the effects of the division of powers, co-operation is needed to ensure that co-ordinated and complete administration of the divided fields is attained. Then there is the area of inter-regional relations, the relations of state and state, or province and province. If each regional government keeps completely to itself, many matters will suffer from diversity of regulation, and government itself will be less efficient because the experience of other states will have been neglected. In both these spheres some attempts at co-operation have been made in the United States, Canada and Australia and in some cases the same machinery operates in both spheres.

An outstanding usage is the meeting of the chief executives of the general and regional governments in periodical conferences. In the United States there is the Governors' Conference which has met annually since 1908; in Australia there is the Premiers' Conference which has met in almost every year since the establishment of the Commonwealth; and in Canada there is the Dominion-Provincial Conference which has met from time to time since 1906, and also the Inter-Provincial Conference, at which the Dominion does not participate, or does so only by invitation.

Of these institutions the Australian Premiers' Conference appears to have become most influential. It has no regular *independent* secretariat to prepare the agenda or to maintain continuity between Conferences.[1] By a resolution at a Conference in 1929 it was decided that meetings should be held annually at some date in May and that the Prime Minister of the Commonwealth and the Premiers of the states should attend. But beyond this there is little organization. The main topics which have been discussed are the financial relations of the Commonwealth and the states, uniformity of railway gauges, the exercise of industrial powers by the Commonwealth, aviation, health and constitutional reform. It was at a series of Premiers' Conferences that the states were finally persuaded to accept the Financial Agreement of 1927. In the economic depression through which Australia passed in the years from 1930 to 1934 the Premiers' Conference reached its highest level of efficiency and prestige. All means to deal with the depression were finally settled in the Conference and it was the 'Premiers' Plan', as it was called, which in the end was adopted and was successful in guiding Australia through the depression. It is not an exaggeration to say that in these years of economic crisis the Premiers' Conference was more important and more effective than any single government was or could have been.

It is important to mention that the reason for its effectiveness in these years was not merely that the desire to co-operate was strong in a time of crisis. There was also the fact that the Premiers' Conference is closely connected with another institution of co-operation

[1] From 1908 New South Wales provided a small secretariat.

in Australia—the Loan Council. Now the Loan Council, which is composed of the Treasurer of the Commonwealth and the Treasurers of the states, that is, of the finance ministers, was originally based upon agreement between the Commonwealth and the states to co-operate. It had no legal status or powers. From 1923 to 1927 it functioned in this way. But in 1927 it was decided to give the Loan Council legal status. As a result of the constitutional amendment of 1928 and the Financial Agreement which it validated, the Loan Council is given legal powers. Its basis is, therefore, different from that of the Premiers' Conference. Yet, since both are political bodies, the Loan Council and the Premiers' Conference will think alike on financial matters, and the former is able to give effect to the decisions of the latter. The integration of the two bodies was even closer in the depression years for in most cases the Premiers were holding the Treasurer-ships also, and the personnel was practically identical. The Loan Council, too, has come in practice to act as a sort of National Production Council, co-ordinating economic development by informal co-operation at its meetings, although its legal powers do not extend so far. Australia therefore provides, through its Premiers' Conference and its Loan Council, two interesting types of co-opera-tive institution, the one on a basis of usage or convention, the other established with statutory powers, and each the more effective through its association with the other.

The degree of co-operation achieved in Canada and the United States by this type of agency has not yet approached that of Aus-tralia. But in both countries there are signs that more use is being made of it. In Canada in the period from 1906, when the first Dom-inion-Provincial Conference was held, to 1963 there have been sixteen such conferences, and the great majority of these have been held since 1926. They have discussed constitutional reform, financial relations between the Dominion and Provinces, the Statute of Westminster, road and rail transport, unemployment relief, company law, agriculture and marketing, the social services and the develop-ment of tourist traffic. At some of these conferences agreement was reached. That held in 1906 adopted substantially the recommenda-tions of an inter-provincial conference of 1902 about subsidies to be paid by the Dominion to the provinces, and this agreement was later carried into effect by Dominion and United Kingdom legislation. That held in 1931 produced an agreement about the provisions which should be inserted on Canada's behalf in the Statute of West-minster. In 1940 the Dominion and the Provinces were able to agree that unemployment insurance should be transferred to the control of the Dominion and this was carried out later in the year by legislation at Westminster. But in the Conference called in 1941 there was a great deal of disagreement and the representatives left with most major questions unsolved and even undiscussed. The Conference of

1945–6 on financial relations adjourned *sine die*, without agreement. The Conferences of January and September 1950 on constitutional amendment produced general agreement, but no action followed. They were called 'Federal-Provincial Conferences', a change of name intended to be permanent. The Rowell-Sirois Commission in its report of 1939 recommended that Dominion-Provincial Conferences at regular intervals and with a permanent secretariat should form part of the machinery of Canadian government. In so doing they were adopting a suggestion of the Government of Nova Scotia, supported by that of Prince Edward Island and of New Brunswick. The recommendation seems likely to be acted upon in course of time, but a good deal will depend upon the willingness of some of the provincial governments to co-operate. This has been lacking in recent years, particularly in Ontario and Quebec, without whom no progress can be made.

The Governors' Conference in the United States has so far not achieved a record of effective co-operation as great even as that of the Canadian Dominion-Provincial Conference. The first Governors' Conference met in May 1908 at the White House, on the invitation of President Theodore Roosevelt, for the purpose of considering the conservation of national resources. The Conference agreed upon a scheme of action and some of it was put into effect. But the future history of the Conference did not live up to its beginnings. Meetings were held as a rule once or twice a year, but until 1931 the usual practice appears to have been to avoid controversial issues entirely and to confine the discussions to broad and uplifting themes. In 1931 three Governors—one of them was Franklin D. Roosevelt of New York State—broke the custom and embarked on some controversial issues and at the same time urged their colleagues to make the Conference a more effective and useful body by encouraging the discussion of such issues. But their example was not followed in 1932 or 1933. The chief characteristic of these conferences and of those that had preceded them was that the Governors had a good time. States vied with each other to provide record hospitality. The meetings were not really business meetings. Attendances began to drop; the average was about fifty per cent of the total. Yet it seems that there is hope that the body may become useful. On President Roosevelt's inauguration in 1933 he proceeded to call the Governors' Conference together; and the meeting of 1934 was held at Washington. He expressed his belief in the value of the Conference and in the necessity of making it more effective. Yet experience since 1934 gave little hope that much could be expected from the Conference in the way of constructive co-operation as between the states or with the general government.

At these meetings of the general and regional governments it is to be expected that the principal topics to be discussed are those which involve the relations of both sets of authorities with each other. But there are opportunities also for inter-regional relations to be discussed. These have always found some place, formally or informally, in Premiers' Conferences, Dominion-Provincial Conferences and Governors' Conferences. In Canada it has been the practice also to hold inter-provincial conferences from time to time. The Governors' Conference in the United States is really a states' conference, for the usual practice has been that the President of the United States does little more than deliver an address. Further there have been regional conferences of Governors for certain groups of states called to deal with particular common problems. Indeed the conferences of Western Governors and Southern Governors are well established institutions and have become of some political importance.

Co-operation in these three federations is not confined to the chief executives. Other ministers and permanent officials meet from time to time to discuss common problems and their mutual relations. Ministers and administrators of the health services, Commonwealth and State, meet in Australia. Similar meetings are held by those responsible for the administration of agriculture, education, police and railways, to name a few. In Canada such co-operation is growing, and the most hopeful indication of it in recent years has been the establishment of the National Conference of Labour Administrators.[1]

In the United States the organization of co-operative institutions has gone far. There exist national organizations of officials engaged in administering a wide variety of governmental activities and through the regular meetings of these bodies some co-operation is achieved. There are, for example, the National Associations of Secretaries of State; of Commissioners, Secretaries and Departments of Agriculture; of Marketing Officials; of Dairy, Food and Drug officials; of Supervisors of State Banks; of State Aviation officials; of State Superintendents and Commissioners of Education; of State Highway officials; of State Attorney-Generals; of Chiefs of Police and so on.[2] Many of these associations are sub-divided into smaller sections which cater for the problems of particular groups of states. No detailed account of the work of these bodies can be given here. The impression one obtains from a study of what they have achieved is that although they are aware of their problems and discuss them, they are relatively ineffective where action is needed.

There is another field where the United States has achieved a little in the way of promoting uniformity between states. In 1878 the American Bar Association was established, and in 1892 it organized the National Conference of Commissions on Uniform State Laws. The Commissioners are lawyers, appointed by the Governors of the

[1] See above, Chapter VIII, pp. 162–3.
[2] A list is given in Appendix B of W. B. Graves, *Uniform State Action.*

states, and they meet annually for one week. Their task is to prepare drafts of uniform laws on particular matters for submission to the state legislatures. It was reported in 1943 that the Conference had provided eighty-three uniform and model acts, most of which have been approved later by the American Bar Association and presented to the various state legislatures. The total number of adoptions of these laws was 935,[1] out of a possible total of something over 4,000. The need for uniformity appears to have been recognized increasingly since 1920. In 1925 the total number of adoptions to date was less than 400, in 1932 it was 600. Yet the amount of uniformity achieved has not been great. In 1940 a writer declared that only one act had been adopted by all the states and territories (the Uniform Negotiable Instruments Act); only eight others had been adopted by half the states and territories;[2] and only twenty-three had been adopted by one-fourth of the legislatures. One-fifth of the work of the Conference had not resulted in any uniformity at all, while only one-tenth had any substantial effect.[3]

An institution which may do something to make the movement for uniformity in state legislation more effective in the Council of State Governments. This body was first organized in 1937 to serve as a clearing house for inter-state activities and to promote inter-state co-operation by conferences and commissions. It is representative of nearly all the states and it has established itself as an important institution in planning the relations of states with each other and with the general government. It publishes a monthly journal, *State Government*, which reports and encourages inter-state co-operation, and provides information about the Governors' Conference, and the Conference of Commissioners on Uniform State Laws. The experience of the war gave the Council of State Governments an opportunity to co-ordinate state plans, and it played a useful part in the discussion of proposals for uniform laws, chiefly put forward by the general government, for promoting the war effort on a common plan. Whether the needs of peace will give the Council further opportunities for co-operative action it is too early to say. In addition to the Council there may be mentioned the American Legislators' Association which represents officially the state legislatures and arranges conferences and research on matters of common concern. The Association is naturally a more unwieldy body than the Council, but it has a function to perform in promoting co-operation between the states.

But the most effective method of promoting co-operation in the legislative and administrative fields appears to be, in all four

---

[1] *State Government*, December 1942, p. 236.

[2] Sales Act, Warehouse Receipts Act, Bills of Lading Act, Veterans' Guardianship Act, Declaratory Judgements Act, Narcotic Drug Act, Proof of Statistics Act, Stock Transfer Act.

[3] Rodney L. Mott, 'Uniform Legislation in the United States', *Annals of the American Academy of Political Science*, January 1940, p. 84.

federations, the use by the general government of its powers to make grants in aid and to require of the regions which accept the grants that certain uniform standards be imposed in legislation and administration. Some account of this co-operation has been given already in the discussion of the social services.[1] in Canada, for example, the Dominion provided 75 per cent of the sums necessary for old-age pensions, and the provinces provided the remainder and administered the service. In Canada and Australia unemployment relief in the 1930s was financed jointly by the general and regional governments, but administered by the latter. In the United States President Roosevelt's New Deal induced the states to adopt uniformity in many spheres. In soil conservation, in state planning and, above all, in the sphere of social security, the states were invited to fulfil certain general requirements in return for financial or technical assistance. All or most of the States have passed legislation regarding unemployment insurance, old age assistance, relief to the blind, and aid to dependent children. The method by which the general government secured this uniformity in the sphere of unemployment insurance is interesting. Congress imposed a tax upon employers and provided that 90 per cent of this tax would be refunded to employers who contributed to a state scheme of unemployment insurance embodied in an act the terms of which were approved by the Social Security Board. States were thus virtually coerced into passing legislation and into passing uniform legislation. But the Social Security Board was flexible in its requirements; it suggested two forms of model statutes; and it accepted a variety of modifications from states, provided certain essentials were met. The Social Security legislation is a most successful example of co-operation in the American federal system and it is also the most significant. It indicates a method by which states may be impelled towards uniformity through the predominant financial position of the general government. Similar powers are available to the general governments of Australia, Canada and Switzerland, but so far they have not used them to the same extent as the United States.

5

The factors making for flexibility in federal government so far discussed have been either legal or non-legal. The processes of constitutional amendment and of judicial review were legal, the process of modification by usage and convention was non-legal. But there are other methods by which flexibility can be promoted which combine legal and non-legal elements. One such method is the temporary delegation of powers by regional to general governments, or vice versa. The adjustments made depend upon a will to co-operate, but they can be given effective legal form only by what amounts to a

[1] See above, Chapter VIII.

temporary amendment of the Constitution. Such a delegation, too, may be carried out by one region only or by a few regions. It does not require complete agreement. It may be for a long or short period, for a few or for many topics. It allows for adjustment to the differing needs of different regions, and it provides an opportunity for experiment. Moreover, since the changes made need not be permanent and irrevocable, the regional governments may not feel so nervous about making the delegation.

But it may be said at once that, so far, delegation has not been used to any important extent in the four federations. In Australia alone is the exercise of delegation possible. The Commonwealth Parliament was given power to make laws with respect to 'matters referred to the Parliament of the Commonwealth by the Parliament or Parliaments of any State or States, but so that the law shall extend only to States by whose Parliaments the matter is referred, or which afterwards adopt the law'.[1] Several attempts have been made to achieve delegation under this section but up to 1963 few have been successful. There was some doubt about the limitations upon the power. Could a state having once delegated a power, revoke the delegation? How far could states impose limitations upon the grant? Doubts on these points assisted the reluctance of the states to surrender powers. Agreements were made, usually at Premiers' Conferences, to promote legislation in the state parliaments and delegate various topics, but these agreements were never completely fulfilled in the end. In 1909, 1912 and 1915 attempts were made to obtain delegation by the states to the Commonwealth of powers over industrial conditions, so as to produce uniformity. In 1920 and 1929 it was proposed that powers over aviation should be delegated, so that the Commonwealth might be able to extend its control in this sphere. But in none of these cases were the necessary steps finally taken by all states.

In 1942 and 1943 a comprehensive attempt to use the delegating power was undertaken. The Commonwealth government had initiated a proposal in 1942 to amend the Constitution by inserting a new section conferring power on the Commonwealth parliament to make laws on a variety of subjects connected with economic and social reconstruction after the war. A convention, consisting of 24 members, twelve representing all parties in the Commonwealth parliament, and the Premier and Leader of the Opposition from each of the six states, met towards the end of the year to discuss the proposed amendment. It became apparent that there was considerable opposition to the holding of a referendum during the war. Instead it was proposed by the Labour Premier of Tasmania that the states should agree to delegate to the Commonwealth, for a period expiring at the end of five years from the cessation of hostilities, such powers as were necessary for post-war reconstruction, and

[1] Constitution, s. 51 (xxxvii).

that such a delegation should not be revoked or amended during that period, without an affirmative vote of the electors in the state. The Convention adopted this proposal unanimously; it agreed upon the list of subjects to be delegated; and upon a bill in common form to be introduced into the state legislatures. The list of subjects included employment, unemployment, profiteering, prices, production and distribution of goods (but primary production only with the consent of the state concerned), organized marketing of commodities, combines, monopolies, and family allowances, and certain additional financial matters to complete the Commonwealth's power to control investment and exchange.[1] It may be seen that the list was comprehensive and that the opportunity was being taken to obtain control for the Commonwealth over a number of matters which in previous attempts at constitutional amendment had been denied to them.

Yet in spite of all this agreement, when the Bill came before the state legislatures difficulties were encountered. Two states—New South Wales and Queensland—passed it in agreed form; Victoria passed it but with an amendment precluding the Governor from proclaiming it unless all the other states passed a substantially similar measure; South Australia and Western Australia passed it with substantial and different amendments; Tasmania rejected it. The legislatures, and in particular the upper houses, refused to follow the lead of their representatives in the Convention. And there the matter rested in August 1943, when the Labour Government fought a general election and won it by a record majority. On reconsideration, they dropped the proposals for delegation and decided to put forward a direct amendment of the Constitution.[2]

The Australian experience of delegation does not encourage one to think much flexibility can be obtained by this method. It is true that there are great difficulties in getting agreement between states and, if the agreement is obtained, in delegating powers for a period only. In practice it would be impossible or chaotic to withdraw the powers after a few years. It is almost impossible, also, to persuade one state to delegate powers unless the others are prepared to do so. Yet there are possibilities along this line. There are some services which one state may be unable to perform and which it may prefer to delegate to the general government. Others might follow its example. The Royal Commission on Dominion-Provincial Relations in Canada felt sufficiently impressed by the possibilities of delegation to recommend that it should be made available in the Canadian Constitution. In their view 'a general power of delegation for both the Dominion and the provinces should provide a measure of flexibility which is much needed in our federal system'.[3] In particular they suggested that

---

[1] See above, p. 143.
[2] See above, pp. 143–4.
[3] *Rowell-Sirois Report*, Book II, p. 73

certain matters might be dealt with most suitably by delegation—that
jurisdiction to make regulations for fisheries might be delegated by
the Dominion to such provinces as could perform this function more
conveniently;[1] that some measure of control over marketing[2] and that
the exclusive control over old-age pensions[3] should be delegated by
the provinces to the Dominion. But up to 1963 no action along these
lines had been taken.[4] So far as old-age pensions were concerned,
indeed, the Dominion parliament had been given power to legislate
by constitutional amendment in 1951,[5] but the power was concurrent,
not exclusive, and provincial laws were to prevail in case of conflict.

6

From this brief survey of the methods by which federal governments
may be modified and adapted, some conclusions may be suggested.
The first conclusion is that for some purposes federal governments
have a high degree of adaptability. In war-time all four federations
have been shown to possess the power to adjust their pluralistic
structure to the necessities of unified and total war effort. This proved
possible from the terms of their constitutions as interpreted by the
courts. Constitutional amendment was unnecessary in all cases
except Switzerland. It proved possible also because of the willingness
of regional governments to co-operate and to supplement the legal
powers of their general government with their co-ordinated efforts.
The working of federal governments in war-time demonstrates quite
clearly that in some situations at any rate there is ample adaptability
in a federal structure.

In times of economic crisis the degree of adaptability has not been
so great. Canada has been largely unable to modify her federal
government to meet the demands of economic depression. But it
must be emphasized here that there was no obvious or overwhelming
majority of Canadian opinion in favour of a New Deal. It was more
the conservatism of the Canadian people than the rigidity of the constitution which left the Canadian federal system largely unchanged.
In Australia, the United States and Switzerland, on the other hand,
there has been considerable adaptation, achieved in the first two
countries largely by judicial interpretation and in the third by constitutional amendment. It is true that many people in Australia and in
the United States think that there has not been sufficient adaptation;
that the Constitutions still embody an out-of-date division of powers.
But this should not blind us to the fact that considerable adjustment
has been made.

It has been interesting to notice how different methods of adaptation have operated in the different federations. Constitutional

---

[1] Ibid., p. 59.   [2] Ibid., p. 56.   [3] Ibid., p. 32.
[4] An attempt at delegation was declared invalid by the Canadian Supreme Court in 1950.
Att.-Gen. for Nova Scotia v. *Att-Gen. for Canada*, 4 D.L.R. 369.
[5] British North America Act, 1951.

amendment has been most influential in Switzerland; judicial review and governmental co-operation in the United States and Australia. In Canada the paradoxical situation arises that the country which, of all four, has the least federal constitution, is the one in which the factors which make for rigidity and a strict application of the federal principle appear to have been strongest.

In judging the degree of adaptability in a federal government, the student must beware of applying standards which are customary in judging a unitary government. It is not sufficient to say of a federal government that it should be so adapted to its times that the general government has power to regulate any matter which a majority of the people think it should regulate. If the opinion of a majority of the people is a sufficient guide in a community, then it is likely that that community does not need federal government; that it will be most satisfactorily served by a unitary government. But if federal government is really appropriate to a country, it is most likely that government by a majority of the people is not usually enough. Majorities of regions as well as majorities of people may need to be consulted. The degree of adaptability which a federal government should possess will depend, therefore, on a variety of factors in situations that are at times complex and dangerous.

On the whole the line along which flexibility and adaptability must be sought seems to be that of co-operation through some of the methods which have been described. As these methods are developed, constitutional amendment becomes easier. Meanwhile the habit of working together has become established. Something further may be said on this topic when we come now to consider the prospects of federal government.

Chapter XII

FEDERAL GOVERNMENT:
TENDENCIES AND PROSPECTS

1

THERE is one general tendency in all federal governments which is apparent from the exposition of this book. The general governments in all four federations have grown stronger. But it is well to consider what this increase in strength means. It has not meant in all cases that the general governments have acquired new fields of jurisdiction in addition to those which were originally conferred upon them at the initiation of the federal union. As I have shown, Switzerland alone among the federations has conferred new areas of jurisdiction upon the general government to any considerable extent. Australia and Canada have each made one important change of this kind: in the United States three amendments—XIV, XVI and XVIII—increased the powers of the general government. It is true that in Australia and the United States judicial interpretation of the constitution has enlarged the powers of the general governments, but these interpretations profess to do no more than explain what the constitution means. Though they may be thought to be misinterpretations by some people, they cannot be regarded as more than a statement of opinion about what powers the constitution has conferred upon the general government. So when it is said that there has been a tendency in federations for the general governments to increase in strength, this does not mean that they have steadily acquired from the regional government fields of jurisdiction which at the establishment of the federation were confided to the exclusive control of the regions.

What has happened in the main has been that the general governments have developed more and more intensively the area which was assigned to them originally. And this is not surprising. For after all when these governments were initiated they began from almost nothing at all. The regional governments theretofore had occupied almost the entire stage and had absorbed the greatest part of the political interest and energies of their peoples. But with the establishment of the general governments it was inevitable that, as they began to exercise their allotted functions, they should gain in importance at the expense of the regional governments. There were certain factors which made the general governments absorb political interest and energies to a very great degree. One was that the control of defence and the power to make peace and war were in their hands. These matters of life and death to the peoples of the federations drew their attention irresistibly to the general government and its doings. So also with their powers over foreign relations and particularly over foreign trade.

The general governments, then, have grown in importance in comparison with the regional governments, because they began from nothing and because they were endowed with control over most of the more important matters with which governments have to deal.

A particular example of the increase of the powers of the general governments is found in the sphere of finance and it is here that the increase has been greatest. But, as will be remembered, this increase has not come about in all cases simply through the development by the general government of the financial powers with which it was originally endowed. In Switzerland amendments of the Constitution were needed to increase the financial powers of the general government; in the United States restrictions were removed by constitutional amendment from the powers of Congress to levy income tax; and in Australia the Financial Agreement was validated by a similar process. But even so in all four countries the general governments owe much of their predominance in finance to the potentialities found in the original financial provisions of their Constitutions. In the sphere of finance it is clear that the general governments have steadily increased their powers at the expense of the states, and it may be said that, with the exception of Switzerland, this increase in power and the predominant positions they now occupy have come about largely by the exploitation of the powers originally granted to them by their Constitutions.

2

Here, then, is one tendency. What is the prospect? Some students have concluded from the way in which general governments have increased in importance and strength at the expense of regional governments that federal government is really no more than a stage towards unitary government. This is a prophecy, not an historical judgement, for, so far, no federal government—as I define it—has become a unitary government. Two federations indeed, Rhodesia and Nyasaland and the West Indies Federation, have disintegrated. But it is worth while to examine the evidence upon which such a prophecy can be based.

The chief forces which have caused general governments to increase in strength at the expense of the regions—whether by the fuller exploitation of their existing powers or occasionally by the acquisition of new powers—seem to have been four-fold. They are war, economic depression, the growth of the social services and the mechanical revolution in transport and industry, the last named so familiar that its existence and significance are often overlooked.

To express the same things in different words, they were power politics, depression politics, welfare politics and the internal combustion engine. War and economic depression demand unitary control if their problems are to be effectively treated, and they impose financial strains which only the general governments have been able to bear. Thus, as I have shown in the chapters which dealt with public finance, economic affairs and the war power, all general governments grew stronger in times of war and economic depression. The growth of the social services affects the general governments by slightly different routes. To some extent the cost of social services has been greatly increased in times of economic depression and by war, and this meant that the general governments had to come to the assistance of the regions. But the growth of the social services went on quite independently of war and economic depression. Educational and health services were developed in times of peace. In most federations these matters were under the control of the regions, but in all it was found that the regions required financial assistance from the general governments. And finally the revolution in transport and industry made so much of life inter-state instead of intra-state, that large areas of activity came within the ambit of the general government's control, until finally, in the United States, crime itself becomes a matter for Congress. And thus the powers of the general governments increased.

How do these considerations affect the prospect? First of all it seems clear that the revolution in transport is a permanent and fundamental factor in the situation and to that extent the increase of power in the general governments is fairly certain to continue—and necessarily so. War and economic depression unavoidably produce an increase in the powers of general governments. If federations are to survive these crises successfully they must submit to a large measure of unitary control while the crises last. The price of victory in war and the price of economic recovery is at least temporary unification. Consequently war, or power politics, and economic crisis, or depression politics, are the enemies of federal government. Peace and prosperity are in truth prerequisites for the successful working of federal government. It may be said, therefore, that if wars and economic crises are to recur frequently the prospect is that federal government will not survive for long. It may be doubted, for example, whether the federal system in Australia could survive another war or another severe economic crisis. The two wars of 1914 and 1939 and the economic crisis of the 1930's have already gone far towards converting Australia's federal constitution and federal government into a quasi-federal constitution and a quasi-federal government.

So far as the growth of the social services is concerned, it would appear to me that although this has led to increased control—especially on the financial side—by the general governments over the regional governments, there is no need that this should continue to be so. There is, as I have argued in the chapter on social services, a good case for putting the administration of most social services in the hands of the regional governments to a large extent. It is only those services concerned with unemployment which seem obviously to demand control by the general government. The defect in the federal systems in the past has been largely that the regional governments lacked the financial resources necessary to carry out the social services which had been committed to their jurisdiction by the constitutions. This may be remedied by a re-allocation of financial powers, and the federal principle can be safeguarded even if grants from the general governments are part of the re-allocation, provided that the grants are guaranteed by the constitution so that the regional governments are not left to depend upon the good will of the general government. In my view, therefore, the growth of social services need not prove destructive of federalism, whereas war and economic depression must. Welfare politics has increased the powers of general governments in the past and it may continue to do so, but it need not. But in no federation has a general re-allocation yet been carried through. In Switzerland the cantons have transferred many powers, but they lack financial autonomy. In Canada alone has a plan for re-allocation been proposed; in Australia increased dependence is the prevailing tendency; in the United States the problem is only slowly coming forward for treatment.

3

I have indicated that war and economic crisis, if they recur frequently, will almost certainly turn federal governments into unitary governments, and I have suggested that the growth of social services may, but need not, tend towards the same end. But that is not the whole picture, because that prospect is based upon the consideration of one tendency only—the tendency of general governments to grow at the expense of the regional governments. One other tendency at least must be noticed. It has not been the general governments alone which have grown in strength. The regional governments also have expanded. In all the federations the regions now perform functions which, at the establishment of the federations, they performed either not at all or to a much less degree than now. Take the police services. Fifty years ago these services were more narrowly conceived than they are at present. Then they represented the protection of person and property, and the pursuit of criminals. Now they include protection and welfare services, reformative institutions, advisory services, traffic control and a wider range of helpful rather than prohibitive activities. Education is another service whose scope has increased in the same period. All regional governments spend many times more money on this service now than when the federations began. Health and destitution services have similarly expanded. The regional governments have all extended their activities in these spheres, and although it is true that many have found their financial resources insufficient to meet the total cost, they have none the less spent to their limit. Thus while the relative strength of general and regional governments has changed strongly in favour of the general governments during this period, the regional governments themselves have made a considerable increase absolutely.

This is one element in a tendency which may be broadly stated by saying that there has been a strong increase in the sense of importance, in the self-consciousness and self-assertiveness of the regional governments. This has gone on side by side with the growth in importance of the general governments and it has obviously been stimulated by it. It has led to a sense of grievance in the regional governments. They have felt that their position is imperilled; that they are becoming mere pensioners of the general governments. And in some cases they have felt so unjustly treated by the general governments that they have talked of resigning from the federation. The secession movement of the State of Western Australia was one example. Here in the federation where the increase in the power of the general government was most marked, it is significant surely that the resentment of a regional government was, for a time, most violent. And the resentment has not been confined to Western Australia. South Australia and Tasmania have felt similar fears and hostilities. The Prairie Provinces and the Maritime Provinces of Canada have also been anxious about their status and existence. But it is not the small and less populous regions alone which have exhibited an increase in self-assertion. Quebec and Ontario equally resist the encroachments of the general government. The increase in the power of the general government in the United States has led the fifty state governments to work more closely together to safeguard their powers.

Nor should it be imagined that the reasons which originally led the regions to make a federal and not a unitary union have by now entirely ceased to operate. Quebec is the most striking example of this fact. The desire of that province to safeguard her distinct language, race and religion and her historical identity as a distinct government, led her to insist that the federal principle be embodied in the Canadian Constitution. Those forces still prevail. Indeed they are stronger than ever. Whatever modifications may be introduced into the Canadian federal government it can be prophesied that the federal principle could not be removed entirely from the government except at the price of Quebec's secession from the union. The Swiss cantons similarly cherish their identity, based upon religion, language and race, and they would be slow to surrender it in a unitary government. What could persuade the Southern States of America to sink their identity in a unitary union dominated by northern industrialism? these are a few examples of the strong desire to be separate and independent—albeit within a union—which still animates some, at least, of the regional governments within the modern federations. The strength of this desire is sometimes under-estimated or over-looked by those who prophesy about the future of federal governments. People say that 'state rights' are dead; that nobody cares nowadays about the independence of the states; that federalism is obsolescent. There is a sense in which it is true that the old state loyalties are not as strong as they were. It is true also to say that the rights of the states are often used to defend those economic interests which do not desire to be controlled by the general governments or by any other governments. It is true that it is nowadays groups of states in America, for example, and groups of provinces in Canada which form a common interest rather than separate states. But in spite of these modifications from the original status of the regions, it remains true that strong forces still operate to maintain their independence and to resist the imposition of uniformity and the unitary state. Not every region in a federal system feels the desire for independence to the same degree. But in every federation a few regions feel it so intensely that no attempt could be made to impose uniformity without bringing into view the possibility of breaking the union in pieces.

It is with these considerations in mind that I say that the prospect for federal government is not so short as is suggested by those who concentrate entirely on the tendency of the general government to increase at the expense of the regions. Federal government is still desired by some regions in all the federations. There is no conclusive evidence that federal government is to be no more than a stage in the process towards unitary government.

4

Yet there remains one strong element in the tendency of general governments to increase their powers and that is the financial pre-dominance which they have attained. The regions have not succeeded in resisting this, and it is noticeable that, with all their assertions of independence and of their determination to resist unification, there is a tendency to accept at the same time a large measure of financial assistance from the general government. In Canada and Australia particularly the tendency is to be noted. The provinces and states are reluctant to give up jurisdiction but they demand grants and subsidies to enable them to perform the functions within their jurisdiction. At the same time it is unlikely that the general governments will be ready to surrender or to return financial resources to the regions. The present predominance is likely to be permanent. The prospect for federal government, so far as this tendency is concerned is, in my view, that a plurality of jurisdiction is likely to be combined with some measure of financial unification. The regions will cling to their areas of independent power, to the topics over which they have

legislative and executive control, but in return for this they will have
to accept from the general government some degree of financial
assistance and with it a greater or less degree of control. This means a
modification of the federal principle to some degree, though it need
not mean a complete denial of federalism. It will mean, too, that the
independence in jurisdiction of the regions in law may be unreal to
some degree in practice. But such a combination may well prove
workable, and it may produce better government than complete
independence in finance and jurisdiction.

This combination of regional jurisdiction and general finance
has already developed into a system of co-operation of which something was said in the last chapter. It enables the two sets of authorities
to work together in such a way that neither is completely independent
of the other, though each is exercising its own independent powers, as
allotted to it by the constitutions. The working of the social security
legislation in the United States is an outstanding example of this form
of co-operation.

It is this co-operative tendency in federal government which provides its most hopeful prospect. Through co-operation the tendency
of the general governments to grow in strength, especially in finance,
is associated with the desire of the regions to maintain the right to
make laws for themselves on the matters confided to them by the
constitution. The machinery of co-operation is so far rudimentary in
most federations. In Australia both the Loan Council and the Premiers'
Conference provide examples of a kind of institution which offers a
prospect of success. There is a flexibility about the co-operative method
and the co-operative institutions, too, which can help to harmonize the
legal divisions and conflicts which are unavoidable in a federal system.

Yet it is wise not to speak too optimistically about the prospects of
co-operation. General governments are not anxious to share powers
if they can acquire them entirely for themselves. Increased financial
resources breed a desire to keep what one has got and if possible to
get more. It is always to this financial predominance that the problem
returns. So far the making of grants by the general to the regional
governments has been allowed to grow haphazardly and it has
encroached steadily upon the federal principle. General governments
have not been sorry to see this happen; regional governments have
not been able to prevent it, or have not wished to refuse money when
it was offered. But unless some machinery is adopted by which assistance from the general government can be combined with some
independence in finance for the regions, co-operation will be something of a screen behind which unification is practised.

5

But supposing that, under the stress of financial pressure, federal
government does disappear in some of the countries we have studied

—what of it? I have said already that I think it unlikely—except in face of continued wars and economic crises—that federal government will disappear in these countries, and, in my view, that is the prospect. But I may be permitted to add in conclusion a word on this theme: Is it worth while to preserve federal government? I am prepared to answer, in general terms, that it is, and to justify that answer by one reason.

It is often argued against federal government that it is out of date because, in a world where economic, and indeed, social, life is becoming more and more a single whole, federal government preserves hard and fast regional divisions. Where unity is the predominant characteristic and tendency of life, where a world unity is so ardently desired, federalism offers multiplicity and plurality. To this I answer that mere unity is no virtue in itself; that if large-scale economics in the modern world is making all people one, it need not follow that it is a good tendency or that it is a tendency which should be assisted by governments or extended to all spheres of life. I can see that to deal with this unified and interlocked economic life, a government with large powers is needed, and it has been evident that federations have not always allocated sufficient powers to their general governments to deal with modern economic crises. This calls for readjustment. And such readjustment can be made. Federal government, after all, does not stand for multiplicity alone. It stands for multiplicity in unity. It can provide unity where unity is needed, but it can ensure also that there is variety and independence in matters where unity and uniformity is not essential.

It will have been obvious from the preceding chapters that an ideal division of powers between general and regional governments has not always been achieved in modern federations and that it is difficult to make readjustments in some cases. Yet the federal principle does not prohibit such readjustments. And, if they can be made, then there will be sufficient unity to cope with modern economic life.

Within this unity there is room under federalism for each region to govern itself in its own way. This exercise in self-government is sufficiently valuable to be worth the cost it entails. If a region cannot support itself, then it is entitled to be guaranteed in a federal constitution access to sufficient resources under its own control to help it to perform its functions. It is not enough to say that only those who can afford to pay for self-government deserve to have it. The federal principle of equality of status between the regions which form the federal union and between those regions and the general government, ensures, when it is applied, that each region, whatever its resources, will be enabled to govern itself and regulate its life in its own way.

One of the most urgent problems in the world to-day is to preserve diversities either where they are worth preserving for themselves, or where they cannot be eradicated even if they are not desirable, and at the same time to introduce such a measure of unity as will prevent clashes and facilitate co-operation. Federalism is one way of reconciling these two ends, and this book has tried to show in what circumstances it is likely to succeed. It is not the only device we need; for the world as a whole, we need, I believe, different machinery, but it will be designed to secure the same general ideal, of making the combination of diversity and unity, independence and interdependence safe and workable. In fact, federation in the strict modern sense which has been given to it in this book is one species of a wider genus, which was often called 'federation' before the word got its specialized meaning. It is therefore one device, appropriate in certain circumstances but not in all, for achieving a high and necessary ideal in the sphere of government.

SELECT BIBLIOGRAPHY

GENERAL

THE classic discussion of federalism is to be found in A. V. Dicey, *Introduction to the Study of the Law of the Constitution*, first published in 1885. In successive editions Dicey devoted an increasing space to federalism and all that he says is lucid and penetrating. There is a good chapter in J. S. Mill, *Representative Government*. E. A. Freeman published in 1863 the first and only volume of his projected *History of Federal Government from the foundation of the Achaian League to the disruption of the United States*. He carried the story down to the dissolution of the Achaian League in 145 B.C. In a second edition published in 1893, after Freeman's death, there was added an additional chapter, dealing with certain defective forms of federalism which had appeared in Italy, and a fragment on the German Confederacy. The title of the book was changed to *A History of Federal Government in Greece and Italy*. Much of what Freeman discusses is not federal government as I have defined it in this book, but none the less his work is of value to any student of modern federal government. There are two introductory chapters on the nature of federal government which are of particular interest and importance, and there are many observations dispersed throughout the work which illuminate the subject.

M. Venkatarangaiya has written a short and illuminating study entitled *Federalism in Government* (1935) of which a second edition is to be hoped for. Sobei Mogi, *The Problem of Federalism, a study in the history of political theory* (2 vols.), gives extended summaries of what American, British and German statesmen and writers have thought about federalism, but there is no study of the working of federal government. The book is useful for reference, but, as Professor Laski says in his foreword, 'Mr. Mogi has traversed ground which it is unlikely any scholar will travel again, at least in quite the same way.' D. Karve, *Federations*, gives a comparative summary of constitutional provisions. A. W. Macmahon, ed., *Federalism, Mature and Emergent* (1959) is an interesting symposium. One aspect of the working of federal government which has received substantial study is its public finance. In this field there is B. P. Adarkar, *The Principles and Problems of Federal Finance* (1933), an illuminating introductory book, and G. F. Shirras, *Federal Finance in Peace and War* (1944), more detailed but not so lucid. The amending process is fully examined in W. S. Livingston, *Federalism and Constitutional Change*

(1956) and A. H. Birch has dealt with *Federalism, Finance and Social Legislation* (1955) in an illuminating way. There is valuable source material in R. R. Bowie and C. J. Friedrich (ed.), *Studies in Federalism* (1954). A useful book of documents is A. P. Newton, *Federal and Unified Constitutions.* H. E. Egerton, *Federations and Unions in the British Empire,* and W. I. Jennings, *Constitutional Laws of the Commonwealth,* Vol. 1, print the Canadian and Australian Constitutions with some commentary. The Constitutions of Canada, the United States and the Latin American federations are included in R. H. Fitzgibbon. *The Constitutions of the Americas* (1949). Most federal and quasi-federal constitutions can be found in such collections as Amos J. Peaslee, *Constitutions of the Nations* (3 vols., 1950); F. Dareste, *Les Constitutions Modernes* (4 vols.), and W. F. Dodds, *Modern Constitutions.*

UNITED STATES

The classic account is James Bryce, *The American Commonwealth,* first published in 1888. After more than seventy years it still stands as the greatest book on American government. The best way to study the American federal system is to read Bryce's book and then to bring it up to date with recent works. Among these may be mentioned: C. A. Beard, *American Government and Politics*; W. B. Munro, *The Government of the United States*; Ogg and Ray, *Introduction to American Government*; and H. Zink, *Government and Politics in the United States,* all written by Americans. The principal British student of American institutions in modern times is D. W. Brogan, whose *The American Political System* has been regarded by some as a successor to *The American Commonwealth.* Of more value to the student who is beginning his reading is M. J. C. Vile, *The Structure of American Federalism* (1961). A collection of essays published in 1938 under the title *Bryce's American Commonwealth* (ed. R. C. Brooks), to commemorate the fiftieth anniversary of Bryce's book, has some interesting comments, but it is uneven and on the whole disappointing. The best study of the financial aspects of American federalism is found in J. A. Maxwell, *Fiscal Impact of Federalism in the United States.*

A thorough study of the working of American federalism was carried out from 1953 to 1955 by the Commission on Intergovernmental Relations, appointed jointly by President Eisenhower and the President of the Senate and the Speaker of the House of Representatives. It was the first official undertaking of its kind since the Constitutional Convention of 1787. The Commission, known sometimes as the Kestnbaum Commission from the name of its chairman Meyer Kestnbaum, published a report in 1955 which is full of interest and information for the student of federalism. It published also fifteen additional reports on a wide variety of topics, with particular emphasis on the nature and extent of federal aid. These publications are available from the Superintendent of Documents, U.S. Government Printing Office, Washington, 25, D.C.

No one can understand American government without some study of the making of the Constitution. This can be undertaken best in Max Farrand, *Records of the Federal Convention* (4 vols.), and Alexander Hamilton, John Jay and James Madison, *The Federalist*, with the assistance of such books as R. L. Schuyler, *The Constitution of the United States*; C. A. Beard, *The Economic Interpretation of the Constitution*; Charles Warren, *The Making of the Constitution*, a day-by-day account of the proceedings of the convention which framed the Constitution; and Max Farrand, *The Framing of the Constitution*.

Some knowledge of the law of the American Constitution—as of all federal constitutions—is essential. Among histories reference may be made to A. C. McLaughlin, *A Constitutional History of the United States*, in one volume; H. Hockett, *Constitutional History of the United States*, in three volumes; C. B. Swisher, *The Growth of Constitutional Power in the United States*; and B. F. Wright, *The Growth of American Constitutional Law*. Among short studies of the law of the Constitution, the most useful introductions are E. S. Corwin, *The Constitution and what it means to-day*; J. M. Mathews, *The American Constitutional System*; and M. Amos, *The American Constitution*, the latter a short study in lecture form for English readers. The standard larger work is W. W. Willoughby, *The Constitutional Law of the United States* (to 1929 only). Of other studies, the best appear to be H. E. Willis, *Constitutional Law* (1936), H. Rottschaeffer, *American Constitutional Law* (1939) and B. Schwartz, *American Constitutional Law* (1955). A most valuable collection of cases is C. Fairman, *American Constitutional Decisions*.

The law of the constitution is only a part of any country's system of government. Much is effected by constitutional customs and conventions. In this respect, H. W. Horwill, *The Usages of the American Constitution*, has opened up the field.

For a history of the United States there is no better book than S. E. Morison and H. S. Commager, *The Growth of the American Republic* (2 vols.). It is full of interest, never heavy-handed, and contains excellent bibliographies. Hardly less good is S. E. Morison's own *History of the United States* (2 vols.). Excellent short histories are A. Nevins, *Brief History of the United States* and A. Nevins and H. S. Commager, *America: The Story of a Free People*.

Among collections of documents illustrative of the working of American government the best is H. S. Commager, *Documents of American History*, and R. Birley, *Select Speeches and Documents on American History* (4 vols. World's Classics), based to a large extent on Commager's collection, but shorter.

There are, finally, among periodicals, *The Political Science Quarterly, The American Political Science Review* and the *Journal of Politics*, all indispensable to the study of American government. Moreover, they contain, from time to time, articles and bibliographical material which are most valuable for the study of other federal and quasi-federal governments.

SWITZERLAND

The best account of the Swiss system is in Christopher Hughes, *The Federal Constitution of Switzerland* (1954), which contains the German text with a translation and commentary. The same author's *The Parliament of Switzerland* (1962) is also most valuable and interesting. Reference may be made also to George A. Codding, Jr., *The Federal Government of Switzerland* (1961) and to such earlier works as W. E. Rappard, *The Government of Switzerland* (1936), R. C. Brookes, *The Government and Politics of Switzerland* (1920), and G. D. Adams and C. Cunningham, *The Swiss Confederation* (1892). A full length study of the development of the constitution is W. E. Rappard, *La Constitution fédérale de la Suisse, 1848-1948*. The reader who has used these books will find that he can extend his knowledge usefully by consulting the informative *Statistisches Jahrbuch der Schweiz (Annuaire statistique de la Suisse)*.

CANADA

Canada was the first of the federations to conduct a thorough investigation of the whole working of the federal system. Here the student has available to him a great mass of information on every subject likely to interest him in the 70 years' working of the Canadian federation from 1867 to 1937. *The Report of the Royal Commission on Dominion-Provincial Relations*—known as the *Rowell-Sirois Report* from the names of its two successive chairmen, Chief Justice Newton Rowell and Professor Joseph Sirois—was published in three books. Book I contains a survey of the social and economic developments in Canada for the seventy years from 1867, and their bearing on the working of the federal system. Book II contains recommendations based on evidence in public hearings, on the facts set out in Book I and in certain special research studies undertaken under the auspices of the Royal Commission. Book III contains statistics. The special research studies are also published. They may be listed here as a whole in order to give an idea of the scope of the material available for the student of Canadian government.

Eight studies are made available in printed form: 1. *A Summary of Dominion and Provincial Public Finance Statistics*. 2. D. G. Creighton, *British North America at Confederation*. 3. W. A. Mackintosh, *The*

Economic Background of Dominion-Provincial Relations. 4. D. C. MacGregor, J. B. Rutherford, G. E. Britnell, J. J. Deutsch, *National Income.* 5. Esdras Minville, *Labour Legislation and Social Services in the Province of Quebec.* 6. A. E. Grauer, *Public Assistance and Social Insurance.* 7. J. A. Corry, *Difficulties of Divided Jurisdiction.* 8. L. M. Gouin and Brooke Claxton, *Legislative Expedients and Devices adopted by the Dominion and the Provinces.*

Eleven studies are made available in mimeographed form: J. A. Corry, *Growth of Government Activities since Confederation.* 2, 3 & 4. Three studies by A. E. Grauer, *Labour Legislation, Public Health* and *Housing.* 5. Stewart Bates, *Financial History of Canadian Governments.* 6. H. C. Goldenberg, *Municipal Finance in Canada.* 7. F. A. Knox, *Dominion Monetary Policy,* 1929–1934. 8. W. J. Waines, *Prairie Population Possibilities*: 9. S. A. Saunders, *Economic History of the Maritime Provinces.* 10. W. Eggleston and C. T. Kraft, *Dominion-Provincial Subsidies and Grants.* 11. W. Henry, *Railroad and Transportation Charges in Canada.*

In addition to the report and studies, there are available copies of the evidence and submissions placed before the Commission by provincial governments and by a wide variety of persons and public bodies; and there are the proceedings of the Commission itself, the last named not published, but available in some libraries, such as that of Rhodes House, Oxford.

The difficulty of a student beginning the study of Canadian federalism is to find his way through the mass of material. He will obtain great help from R. Mc. G. Dawson, *The Government of Canada* (1947), and A. Brady, *Democracy in the Dominions* (2nd ed., 1952). W. P. M. Kennedy, *The Constitution of Canada*, is the best written book about Canadian government, but it is primarily a history and not an analysis. The problem of amending the Canadian Constitution is dealt with authoritatively by P. Gerin-Lajoie in *Constitutional Amendment in Canada* (1950). H. McD. Clokie's *Canadian Government and Politics* (1944) provides a good general survey of Canada's government. There is much factual material in A. E. Buck, *Financing Canadian Government* (1949). There is a chapter on the constitution and its working in the *Cambridge History of the British Empire*, Vol. VI, *Canada*. On the law of the constitution Bora Laskin, *Canadian Constitutional Law* (2nd. ed., 1960), may be supplemented by articles in *The Canadian Bar Review* or *The University of Toronto Law Journal.* Special attention should be drawn to the issue of *The Canadian Bar Review* for December 1951 (Vol. XXIX, No. 10) entitled 'Nationhood and the Constitution', and to A. R. M. Lower *et al.*, *Evolving Canadian Federalism* (1958).

It may be expected that, with so much raw material now made available by the Rowell-Sirois Commission, further studies in Canadian federalism will appear. In the meantime the most helpful treatment is to be found in articles in *The Canadian Journal of Economics and Political Science* or in *The Canadian Bar Review*.

There is a valuable book of documents *British North America Acts and Selected Statutes, 1867–1943* (King's Printer, Ottawa, ed. Dr. M. Ollivier). The making of the federation can be studied in Joseph Pope, *Confederation Documents*, though this source is meagre in comparison with similar material for the United States and Australia.

For further bibliography reference may be made to *Cambridge History of the British Empire*, Vol. VI, *Canada*.

AUSTRALIA

The Australians also conducted an investigation of their federal government by royal commission, but it was not so thorough nor so wide in its range as the Canadian or the American. None the less its report is valuable and the printed minutes of evidence contain even more that is interesting. *The Report of the Royal Commission on the Constitution* was published in 1929; it contains a majority report and a minority report. The latter advocated greater unification in Australia; the former accepted federalism. In the minutes of evidence, perhaps the most valuable contribution is that of Sir Robert Garran. Australia lacks any thorough study of her federal system. The standard work on the making and early development of the constitution is W. Harrison Moore, *The Commonwealth of Australia* (2nd ed., 1910). There is also J. Quick and R. R. Garran, *Annotated Constitution of the Commonwealth of Australia* (1901), which makes very interesting comparisons and is informative in exposition. G. S. Knowles has brought out an annotated text of the Commonwealth Constitution, as amended, and this is kept up to date. It is published by the Commonwealth government. The modern development of the law is best shown in W. A. Wynes, *Legislative, Executive, and Judicial Powers in Australia* (2nd ed., 1956), G. Sawer, *Australian Constitutional Cases* (1948) and G. W. Paton (ed.) *The Commonwealth of Australia: the development of its laws and constitution* (1952)—books for lawyers rather than for students of political institutions. The latter will find most help in the short essays contained in G. V. Portus (ed.) *Studies in the Australian Constitution* (1933), W. K. Duncan (ed.) *Trends in Australian Politics* (1935), G. Sawer *et al.*, *Federalism in Australia* (1949), *Federalism—an Australian Jubilee Study* (1952) and L. F. Crisp, *The Parliamentary Government of the Commonwealth of Australia* (1949). A. Brady's *Democracy in the Dominions* has some valuable discussion of federalism in Australia as well as in Canada. Criticisms of the whole system are A. P. Canaway, *The Failure of Federalism in Australia* and G. Greenwood, *The Future of Australian Federalism*. Some of the most interesting discussions of the working of Australian federalism are found in the *Reports of the Commonwealth Grants*

Commission. The third report of the Commission (1934) was particularly illuminating. These reports are, unfortunately, difficult to obtain outside Australia. There is also the annual *Year Book* of the Commonwealth of Australia which is full of essential information.

For the study of the making of the Australian Constitution there are fuller records available than for any other federal government. The debates of the conferences of 1890 and 1891 are to be found in the *Record of the Australasian Federation Conference*, 1890 (Melbourne), and in the *Official Record of Proceedings and Debates of the National Australasian Convention* 1891 (Sydney). This was abortive but in 1897–8 there met the convention which succeeded in drawing up the Constitution. Its records are well worth study. There are four volumes: *Official Report of the National Australasian Convention Debates* (Adelaide) 1897; *Official Record of the Debates of the Australasian Federal Convention* (2nd session, Sydney) 1897; and *Official Record of the Debates of the Australian Federal Convention* (3rd session, Melbourne) 1898, 2 vols.

Some useful articles on the working of Australian federal government appear in *The Australian Quarterly* (1929 *et seq.*) and *The Economic Record* (1926 *et seq.*).

For a bibliography see *Cambridge History of the British Empire*, Vol. VII, *Australia*, where there are also chapters on the making and working of the constitution, in particular the brilliant survey in Chapter XVI by W. Harrison Moore.

WESTERN GERMANY

The making of the basic law of the Western German Federal Republic is described in J. F. Golay, *The Founding of the Federal Republic of Germany* (1958). There are useful chapters on the federal aspects of West German government in R. Hiscock's *Democracy in Western Germany* (1957), and E. Plischke, *Contemporary Government of Germany* (1961). An illuminating short article by G. Sawer entitled 'Federalism in West Germany' appeared in *Public Law*, Spring 1961, pp. 26 et seq.

INDIA

How far the framers of the Indian Constitution of 1950 intended the federal principle to be embodied in it may be studied in the debates of the Constituent Assembly, 1946–9, published in twelve volumes. More illuminating are the reports of certain committees of the Assembly, which are published in three series, particularly the Union Powers Committee, the Union Constitution Committee, the Expert Committee on Financial Provisions, the Linguistic Provinces Commission, and the Drafting Committee. On the working of the Constitution so far as relations between the centre and the states are concerned, it is important to consult the reports of the States Reorganization Commission of 1955 and of the Finance Commissions of 1952 and 1957; and V. P. Menon, *The Integration of the Indian States* (1956) and K. Santhanam, *Union–State Relations in India* (1960). Whether the Indian Union is federal or not is discussed in C. H. Alexandrowicz, *Constitutional Developments in India* (1957) and D. N. Banerjee, *Some Aspects of the Indian Constitution* (1962). D. D. Basu, *Commentary on the Constitution of India* (4th ed., 1961) is useful for reference.

PAKISTAN

The shortlived quasi-federal constitution of 1956 may be studied in K. Collard, *Pakistan, a political study* (1957), H. Feldman, *A Constitution for Pakistan* (1955), and K. J. Newman, *Essays on the Constitution of Pakistan* (1956).

MALAYA

The best source on federal government in Malaya is the Report of the Federation of Malaya Constitutional Commission (the Reid Commission), published in 1957 (Col. No. 330 of 1957) upon whose recommendations the Constitution of 1957 was based. The Constitution itself is found in Statutory Instruments, 1957, No. 1533, Annex, First Schedule. *Malaya and Singapore*, by L. A. Sheridan and others (which is volume 9 in G. W. Keeton's series on the laws and constitutions of the British Commonwealth) is useful.

NIGERIA

The federal Constitution of 1960 is found in Statutory Instruments for 1960, No. 1652, The Nigeria (Constitution) Order in Council, 1960. Two useful books are D. Rothchild, *Towards Unity in Africa* (1960) and J. S. Coleman, *Nigeria, Background to Nationalism* (1958). Reference may be made also, for constitutional history, to K. Ezera, *Constitutional Developments in Nigeria* (1960), which is mainly concerned with the period before 1954. There is a lucid exposition of Nigerian federalism and of the Constitution of 1960 by Taylor Cole in *The Nigerian Political Scene* (ed. R. O. Tilman and Taylor Cole), 1962. A valuable discussion of federal finance, of wider concern than the particular problems of Nigeria, is found in the report of the Hicks-Phillipson inquiry of 1951 entitled *Report of the Commission on Revenue Allocation* (published at Lagos by the Nigerian government).

WEST INDIES

The Constitution of 1957 is found in Statutory Instruments for 1957, No. 1364, The West Indies (Federation) Order in Council,

1957. Among the numerous blue books on the movement for federation, the most valuable are *Closer Association of the British West
Indian Colonies* (Cmd. 7120 of 1947); *Proceedings of the Conference
on the Closer Association of the British West Indian Colonies* (Col.
No. 218 of 1948); the *Report of the British Caribbean Standing Closer
Association Committee* (Col. No. 255 of 1950) and the reports of the
constitutional conferences of 1953 (Cmd. 8837 and 8895 of 1953) and
of 1956 (Cmd. 9733 of 1956). Some valuable articles are found in the
special issue of *Social and Economic Studies*, vol. 6, No. 2, June 1957.
An illuminating study of the making and the break up of the federation is given by Hugh W. Springer in his *Reflections on the Failure of
the First West Indian Federation* (Occasional Paper No. 4, July, 1962,
of the Harvard Centre for International Affairs).

RHODESIA AND NYASALAND

The Constitution of 1953 is found in Statutory Instruments for
1953, No. 1199, The Federation of Rhodesia and Nyasaland (Constitution) Order in Council, 1953. The best source materials are blue
books, particularly *Central African Territories: Report of Conference
on Closer Association* (Cmd. 8233 of 1951); *Closer Association in
Central Africa* (Cmd. 8411 of 1951); *Southern Rhodesia, Northern
Rhodesia and Nyasaland: Report by Conference on Federation* and
The Federal Scheme (Cmd. 8753 and 8754 of 1953). On the working
of the federation the Monckton Report of 1960 and its appendices
should be consulted. Appendix VI and appendix VII are particularly
useful. (Cmnd. 1148 and 1151 of 1960).

TABLE OF CASES

UNITED STATES

INDEX